WENDY M. WILSON

A Cold Wind Down the Grey

Copyright © 2018 by Wendy M. Wilson

All rights reserved. No part of this publication may be reproduced, stored or transmitted in any form or by any means, electronic, mechanical, photocopying, recording, scanning, or otherwise without written permission from the publisher. It is illegal to copy this book, post it to a website, or distribute it by any other means without permission.

First edition

This book was professionally typeset on Reedsy. Find out more at reedsy.com

Contents

Dedication and Details	v
Wanganui, 1888: A Testimonial for Inspector James	1
Greymouth, 1866: Finding George Dobson	10
Greymouth, 1866: Down the River to Town	18
Greymouth, 1866: The Autopsy	25
Greymouth, 1866: The Inquest: Day One	35
Greymouth, 1866: The Funeral	44
Greymouth, 1866: The Coach Returns	52
Greymouth, 1866: The Inquest: Day Two	58
Wanganui, 1888: The Boatman's Steps	65
Greymouth, 1866: The Suspect	69
Greymouth, 1866: The Warning	79
Greymouth, 1866: The Arrest	91
Greymouth, 1866: The Reporter	97
Greymouth, 1866: The Interview	104
Greymouth, 1866: The Body	112
Wanganui, 1888: The Maungatapu Murders	121
Greymouth, 1866: Neither Man Nor Boy	127
The Arnold Track, 1866: More Bodies	134
Maori Gully, 1866: George Dobson's Last Walk	146
Greymouth, 1866: The Skittle Alley	157
Greymouth, 1866: The Criterion Hotel	170
Hokitika, 1866: The Accessories	181
Greymouth, 1866: Burgess Confesses	191
Wanganui, 1888: The Executions	196
Greymouth, 1866-67: Sullivan Returns	202
Hokitika, 1867: The Trial: Day One	212

Hokitika, 1867: The Trial: Day Two	225
Greymouth, 1867: A Letter to the Editor	238
Greymouth, 1867: A Cold Wind Down the Grey	243
Wanganui, 1888: Memento Mori	248
Afterword	254

Dedication and Details

Dedicated to the memory of William Henry James, 1827 to 1907

This book is a fictionalized account of an actual crime and the police inspector who investigated that crime: the murder of George Dobson, a young surveyor whose extended family have left their names all over the South Island of New Zealand.

I have kept as close as possible to real events, but have made some guesses regarding motivation and emotions. I investigated Inspector James' life before 1866 closely, using the Australian newspaper database Trove, and the genealogical database Ancestry. The events of 1866 and early 1867 were covered closely in the newspapers of the time, and I relied on them for many of the details in this book. Inspector James' personal life came to me in pieces, from a notation on a cue card in the Greymouth History Museum, to cemeteries in Wanganui and Timaru, and by the time I had finished my research I felt I knew him well.

My primary source of research for events in this book was the online New Zealand government database Papers Past, especially the newspaper *The Grey River Argus*. For a bibliography with links to the database please check my website: www.wendymwilson.com.

The title of this book is taken from a description of the **Barber**: A chilly damp wind that blows down the Grey Valley and seen only in a handful of places in the world the 'Barber' is the local name for a katabatic wind formation.

Cover image used with permission from The Hocken Collections at the University of Otago:

William Marshall Cooper (1833-1921), Greymouth, 1866-1871, chromolithograph by Harnett & Co., Hokitika, Lithographers, 210 x 330mm, accession 12,729 Hocken Collections - Uare Taoka o Hākena, University of Otago

1

Wanganui, 1888: A Testimonial for Inspector James

He knew as soon as he walked through the door of the station that something was up. Constable Crozier, seated nearest the door, said a quick, "Morning Mr. Inspector James," then refused to meet his eyes, shoving something under his desk. The rest of his men stopped talking suddenly and watched him, grinning. He sighed. He'd come by arrangement to pick up his personal effects and his men were waiting to pounce on him and force another one of those bloody framed testimonials on him. That imbecile from *The Herald* was there as well, perched on his usual wooden stool. The reporter caught his eye and winked, pleased to have been proven right.

He'd run into the reporter in court recently while testifying against a young lad who'd been terrorizing his neighbourhood. The boy on trial, Joshua Bason, was a bad seed—two brothers already at the industrial school up in Burnham, and his father in court that same day, charged with going about carrying a loaded gun and using insulting language when not in a sober state. The reporter had come up to him afterwards to discuss the case. They'd spoken briefly, but as he moved away the reporter had asked, "What will you do, Inspector James, now that you're retiring?

"Retiring? I'm not...where did you hear that?"

The reporter's expression had changed – he'd smelled blood. "We heard Pardy from New Plymouth was taking over this district in addition to his own."

"I've received no intimation of such a change," James had said, worried. Surely it could not be true—but what if it was? Was the bloody government trying to save money again? Why did the force always take the first cuts? And why him?

The next day the rumour, accompanied by his denial, had appeared in the paper, and a week later he'd received the official letter telling him he was to be retired with six month's salary. He'd felt like a fool. Six month's pay, they'd offered, in lieu of the pension he'd been promised when he left Victoria to come to New Zealand. He had some savings, but how would they manage, the two of them? And what would happen to the new house?

Constable Crozier made a sudden move, rising to his feet, almost knocking over his chair. Clutched in his large awkward hands was a letter encased in a massive gilt frame. A testimonial, as he had surmised. Others were rising as well, and the young recruit appeared like Aladdin from the kitchen wheeling a tea trolley loaded with a battered silver tea pot, tin mugs, and a plate of buttered pikelets from Woolley's.

James stood there, a smile frozen in place, as they sang an enthusiastic round of "For he's a jolly good fellow," wondering what to say in response. Perhaps he should let out his house and move to something cheaper, up north, leave behind his wonderful new home here… But Elizabeth would be distraught. She'd finally started to enjoy life here, to fit in…

"…and so say all of us…"

The voices faded, and Detective Benjamin stepped forward rubbing his hands together in that annoying way of his. Benjamin was being transferred as well, to Wellington, the Gazette said. Last night, Benjamin's friends had presented him with a gold watch chain. Very nice. Better than the testimonial James' men were about to foist on him, he was sure. But Benjamin was not a chain-of-command type; he treated everyone as equals, regardless of stature. He'd never be given his own command with that attitude.

"Inspector James," said Benjamin. "I've been commissioned by the police of Wanganui, and the surrounding district, to hand you this letter, expressive of the regard with which we all hold you, and to express the regrets of those who are unable to attend."

Benjamin gestured towards Constable Crozier, who cleared his throat and thrust the framed testimonial forward. "Inspector James, when you took over Wanganui District in 1880, I was stationed in Hawera," he said. "I was serving under an officer second to none in the force as a policeman, but his conduct towards the men was different to that of yours, and when you came we all felt as if we had…as if we had been let out of prison."

James attempted to look appreciative. They tolerated him because he was decent to them, impartial, severe only when necessary—certainly much less severe now than he'd been as a younger man. But he didn't believe they admired or respected him.

"I've been in the service twenty-three years," Crozier continued. "and served under many different officers, but none as considerate as you, sir."

He held the framed testimonial forward and James took it, making a show of turning it around and reading it carefully. The frame was excellent, anyway. It would look good with one of his Indian ink sketches - replace those oils he was going to have to sell. Maybe he would frame the sketch he'd done the day of young Dobson's funeral, of the diggers on the beach silhouetted against the waves. Always been a favourite of his, that one. He'd discovered it in the side drawer of his Davenport when he was clearing it out for the move to the new house, tied up with a couple of newspapers from back then he'd forgotten about.

"I have to return you my sincere thanks for the kindly expressions embodied herein." He looked around the room, briefly holding the eyes of each man. They had all signed the testimonial, even those who weren't present. "Until this moment, I never knew I was held in such esteem, but I take your kindness as evidence of your appreciation of my conduct during the time I have been in command of you and the feeling that I have gained your respect is something…is something to be thankful for."

They clapped politely and he saw his sergeant glance over at the clock.

"I've been in service for thirty-seven years…"

Constable Crozier grimaced. The old bugger's going to tell us about his whole entire life, his face telegraphed. Well, dammit, he wanted to tell them. He deserved that at least. Pushed out of the force after that length of time, with nothing but a handwritten testimonial in a, well, in a good frame, although probably picked up cheap at Jackson's Auction House.

"Thirty-seven years," he repeated. "Although nine of those years were in Victoria. I joined the force in Victoria in '54, right off the boat from London. That was the year to join. Any of you could have joined, even…" He caught Crozier's eye and stopped himself. "They took anyone over five foot seven who could ride, and was of good character. That was after the defeat of the miners at the Eureka Stockade. Broham was there, and Hickson, Shearman, of course…"

His mind started to wander back to those times. Shearman had brought him to New Zealand. Commissioner Shearman of the Province of Canterbury he was back then. A good man, who'd had James' back during the incident in Timaru. Said he had the "toughness of character" to be a strong leader, and for that reason had later given him the gold escort to lead. Their careers had stayed in tandem for years, Shearman always a step or two above him, until James had been given command in Wellington. But when the cuts came at the end of his first year, Shearman had pushed him out and taken the job for himself, the job he'd worked so hard to get. The government had fobbed him off with a new position up here in Wanganui, still a first-class inspector, but with lowered stature. Shearman's betrayal had stung; Elizabeth swore never to speak to Helen Shearman again.

He shook himself, and pulled himself back to the task at hand. "I started out in Timaru, as Sergeant of Watch." He saw Constable Crozier's shoulders slump in dismay. "In '64. Then in '65 I was promoted to inspector in charge of the gold escort. We rode from Christchurch across the mountains to Hokitika, myself and some troopers—and Shearman, the Commissioner of Police. A hell of a ride, it was. No roads then, of course, they were still being built, but Cobb's Coaches started running later the same year. Shearman was in the first coach to cross, and so was Edward Dobson, the provincial engineer, George Dobson's father…"

He realized he was starting to ramble, and stopped. The reporter was tapping his pencil on his knee, an irritated expression on his face, no longer taking notes.

He felt foolish.

Detective Benjamin helped him out. "Did that for a while, did you, sir?"

"What? Oh, the gold escort? No. Just one trip. The bloody … the miners started sending their gold by sea around the Bluff to Melbourne after the government refused to insure the stuff." Lucky really. The route through the mountains was treacherous…easy for bushrangers to hide in the dense bush and assault them, even with the fortifications added to the gold coach. The "perambulating, impregnable, gold-escort redoubt," the papers laughingly called it…

His men were all frowning now, wanting to get at the food. Better finish this thing then.

"I worked my way up through the ranks," he said, looking at Constable Crozier, still a constable after twenty-three years on the force, "principally by sobriety, truthfulness and perseverance, and I trust you will advance the same way, if you apply yourself." Crozier blushed and looked at his feet. Benjamin was frowning disapprovingly.

James felt a brief pang of guilt about what he'd said, and changed the subject. "Let's all get at that tea, shall we?"

He poured himself a mug, folded over a couple of pikelets in his left hand, and went into the small room beside the kitchen he used as an office, holding the framed testimonial under his right arm. He leaned the frame against the wall and lit himself a Scotch Cap, staring at the testimonial as he drank his tea, thinking back on his career. Left-handed. Who was that, and why was it important? Something twigged in his mind and then disappeared. Left hand, right foot. Connected with something he had….

It was a damned shame that he'd just closed on the Halswell Street property. They had both been so happy with the new house, pleased to be moving from the cramped quarters of Sydney Place, Elizabeth ready to entertain more, to hold *soirées*. She'd already made an appointment with Mr. Harding to have a photograph taken for her *carte de visite*. He would let out the Sydney Place house—the lease still had some time before it expired. But what work could he do? All he knew was policing.

They would move to Halswell Street, he decided, and not go north. He would pick up some work as a justice of the peace, sell his sketches, do something. He could take up writing - write a book about his experiences. They deserved Halswell Street after all they'd been through. He'd spent the last twenty years collecting furniture and fittings, and they were finally going to have a place worthy of them: his beautiful Schwechten piano, the velvet drawing suite, the Brussels carpets, the dinner service Elizabeth loved, the Davenports, and his art pieces: the over mantel oil paintings and the alabaster ornaments.

He drained his tea, lit himself another cigarette and leaned back, still staring at the testimonial. An odd feeling brushed over him momentarily, a feeling that he had been here before, seated at his desk staring at something on a wall.

It all came back to him in a rush. He had been thinking about it all day, without realizing he had. The murder of George Dobson in

'66. He'd been sitting at his Davenport in his house on Arney Street in Greymouth looking at the reward notice he'd pinned to the wall, just as he now sat and looked at the testimonial. That must have been after he found the body.

Poor Elizabeth had been pregnant the whole time he'd been investigating young Dobson's murder – tired, uncomfortable, nauseous. And Thomas' birth was early, partly because of the shock of…. but Thomas had amazed them both from the start; he'd had nothing but success his entire life. Training as an architect now, by god, at Atkins and Clere, the best architects in Wanganui. What a pity Elizabeth couldn't warm to Thomas the way she had the others…he'd never understood it.

He did not want to think about his children, any of them, even now, and focused instead on the murder, and the day he'd found the body. The smell, the gut-wrenching smell, he could almost think it was still in his nose now, so strong had it been. From a body that had lain there for six weeks…with that ugly thing sticking up from the ground, taunting him with its presence…

He took a last draw at the cigarette, enjoying the cleansing burn of it in his lungs, and stubbed it out in the dregs of his tea. He could carry everything home easily, if only he didn't have to cart along the damn testimonial. He would leave it behind and ask Crozier to deliver it to him tomorrow. He'd invite Crozier in for a drink—sit on the verandah with a beer, that was the ticket. He wasn't a police officer now. He could be polite to the man.

As he walked through the station carrying his possessions - an Indian ink drawing of the wharf he'd done when he first arrived in Wanganui, a spare uniform shirt, a bag of pens and papers - he responded to the murmured goodbyes from his men, and opened the door to his new life. The day was sunny and cold, somewhat frosty, and on any other day would be full of potential. How he would miss being a police inspector. The idea weighed on his spirits as he headed down Bell Street towards the courthouse and Taupo Quay.

The past rose from the depths of his memory to meet him. He had spent so much time in courthouses, here and down south in Greymouth. He'd met Edward Dobson for the first time in a courthouse, after Dobson had crossed the mountains from Christchurch by Cobb's Coach to instigate a search for his son, just days after everyone had realized that young George was missing. Someone must have sent a telegram; the electric telegraph was being built across the country around that time. Charles Todhunter, George Dobson's brother-in-law, had arrived soon after to assist in the search. He'd liked Todhunter. A decent man.

James had known that George Dobson belonged to an influential family, connected by blood and marriage, a mob of road builders, surveyors, engineers, men who were building Canterbury and the west coast. In fact, back then very little got built on the west coast of the South Island unless a Dobson or a Dobson relation had his finger on the plan. The family were stunned to learn of the deadly gang of killers who had slaughtered their son and so many other men, to understand that even they had not been immune from such a disaster. If a young man like George Dobson, well-liked and well-connected, could suffer that fate, who was safe?

The cawing of seagulls and the smell of the docks assailed his nose, reminding him once more of that smell, and that thing sticking up from the ground, when he found the body…

"Mr. Inspector James, sir…"

He turned. Constable Crozier was hurrying down Bell Street, holding the testimonial under his arm. Blast. He'd forgotten to ask Crozier to bring it to his house tomorrow, and now everyone would assume he didn't want it.

"You forgot your testimonial, and…"

"So I did." He raised his loaded arms and forced a smile. "But I had no room. I intended to…well. Perhaps you'd be so kind as to accompany me home with it?"

"I'd be happy to, sir," said Crozier. "As I said at the presentation earlier on, when you arrived to take charge, I felt as if…"

"Yes, yes." He glanced at Crozier. Might as well make it up to him. "Now, let's walk along the riverbank. It isn't the fastest way to my house, but it's the prettiest, and today I feel like looking at something pleasant…with a good companion, of course."

They set off along the river, James thinking once more about all the deaths from that time, and the body he had found in his own district when he saw something sticking up from the muddy ground.

2

Greymouth, 1866: Finding George Dobson

Twenty-Two Years Earlier

It was the toe he was remembering…the toe of a scuffed leather boot sticking up from the earth just a stone's throw from the track that told him he'd finally found the body he sought. That and the sickly stench of death that hung in the air, making it hard to breath. Inspector James stood looking at the area, and felt exasperated with himself. The body was buried beneath a high terrace, just thirty yards from where he'd stood on the first day of his search. There was even the appearance of a slight track down to where the body lay. How had he missed seeing it?

He stared at the tip of the boot and felt it pointing back at him accusingly. You could have stopped this, it said. Why did you not arrest them when you had the chance?

Tearing his eyes away from the burial site he squinted towards the river. A group of men were disembarking from a flat boat, clearly about to head his way. He thought he could see Todhunter among them. Cupping his hands around his mouth, he cooeyed. An answering cooey came from the group, and an arm rose in a wave.

He'd calculated the possible burial site using information from Mr. Fox, the gold buyer from Maori Gulley, who had parted from George Dobson at the Arnold River, and a report from a couple who'd seen a group of suspicious-looking men putting up a tent near the iron shanty down towards Greymouth. He and his team had spent the best part of three days searching the bush, wading through icy streams that numbed feet, and deep, rock-strewn gullies that twisted ankles and bruised shins, along the Arnold track, upriver from Greymouth.

By then he knew the time for finding George Dobson alive had passed. But where the hell was the body? He'd been struggling up a blind dry creek, Constable McIlroy behind him, when they had both smelled something putrid, something that caused the constable to stop and gag. He'd gone towards the smell, pushing aside ferns, and had seen the toe of a boot, thrusting up through the damp earth and rotting leaves like a beacon.

The sound of boots knocking on stones made him turn and look back along the track. Matthew Russell, a storekeeper with a supply shack a mile or so away, was hurrying down towards him, a shovel in hand.

"Ya got 'im then, Mr. Inspector James? I heard your cooey and thought I'd come and help. I been looking…"

"More than likely." James nodded towards the burial site. "We've certainly got someone. We'll have to have a formal identification, but…"

"I can do that. I knew him, I knew Mr. Dobson," said Russell. He directed a stream of brown spittle at the ground, then plunged his shovel into the dirt beside the grave. "A wonderful young bloke. I hope you get them bastards who did this to him. You want me to dig 'im up?"

"Thank you, yes. But there's a party on the way down from the river. We'll wait for them. I believe it's Mr. Todhunter, Mr. Dobson's brother-in-law. He'll want to be here."

They stood silently, both now staring at the burial site, waiting for the group from the flat boat to make its way to them. Guilt nagged at the edge of his mind. He'd known about the Burgess gang for some time, had even been warned they were planning a robbery. When he threw them out of town he'd believed his problems with them were over, that Shallcrass up in Nelson, with a much bigger force, would deal with them. Now five men had been reported in missing in Nelson, believed murdered by the gang, and he understood that they may have also murdered the young man in the grave at his feet.

He glanced at the burial site again, then glanced away. Greymouth, his town, was immersed in a massive gold rush that brought with it the loafers and the scoundrels who circled the half-eaten carcass of the rush like vultures, making life difficult for honest men. It galled him that such a good and decent young man could be murdered in his district.

James was confident that Shallcrass would prove Burgess and his crew were guilty of the Nelson murders and see them all twisted. They would die in torment like the four murderers of Reverend Volkner, who had all gone to the gallows not long since up in Gisborne. Of course, those killers were Maori with a grievance. They'd believed Volkner was a spy for the government and were waiting for him. Volkner, the damn fool, had been warned not to go, but leaning on his faith he had gone anyway, and ended up with his head in a bag and pieces of his heart being devoured by his killers.[i]Fortunately, the hostilities and atrocities of both sides in the land wars were confined to the North Island, not down here in the South Island. Until now, all he'd had to put up with were the sins of the dregs of humanity from Victoria…and some stupidity by the diggers, of course: theft, drownings, arguments, drunkenness, and suicides, lots of suicides.

But James had been warned that Burgess might be up to something worse than robbery. One of Burgess's followers, Jimmy Wilson, had come to his house back in May, scared crazy about something, with a story about a plot to rob and kill Mr. Fox the gold trader, and James had gone looking for them. Wilson had claimed the gang had bought a shovel to take Mr. Fox by surprise from behind, because Fox carried a revolver in his hand to fend off bushrangers. Wilson was worried that the gang meant to use the shovel to kill the gold trader and didn't want any part of it. Robberies were common around Greymouth, with all that gold on the move, but murders were not; James had worried about protecting Mr. Fox from harm, not death. But now Wilson's fear of murder had taken on a darker aspect. He must have known—or seen something that spooked him.

He'd acquired an arrest warrant on conspiracy to rob, but the gang had decamped to Nelson by steamer… as James himself had suggested they do. He'd sent an urgent letter to Broham in Hokitika, and Broham sent a formal letter on to Shallcrass in Nelson, eschewing the use of the newly installed telegraph, warning of a possible robbery; but too late. Five men were missing on the Maungatapu track near Nelson and the gang had been arrested under suspicion of murdering them. Shallcrass had already managed to turn one of them against his fellows and a desperate search for the bodies was underway.

James had put Jimmy Wilson in the lockup at the police camp back in June on suspicion of conspiracy to rob Mr. Fox, but had begun to believe he had a murder on his hands, a murder that Wilson knew about. Wilson had denied all knowledge of a murder, had refused to say where the body of George Dobson might be buried. He would get the truth from Wilson, and if he was involved in this crime, if he had been present at the murder of George Dobson, he would go down for it. Let the rest of the gang swing for the Nelson murders; if Wilson was guilty he would swing for this one; Inspector James would make sure he did.

Standing on the stump of a totara tree near the burial site, he surveyed the track towards the Grey River. It was going to be difficult to carry a body along that winding and rocky track, and now a light rain was falling, making the trip even more slippery and treacherous. In the distance, he could see the group getting closer and hoped they had a stretcher with them.

He slapped his pockets to check for his pipe; there was just time for a quick puff to ward off the smell. But the pipe was not there. It must have fallen out at the coal pits when he lay last night, fully clothed, his head against a log, trying to sleep next to a small coal fire. His neck still ached. Wishing he had his pipe, he watched as the group struggled in his direction. They would appreciate that he had waited for them, but would be sickened by what they were about to see, he knew that.

Mr. Todhunter, the victim's brother-in-law, reached him first, hurrying frantically up the last hundred yards of the track. Todhunter had been in the district the entire time, even after Mr. Edward Dobson, George's father, had taken Cobb's Coach back to Christchurch.

"You have found him, Mr. Inspector James? You have found George?"

"Sorry sir, but I believe we have. We smelled something in the area, and at first thought it came from an empty bottle of brandy lying nearby. But we noticed these footprints," he indicated the indentations leading towards the burial site, "and then we saw that."

Todhunter reeled back, seeing the tip of the boot for the first time.

"That," he said, then stopped and took a step towards the toe, stooping slightly to look at it more closely. "That...I believe that to be George's boot. Is his body here?"

Not much of an identification. Most men owned such boots in this district, a good pair of sturdy leather walking boots for the rough mountain tracks. A coroner's jury would need more than a boot.

James nodded at Russell, who began to uncover the corpse slowly and carefully. The earth had been trodden down into a heavy mass of clay and fern, making it difficult to remove. Todhunter stood nearby, his face barely under control, waiting for what was to come, while other members of the search party stood back respectfully, some with handkerchiefs over their noses to mitigate the smell, others trying to look anywhere but at the emerging body.

The two constables knelt beside Russell and scrabbled at the grave with branches and bare hands. One of the constables had arrived from Nelson the day before with the rough map provided by a gang member who had turned Queen's evidence, showing where the gang had pitched their tent to await Mr. Fox. The map had sent them in the wrong direction. James led his team to the spot indicated, and spent a rigorous day scouring the bush and wading through every creek near where the tent should have been, but found nothing. He'd refused to give up. He would find the body, he had to. He took his small group of searchers back to the coal pits above the river, where they passed the night, dispirited and defeated—and bloody uncomfortable to boot.

On the final day, inspired by the dark, bone-chilling night spent at the coal pits, he wondered if the map might be wrong—the memory of the sketcher flawed. The husband and wife who'd passed by the gang shortly before the time Dobson would have been in the area had arrived at the coal pits in the dark. Perhaps the site was closer to the town?

He'd made a decision. One of the constables would go back to Arnold Township and find out who the couple were and, if possible, bring them back to identify the site. James and the other two constables would start searching closer to town, a mile further down the track.

And a mile down the track was where they had smelled that sickening odour, one they knew well, of a decaying body, and, after finding the footsteps, had seen the toe sticking up through the mud.

As the diggers removed the earth, the outline of a body took shape. It lay with the feet pointing up the gully, the head pointing down. The men scraped away the dirt carefully, making sure not to disturb anything, while James stood at the head and looked down, watching for evidence. Once he'd convicted a man with little more than some hair from the back of his head and a smear of blood on his trousers. Nothing should be overlooked.

The first identifiable thing to appear was an Inverness cape, draped across the lower part of the body. Charles Todhunter dropped to his knees and touched the cape gently: "This is George's. I've seen him wearing it many…"

James moved the cape to the side of the gravesite, causing a cloud of blowflies to rise lazily. Next came a prismatic compass in a case and a field book, from between the legs. Surveyors tools—a strong indication this was George Dobson. As he lay the compass and the field book on top of the cape, he noticed something odd. Two leather straps lay each side of the body. Not Mr. Dobson's, by the look of them. He retrieved those as well, for further study.

The three diggers stopped and leaned down to clasp the arms of the body and release it from the earth, keeping it steady so as not to disturb the vestiges of dirt still covering the face; Dr. Foppoly would remove that during the autopsy. As the body came free of its damp tomb, James could see that much of the lower half of the face was missing. The watchers gasped and held handkerchiefs more tightly against their lips. Then, as the diggers lifted the body to drier ground, the skin of one hand slipped off like a glove and dropped to the dirt beside the grave. Todhunter made a choking sound, and two of the watchers dashed into the bush retching loudly, returning a few minutes later wiping their lips.

Given that the lower half of the face was mostly gone, the jaw ravaged, the entirety of the protruding tongue visible, the next best item useful for identification was the timepiece. The courts would certainly agree, especially as Todhunter had already identified the cape and the boots. James removed a gold chain and silver watch from the left-hand pocket of the vest and held them towards Todhunter.

"Can you identify this watch and chain as belonging to your brother-in-law?"

"I recognize the chain." Todhunter sniffed and wiped away a tear with the back of his hand, smearing dirt across his cheek. "But the watch—I'm not sure of the watch. He has one like that, however."

James picked up the field book, opened it, and passed it to Todhunter. You couldn't go wrong with handwriting in court. Forged cheques, threatening letters, the courts saw those all the time. A jury would understand handwriting evidence.

"And do you recognize the handwriting in this field book?"

Todhunter nodded, his face grey and bloodless; no doubt he was thinking about his new wife Caroline, George's younger sister. Todhunter would find it difficult to tell his wife her beloved older brother was dead, murdered.

And murdered he was, that was clear. The wounds on the jaw and neck were man-made, never mind the fact that someone had deliberately buried the body and stamped down the soil that covered it.

The two constables loaded the corpse onto the stretcher, threw a piece of tent canvas over it, and hoisted up the stretcher, one each end, sides raised to stop parts of the body from falling to the ground. As they maneuvered their way along the track, Inspector James followed. The canvas was pulled up to cover the face, leaving the boots exposed. Over the left shoulder of Constable McIlroy, he could see the leather sole of one boot as it flopped from side to side with the movement of the men carrying it, and silently swore he would follow this case to the end. Nobody would get away with it, whatever his part had been. Especially not Jamie Wilson.

3

Greymouth, 1866: Down the River to Town

A group of pipe-smoking boatmen sat waiting for them on the rocks where the boat was moored, and they hopped up quickly as they saw the group approach, gathering around the stretcher.

"Ya got 'im? Ya got 'im?"

Word spread through town as the flat boat pulled slowly abreast of the Greymouth wharf; despite the threat of rain and biting cold wind, a large crowd had gathered, flooding from the shops on Boundary Street and the hotels and offices along the quay. As the constables hoisted the stretcher and carried it on foot to the Union Hotel, the crowd trailed behind quietly. They had all been following the search, wanting the young man found, but dreading confirmation of his death. James nodded to the men of the town as he walked behind the stretcher, confirming he had found Dobson. Some women sobbed quietly, some wailed.

Mr. Edward Dobson, father of the victim, had spent time in Greymouth leading search after desperate search for the missing man, and townspeople had seen the quiet grief etched on the man's face when he had found no clue to the fate of his eldest son. He was not a man to show emotion, but the town had united behind him. One way or another, George Dobson must be reunited with his father.

The autopsy was scheduled for the next morning, followed by an inquest in the afternoon, so he returned to his home in Arney Street to prepare his inquest notes. He would attend the autopsy, as unpleasant as it would be, to learn what he could about the murder. He wasn't obliged to go, but doctors were trained to look for different things than he was, and not everything said in the autopsy room made it to the report. He needed to be there, to see and hear for himself.

Elizabeth was in the kitchen kneading bread for the next day, stopping occasionally to stir a hearty stew of mutton, onions and potatoes for their tea. The first ships since the recent floods had arrived in port and the price of mutton had dropped back to normal, making it the first meal she thought to cook each night. However, she refused to eat stew herself—she said it turned her stomach. Often a little bread dipped in gravy was all she could manage. Perhaps things would improve in the coming months—they had every other time. But perhaps not, at her age—nearly forty.

"Did you find him?"

He nodded without speaking.

"Oh dear."

He went to his Davenport thinking about the details he needed to cover in his notes. What a pity the soil had been so damp, causing the grave to fill with water once the body was removed. He'd marked the area, but any preservation of material was increasingly unlikely after the six weeks it had taken to find the poor young gentleman lying in his water-soaked grave. The leather straps were interesting, however. He had a theory about those—he'd seen them before…

He'd noticed a rat hole not far from the grave. Could that be the reason the face was so damaged? Rats were everywhere on the coast, both in the towns and in the bush, and no amount of strychnine would reduce the numbers.

And why had the murderers not taken George Dobson's watch and chain, which must be worth a quid or two? All that was missing, as far as Charles Todhunter could tell him, were the few bank notes

George usually carried in his pocket book. Hardly worth killing a man for—although Old Jamie, James Battle, one of the five murdered by Burgess and his gang up in Nelson, had carried just three pounds on his person.

The Burgess gang, who were certainly implicated in the murder, had followed a similar path to his own—from England to the goldfields of Victoria, through the port of Lyttelton and down to the first rush at Gabriel's Gully in Otago, where they had been jailed briefly for attempted murder after a shootout with the police. Escorted out of Otago by the force, they'd crossed the mountains to the West coast, accompanied by alerts from the Otago police.

In Hokitika, Broham had kept an eye on them, even following them to the Opera House. And now after James had moved them along once again, they'd gone to another district and murdered five people. That was bad enough. But worse, he hadn't realized what they'd already done in his district. He'd sent them on their way when he should have put them in gaol. Because of that, he had a personal stake in this crime. He could not punish the fiends who had done this to George Dobson – they would hang for the crimes they had committed in Nelson – but he would make sure that at least Jamie Wilson would pay.

He sat at his desk, pulled out some foolscap and started to write his notes for the inquest, being careful not to omit any details.

He was up early the next morning, ready for the inquest. Elizabeth had left a copy of the newspaper lying open on the kitchen table, and he carried it in to his study and read it as he ate his breakfast.

We cannot conclude this notice without stating that the best thanks of the community are due to Mr. Inspector James, and the other members of the police force who were engaged in this search, for the hearty and determined manner in which they both entered into and prosecuted the search, and we must congratulate them upon its successful termination. Grey River Argus, Issue 76, 7 July 1866

Kerr, the editor, was laying it on a bit thick, probably with the trial in mind—he'd want to keep a tight grip on James' ear, to see if he could scoop the other papers whose reporters were circling like vultures. He shook his head as he folded the newspaper and put it in the drawer of his Davenport to read later. Kerr wasn't fooling him with his false flattery.

He pinned Shearman's reward notice on the wall above his desk, and glanced up at it, wondering if he could claim it. The reward was generous: two hundred and fifty pounds—almost a year's salary for James—along with her Majesty's Free Pardon extended to anyone giving information that led searchers to the body, if they weren't personally involved. The man Shallcrass had turned in Nelson, Joseph Sullivan, would be hoping to claim it, he was sure. Why else would he turn Queen's evidence?

George Dobson, the notice said, was *"About 26 years of age 5ft. 7in. high; slight build; fair complexion; fair hair; small fair whiskers; small moustache thin face; dressed when leaving Greymouth for the Arnold Township in light colored coat and trousers, the latter worn inside his boots; dark colored vest; wore strapped on his shoulder a black glazed leather despatch bag."*

The description certainly matched the clothing and the despatch bag he'd found on the body.

He could hear Elizabeth clattering around in the kitchen, and for a moment thought of calling to her to show her Kerr's comments, but decided against it. She was mopey these days, often tired and peevish. She had follow him loyally from Victoria to Timaru to Greymouth, but had come here grudgingly. Why could they not go to a larger city, somewhere like Christchurch or Dunedin? The diggers here alarmed her, and she found it difficult to be in such a remote place, even though she came from the wilds of Dartmoor herself. A whimper came from the upstairs, where the girl who did for them was putting young Harry down for a nap - he was a quiet, fussy child, lacking the spirit and energy one expected in a two-year-old – but the girl was gentle and the whimpering soon stopped.

James had met Edward Dobson, George's father, in early June when he'd come to search for his son. James had been up near Stillwater dragging the river when Mr. Dobson arrived and took over the search, enlisting his son's mates from the survey department, desperate to find their friend, experienced Maori trackers familiar with the area and even men with sniffer dogs; he understood it was a corpse he sought.

The newspapers agreed with Edward Dobson. "The impression," the reporter from the Grey River Argus had written four weeks into the search "is becoming more strong that Mr. Dobson has been waylaid and murdered upon the cut track between the Arnold and Greymouth, about seven miles from Arnold township, somewhere between twelve and one o'clock on the 28th May, and that the body has been buried." Dobson was last seen shortly after separating from Mr. Fox at the Arnold River. If he'd gone much further they would surely have had a report from one of the supply stores along the way. He would have at least stopped in for a pipe and a chinwag, everyone knew that.

James had learned something about George Dobson during his search, most of it positive. There'd been complaints—there always were; a letter writer in the Argus had grumbled: "The road from Greymouth is in a disgraceful state, and should be made passable at once, as the traffic is very considerable. Why not have a gang of men at work in fine weather? What is Dobson about?" The Argus enjoyed a good complaint from a reader. He should complain about the *Argus*, for all the trouble they'd given him.

As he placed the Argus in the drawer of his Davenport, James noticed he still had an old copy of the Lyttelton Times from his days as a sergeant in Timaru. He'd originally kept it because it contained an account of the Canterbury goldfields; there'd been some talk back then on the necessity of a gold escort, the job that had initially brought him to Hokitika and eventually to Greymouth. He'd been interested in a new posting after a run-in with his superiors in Timaru. He found the article on the second page: Canterbury Goldfields. Latest Intelligence. He browsed through the rest of the paper as he finished his tea, and realized that the same paper contained a long letter, accompanied by a report, from George Dobson himself. When he put it in his drawer, back in Timaru, he'd not even known of the existence of the Dobson family, let alone of George Dobson. He spread the paper out and looked at the article with interest. When he had time, he would read it. For now, he returned it to the drawer.

He folded his notes, put them in his inside pocket and stood up, stretching. Time for the autopsy. Autopsies were unpleasant to watch, but he had strong nerves and found the dissection of a human body interesting, especially when the body belonged to someone with whom he was unacquainted, although the autopsy of a fine young man like George Dobson would be more difficult than most.

He took his empty mug into the kitchen. Elizabeth was leaning over the sink, her face buried in her apron, holding her belly. His heart stopped briefly, then he realized she had a letter clutched in her hand. Louisa sat in the corner watching her mother nervously; she exchanged glances with James. She had one arm around Charlie, the large black Newfoundland James had brought with him from Victoria and trained to protect his family. Charlie had helped comfort Louisa in bad times, and she treated him like a brother. He went to his wife and put his arm awkwardly across her shoulder.

"My dear, whatever is the matter?"

She took a deep, ragged, breath, wiped her eyes with her apron and leaned her head against his chest. She looked older than her thirty-nine years, her hair starting to grey already, her face pale and lined. He could smell the carbolic soap on her skin and hair, mixed with the musky scent of lavender that clung to her clothes from the sachets she slipped amongst the folded garments in her drawer.

"Constable Boyle was here with some papers for you to sign," she said. "And he said…"

"Something important? Why did you not…"

She sighed and pulled away from him, her eyes fixed on the kitchen floor. "Nothing you needed to see immediately. It was just an excuse to…he thought you might…Sergeant Hickson's son…"

"Has something happened to the child?" Sergeant Hickson, second in command at Hokitika, had recently welcomed a son to his family.

"He had the thrush and went it through him," said Louisa from her spot in the corner. "The funeral is tomorrow, the constable said."

He gave Elizabeth's shoulder an awkward pat, knowing how upset she must be.

"Take the Cobb's Coach to Hokitika with Louisa," he said. "The girl will take care of Harry for the night. Mary Anne will appreciate talking with someone who understands…"

He saw his daughter sit up and stopped. A trip to Hokitika would lift her spirits. No need to talk about her mother's problems right now. He was feeling generous. "Stay the night in a hotel, the Bull and Mouth on Revell Street, and do some shopping at Burke & McHugh's. Buy yourself a new bonnet. Go to the Opera House and see *The Corsican Brothers*…I hear it's very good…" He took a five-pound bank note from his pocket book and handed it to her.

His wife sniffed, straightened her shoulders and nodded to him.

"I shall buy a christening gown for our new little girl," she said. "And some linens." She was convinced that the child inside her was female, and was determined to name the girl Mary Elizabeth. "We'll be needing those before too long."

He did not reply, but nodded agreeably and left for the Greymouth Hospital, where the autopsy was to be performed. Best not to argue with her. She could easily be right.

4

Greymouth, 1866: The Autopsy

On the way along Arney Street he decided to call at the police reserve before the autopsy to see what other business he might have to deal with. His street was still muddy from the floods of the previous month and he walked with some difficulty, his boots drawn into the mire with each step. Every time heavy rain fell, the Grey River rose over the banks and flooded all the homes nearby, including his. The mayor had solicited funds from the provincial government to construct an embankment, and piling work was underway to build a barrier at the end of Boundary Street. He hoped it would help. He was tired of pushing water from the floor of his house every time it rained heavily. Even the pylons that raised his house above the ground were not entirely helpful.

On Boundary Street, he smelled the familiar smell of hogs, and heard a chorus of grunts coming from behind a fence piled high with rubbish. John Heron's place. Heron was the owner of Jack's Nonpareil Pie House where James lunched frequently, but it didn't excuse him from disobeying the law. He shook his head, hoping that Heron was watching from the window. His men had a running battle with Heron, who insisted on keeping pigs inside the town boundary. Mr. Warden Revell had served Heron with a notice saying the pigs were a public nuisance, because of the smell and the noise. Heron had responded with an angry letter to the *Grey River Argus* saying he had "waited upon the author of the said notice (Mr. Revell) and asked him where I was to remove my pigs to, and, in answer, was told outside the town boundary; and yet Mr. Revell can't tell me where that is." He had asked Mr. Revell why Greymouth was not like Victoria, where pigs in town were not interfered with. Mr. Revell had answered, "I don't want to hear anything about Victoria," with which sentiment James heartily agreed. He too was tired of hearing people comparing Greymouth to Victoria, unfavourably. Still, keeping pigs inside town boundaries was the least of his problems. There were too many real criminals for him to deal with.

The police reserve consisted of log huts and calico tents, including sleeping quarters for unmarried troopers, a wash house, a cooking shack, and a horse paddock. His own house on Arney Street backed onto the paddock and he and Mr. Bain, his next door neighbour, were trying to prevent anyone building in the paddock. A station house where he and Sergeant Slattery had their offices, fronted Gresson Street. A new courthouse was under construction on the reserve, which would simplify all their lives. The present courthouse, the government hut beside Mr. Revell's house, had been described by the Argus as a "disgraceful hovel." Fortunately, the Dobson inquest was being held at the Union Hotel, one of the better hotels on Mawhera Quay.

The constable standing outside one of the huts, the armory hut, rifle butt resting on the ground, arm straight out, snapped to attention as he passed. Hardly a week went by without some ruffian trying to break in and steal the guns, and he'd resorted to leaving a constable constantly on guard. It was a damp, bone-tiring task for the constable, with little action, interspersed with sudden flurries of activity when a suspicious character was spotted lurking nearby. No one volunteered for the work and he'd been forced to assign men to it. Some saw it as a punishment. He avoided the constable's gaze as he passed by, knowing it would contain a plea for release.

Sergeant Slattery met him on the steps of the station house, a frown on his broad, ruddy face.

"Morning Inspector. Congratulations on your…"

James silenced him with a wave of his hand. "Joint effort," he said. "Now, what's on for the next few days. The Dobson inquest, I know…"

"And the Rees inquest. That will probably be Monday."

"Mr. Rees, from the Bank of New Zealand?" asked James, surprised. "He's dead?"

"Slashed his own throat last night, he did, died on the floor of his bedroom, covered with blood." Slattery made a slashing gesture across his own throat. "Sergeant Walsh was called in early this morning…blood everywhere, he said. Mr. Rees had a bloody gash across his throat, and the knife was in the middle of the room covered in blood. There was a chamber pot full of blood beside him, apparently."

James put his hand to his own throat and rubbed it instinctively.

"My God, why did he…"

"Because of a woman," said Slattery. "He was living with Ann Fraser, not married to her though. They fought all the time."

James nodded. "I've heard something to that effect."

"And of course, the Bank doesn't look kindly on him for living with a woman who's not his wife."

"What makes you think he did it to himself? Couldn't Ann Fraser have done it?" asked James.

"Doubtful," said Slattery. "He'd told several people he might cut his own throat. Tried to drown himself in the Teremakau River on Friday, before two witnesses, who intervened. And he signed over the house to Mrs. Fraser just recently – he had the Deed of Assignment on his body, as well as a letter to his brother telling him what he was about to do. I have it here." Slattery picked the letter from his desk and gave it to James. "He had overwhelming expenses from some gold speculations, and he felt his position had become so embarrassing that suicide would be the best choice."

"Cut and dried then," said James. "Do you need me for the

examination in court?"

"We do," said Slattery. "Murphy's Hotel, first thing Monday morning." In small towns like Greymouth it was common for the inspector of police to act as the examiner at an inquest, or even as prosecutor at a trial, and James had become proficient at both duties. He would need to move quickly between Murphy's Hotel and the Union Hotel, if the Dobson inquest went into Monday, but Mr. Warden Revell was presiding in both cases so there shouldn't be a problem. For today, he would attend the Dobson autopsy, and then find a glass of ale and a pie at one of the hotels before he went to the inquest. Or he could drop into Jack's Nonpareil Pie House, and have a word with the proprietor, John Heron, about his pig problem.

"Leave your report in my office," he said. "I'll be at the Dobson inquest today, and the funeral tomorrow. I expect the inquest will go on into Monday or Tuesday. But I'll drop by to pick up the report later."

"Watch out for the diggings," said Sergeant Slattery. "There's a rush on the creek on Boundary Street, across the road from Murphy's Hotel, and they've staked claims all along the banks of the creek. A young lad fell into one of the pits yesterday and had to be pulled out by some diggers. The poor woman was hysterical. Thought she'd lost her boy."

He saw the men digging frantically as he went past Murphy's Hotel on the way down Boundary Street to the hospital. Water was filling in the holes almost as fast as they dug them, and he knew it would be a matter of days before they abandoned their claims. There were two reasons prospectors tended to leave a claim: not enough water for the long toms, the sluices that trapped the gold, or water filling the pits. The town was inundated with miners and every possible site where gold might be found had a claim on it. Men were digging along the banks of the river, and the beach and terrace above it had more holes in it than surface. Anyone sighting a bit of black sand, indicating the possibility of gold, jumped on it with claim sticks in hand and sent for Mr. Revell to record the claim. Walking along the beach could be as dangerous as trying to bring a boat in across the sandbar. It was said that in the first six months of the year over 50,000 ounces of gold had been shipped out of the harbour, mostly to Melbourne. Just as well he wasn't still in charge of the ill-conceived gold escort. He and his men had more work than they could handle as it was. Policing Greymouth and the districts nearby was difficult, with all that gold in so many hands, especially the hands of the gold buyers.

Like everything else in Greymouth, the hospital was doing a brisk business. Dr. Foppoly ran it like a military hospital, dressing wounds, removing limbs, bringing children into the world or watching them leave.

Dr. Foppoly had a practice on Albert Street as an Accoucheur and would help Elizabeth when her time came. James preferred a doctor to a midwife although Elizabeth didn't agree. She was nervous about the chloroform Dr. Foppoly might administer, afraid she would fall asleep and never wake up. She had been through childbirth without chloroform before, and would be happy to do it again. Generations of women had suffered, she told him, and she saw no reason to change the old ways now.

They both knew that the death rate for children in town was horrific and the chances of survival for a child in the first three years of life in Greymouth were as low as any town in the colony, which made him worry about his wife. Another lost child would send her to the insane asylum, especially one born alive who survived past infancy. That was something he had blocked from his mind and hoped never to experience again. If it happened to Harry or Louisa, God help them both.

As he passed the lying-in ward he turned away. He could hear the groans and screams of a woman in labour. Elizabeth would have to wait until the last minute for her dose of chloroform. There would be some pain to get through first, despite the soporific…if she decided to take it

The lunatic ward was busy as well; the isolation of the diggings and frequent deaths of young children drove both men and women from their minds. Mr. Rees might have done better to commit himself here, rather than to slash his own throat. But as he passed by the locked doors he heard wailing, groans and guttural sounds. Perhaps Mr. Rees had made the right decision.

He found Dr. Foppoly, a heavy-set, dark-haired, dark-eyed Italian, in his autopsy room, accompanied by Dr. Strehz, the new young doctor who had recently set up a surgery on Richmond Quay, offering vaccinations on request, doing his best to reduce the numbers of smallpox deaths. Why weren't there vaccines against typhoid, and pleurisy, and scarlatina and thrush, and teething pains, and all the other things that killed so many children? Was someone working to develop those right now? The thought of vaccination, with a needle piercing his skin, was unsettling. He'd rather be hit in the arm by a bullet.

Dr. Foppoly nodded to James, tied a heavy cotton butcher's apron over his clothes, then washed his hands briskly with carbolic soap. He was meticulously clean and insisted that everyone in his operating room or autopsy room was as well. He'd taken over temporary management of the hospital in May, and had made it known to the hospital committee that he believed the typhoid outbreak at that time was caused by lack of cleanliness, pointing to the way typhoid and bilious fevers had almost entirely disappeared once winter set in, "confirming," he said, "the theory on malaria during the summer season, and the necessity of the people adopting all the sanitary measures repeatedly suggested by the resident professional men and by the local press."

George Dobson's partially-clothed body lay on a stretcher in the centre of the room, still covered with a layer of soil. A young orderly sat in the corner of the room with a notepad and pencil, ready to take notes. Nearby lay an empty wooden box, while another wooden box, with closed lid, lay on the floor beside the wall. Mr. Rees, probably.

The two doctors started by removing the dirt from the face and body and placing it in a bucket. Then they removed a necktie from around the neck.

"Black silk," commented Dr. Foppoly, glancing at the note taker. "Tied in a sailor's knot by the look of it. Loosely tied." The note taker licked his pencil and began to write furiously.

Foppoly leaned over the body, his face near its face. Dr. Strehz followed suit, almost bumping heads with the older man.

"The muscles have been destroyed from the eye to the chin," Foppoly said, touching the face with his hand and pushing down firmly, causing the face to look as if it was grimacing. "Destroyed to the bone." He pulled apart a wound on the face. "Rats, I should say. Look at these cuts. Caused by the teeth of rats, and not by decomposition. Note that." He nodded in the direction of the note taker.

He took hold of the head and moved it from side to side, staring intently. "Not as much decomposition on the rest of the face as I would expect."

"Something in the soil?" suggested Dr. Strehz tentatively.

Dr. Foppoly shrugged. "Possibly. Help me turn him on his side, if you would." He prodded the head on the left side. "Egg-sized contusion on the temporal bone, extending to the external ear. And here is another one on the top of the head and down the left side. And a third on the back of the head…"

"What size?" asked the note taker.

"I beg your pardon?" asked the doctor, distractedly.

"What size is the contusion on the back of the head?"

"Hmmm," he rolled the body over the other way "The size of a half crown piece, I should say. In the occipital region. And another the size of a crown piece on this - on the left side."

He picked up a knife and James closed his eyes briefly, knowing what was coming. When he opened them again the scalp had been cut through and pulled partly over the face. He took a few deeps breaths to stop himself from gagging. The doctor seemed to sense his unease and grinned at him wolfishly. "Feeling all right, Inspector James?"

"Very well, thank you," said James. "Although I've never cared for that particular sight."

"The contusions pass right through the skull integuments," the doctor continued. "The skull is discoloured, see that Strehz?"

"Most of the body is discoloured," said Strehz, stating the obvious. "Decomposition?"

Dr. Foppoly nodded and pushed back the head, his knife in hand, and started to cut into the neck.

"Here's another wound, you can see from the darker colour on the left side of the neck."

"Exactly where the jugular passes through," said Dr. Strehz, somewhat triumphantly.

"Size?" asked the note taker.

"About the size of, well, I would say about the size of a sixpenny piece," said Dr. Foppoly, continuing his monetary theme. "Made by a thumb, perhaps. And look here, these red stripes running down towards the shoulder."

"More of the same on the right side of the neck," said Dr. Strehz. "About a quarter of an inch apart. But no thumb print on that side."

Foppoly inserted four fingers into the mouth and pried it apart.

"A tooth missing from the upper jaw. Gone for some time I believe. And another one from the lower jaw. The stump still remaining on that one."

"What has happened to the tongue?" asked Dr. Strehz.

"Looks like he bit some of it off," said Foppoly. He let the mouth go and lifted his knife again, making a long cut down the throat. James wondered briefly if Edward Dobson had already seen his son. He hoped he would not have to look at the ruined body on the table.

"Adam's apple has been flattened and pushed up to the chin."

James leaned forward. He'd heard that one before, in Victoria.

Foppoly picked up a small mallet and chisel and attacked the skull, pried it open and commented on the fluid nature of the brain, which was apparently normal.

James' mind started to wander. Dobson had been beaten about the head, probably with the stock of a gun, until he was half senseless, and then someone had strangled him. Someone with a dominant left hand who knew that pushing the larynx up into the throat was an effective way to kill someone. A neophyte would assume merely blocking off the breath with a tight grip would do the job.

Where this man—or these men had purchased - or stolen - their guns was something he should investigate. No place in Greymouth to buy them. He only half heard the rest of the autopsy, with vague words floating in and out of his consciousness: "No skull fracture…lungs congested with blood, especially on the left…intestines, bowel, liver, all healthy." The sight of the doctor removing all these parts caused him to avert his eyes, but he couldn't escape the sound of the shears clipping at the skin and muscle, or the smell of blood and bodily fluids that permeated the room.

He started to pay attention again when the doctor began to state his conclusions, slowly and clearly to allow the note taker time to get it all down: "The alteration we found in the respiratory organs are visibly the effect of the violent pressure of a hand on the throat. The mark on the jugular vein may be caused by a thumb, and the person who committed the deed must have used the left hand. The cause of death was the blows to the head and the pressure on the larynx in an upward direction until suffocation ensued. The handkerchief was not used to strangle the deceased, for if it had it would have caused a circular mark round the neck, but would not have displaced the larynx as was done."

James had one question, which he would ask again at the inquest. "Any use of acid or vitriol on the face that you can tell?"

Dr. Foppoly shook his head firmly. "Definitely not. Now, Strehz, if you can just put the gentleman back together again so we can show him to the jury without all of them fainting, I would be most appreciative. And have the men take him over to the Union Hotel for the inquest. Put him in the lean-to beside the kitchen. I think I shall take some lunch before I'm due in court. Jack's perhaps." He looked at James from the corner of his eye, smiling slightly. "A steak and kidney pie would hit the spot."

He took off his apron and hung it on a hook in the corner, washed his hands in a bowl of water with carbolic soap once more, and carefully selected a clean area of the blood-soaked apron to dry his hands.

5

Greymouth, 1866: The Inquest: Day One

Inspector James was not quite as hungry as the doctor, but decided he would at least have a cup of tea at the Jack's Nonpareil Pie House, and perhaps a small fish pie – or anything that didn't involve organs – if his stomach could handle it, before going to the Union Hotel. The inquest would take some time, possibly even more than a day, as a jury had been empaneled and there were several witnesses who would be taking the stand. The task of the jurors was to deliver a finding about the fate of George Dobson. Had he been murdered, died by accident, or by his own hand? Inspector James knew the answer, but could not lay charges without a finding of murder by person or person unknown.

John Heron, proprietor of Jack's, and owner of the pigs illegally kept within the town limits, served him his pie and hovered by his table, seemingly wanting to say something. "Mr. Inspector James…"

James looked at his pie and waited, his fork poised for action.

"I heard…is the inquest for Mr. Dobson today?"

"I'm going there as soon as I finish my pie," said James, hoping Heron would take the hint.

"Those murderers," said Heron hesitantly. "They were in here back in May – around the time Mr. Dobson disappeared."

"Which ones?" asked James, not wanting to put words into Heron's mouth. He took up his fork and began to eat. No time to be polite.

He had an inquest to attend.

"Burgess and Sullivan – I knew them both – and two fair men. Small men they were, the other two."

Burgess, Levy and Kelly were all short, while Sullivan was an above average height. But both Burgess and Kelly were dark. Levy was short and fair, and the only other short fair man connected to the gang was Wilson.

"Would you recognize the other two if you saw them?"

Heron shook his head. "I don't think I would. I see so many people in here. But the two short fair men stuck in my head for some reason."

"I don't suppose you heard them say anything," said James, wiping up the last of the gravy from the pie with a chunk of bread. If he had an identification he could put Wilson together with the gang in an interesting way, but a comment implying foreknowledge would be very useful.

"I didn't hear anything," said Heron. "But they asked me to do something for them. They asked me to take care of a swag and a shovel. When I picked up the swag to move it behind the counter it was fearfully heavy."

Guns, most likely. "Have you been called as a witness at the inquest?"

Heron picked up James' empty plate. "No. This is the first time I've said anything. Do you think it's important?"

"You're sure you can't identify the two fair men?"

"No. I'm sorry."

"We may call you at pre-trial," said James. "But unless you're willing to identify all four men I'm not sure how useful you will be. Thanks for mentioning it, however."

He stood up to leave, but Heron was not done.

"About my pigs," he said. "Mr. Warden Revell says…"

"You'll have to take it up with Mr. Revell," said James, beating a hasty retreat before Heron tied his pig problem to an identification of the short fair men.

As he entered the Union Hotel later, one of his constables handed him a letter from the police in Nelson that had arrived while he was searching for Dobson. He scanned through it quickly. This was what he had been waiting for. He had half an hour before court was to begin, so went into the billiard room and found himself a seat. He would read as much as he could before the magistrate arrived.

Half an hour later, pleased with how things were going, he entered the room where the inquest was to be held and found himself a seat at the end of a row, a few rows from the front. The letter, as he had hoped, contained a confession from Joseph Thomas Sullivan, one of the murderers from the Burgess gang – the same man who had turned Queen's evidence on the murders up in Nelson. Major Shallcrass had attached a note saying the police in Nelson found Sullivan's description of the murders highly credible and that he expected to bring the other three gang members to justice using Sullivan's statement.

When he came to the murder of George Dobson, the one that now occupied Inspector James, Sullivan had pointed his finger at Jamie Wilson, alias Murray, saying that Wilson, a sometime bellman and petty thief from Nelson, "was concerned with Burgess, Kelly and Levy in the murder." Actual participation – that was more than James had expected, and he felt a strong sense of satisfaction.

Sullivan claimed they had initially left Dobson at the foot of a tree to make it appear he had died of exhaustion, but later decided that would not do and had returned and buried him, adding some details about the contents of the grave, which matched what James himself had seen as the body was uncovered. James knew that Sullivan could tell a good story. He'd arrested Sullivan back in Victoria, for the murder of two Jew hawkers on the Wedderburn Road. The men had been tied to a tree with leather straps, and then burned to death. He hadn't been able to connect Sullivan to that crime and would hate to see get away with another one. But at the time he'd been impressed with Sullivan's memory for the details; in James' experience most criminals were caught out by their own feeble attempts at perverting the truth.

Sullivan knew to stick to the truth most of the time.

Wilson was in the courtroom, guarded by one of James' constables, his wrists fastened with cuffs; he'd been brought up from Hokitika, as per James' instructions. If the inquest went as he expected, he intended to charge Wilson with the murder. He would ask for a remand as well to give him time to make his case. The rest of the gang were beyond his reach in Nelson, but Wilson would pay for what he had done. Wilson tried to catch his eye, looking for understanding and sympathy, but James kept his eyes fixed ahead; he had read Sullivan's confession and knew what he knew.

Mr. Revell, the magistrate, entered and everyone rose. William Revell had started life in Greymouth as the government storekeeper, and was now the government agent, goldfields warden, resident magistrate, coroner, and returning officer.[ii] As a young man, "Big Bill" Revell had been a member of the armed constabulary in Kaiapoi, near Christchurch, and still fancied himself as a police detective. Sometimes that notion of his interfered with James' work.

Once they were all seated again, Revell addressed the jury: "You have been assembled to inquire how, where and when, and by what means the deceased man came by his death," he said, the seriousness of his face signaling the importance of the task before them. "I would ask you to discharge from your minds anything which you might have read or heard outside this room touching this matter, and to return a verdict strictly in accordance with the evidence which will be laid before you."

The jurymen nodded their agreement. They were serious men, shopkeepers, clerks, and landowners, British subjects over twenty-one, with voting rights, which now included anyone with a mining license, although there was a move afoot to stop goldfields suffrage.

"Now, you must proceed to view the body of Mr. Dobson," said Mr. Revell.

As the jury left, James looked around the court. He could see Charles

Todhunter seated at the front of the room, with Mr. Edward Dobson, father of the victim, beside him. Dobson was a fit-looking man a few years older than Inspector James, probably no more than fifty. He'd arrived quickly. James wondered if it was he who had brought the letter from the Nelson gaol, or at least a companion. If so, the Nelson police would have provided him with an armed guard for the journey, no one wishing to see another murdered Dobson.

After some time, the jury returned, some with somber faces, others looking pale. A body that badly decomposed was not easy for a man to look at, even in a town where unexpected deaths were commonplace. He hoped Dr. Strehz had done his best work putting the face back into a semblance of normalcy.

Mr. Warden Revell watched as the jury filed in, then spoke to the court.

"Inspector James, if you would please take the stand?"

James glanced at his notes and addressed the court, as he had done so many times before: "On Tuesday, the 3rd instant, I proceeded up the Grey river, with a party, to search for the body of George Dobson, at a spot about one mile on the Canterbury side below the coal-pits, on the Arnold track. The instructions where to find the body had been received by telegram from Nelson, and were said to have been given by the prisoner Sullivan. For the first three days we were unsuccessful, and on Friday, the 6th inst., I commenced the search at a point a mile below the spot indicated on a tracing which I received from Nelson by special constable O'Brien on the previous day, as the tracing indicated the locality which we had already searched for three days." He paused and looked up from his notes; the members of the jury were taking in every word. "At five minutes to twelve o'clock I was in the act of crossing a log which lay over a blind creek or gully, when I felt a strong smell, and I called Constable McIlroy's attention to the spot, and told him to make a strict search near it."

As he told the court about the brandy bottle they had found, followed by the footprints, and then finally the sighting of the tip of the boot sticking up from the grave, he noticed the jury were all leaning forward, straining to hear every word. He heard a groan from the courtroom, which was crowded with residents of Greymouth, men and women both; he thought it may have come from Mr. Todhunter. The rest of the assemblage were so utterly silent that they might well have been asleep, if not for the fixed stares with which they regarded James.

He continued with his evidence: "When the earth was removed, we found that Mr. Dobson's Inverness cape was lying across the lower part of his body and legs, and that his Albert gold guard was hanging on his vest, and his silver watch in his vest pocket. On removing the cape to one side I found a prismatic compass in a case, a tape, and a field book lying on the legs, and on each side of the body two leather straps were lying. On examining the watch, I found that it had stopped at twenty-seven minutes to four o'clock, but it had been run down."

He dropped his bombshell quietly. "I have today received a copy of Sullivan's confession, wherein he states that the articles found in the grave, and now produced, were buried with the body."

He heard a hum within the court, causing Mr. Revell to frown and tap his gavel gently on the table in front of him. One of the gang had confessed! And it was Joseph Sullivan who had done so, the same gang member who had pointed the search party, unsuccessfully as it turned out, to the site where the body might be buried, the place where the gang had supposedly pitched their tent. The entire courtroom was transfixed.

James next told the court that Mr. Todhunter had identified the body on the spot, using various garments, the general appearance of the body, and the watch chain, and that Mr. Matthew Russell, who was well acquainted with the deceased, had confirmed the identification.

A member of the jury raised his hand with a question. He had seen the face and wondered about the condition of the grave and how that had affected the body in the weeks it had lain there. "The earth was not removed from the face," James answered. "There were no rat holes about, the earth was hard on the surface, having been apparently trodden down. There was a greater depth of earth on the upper than on the lower part of the body. The earth was mixed with fern and clay, and as tenacious as if it had been trodden down."

He concluded by explaining a theory he had in mind that George Dobson's hands or legs had been bound, possibly to a tree, but loosened after the body was placed in its grave. He had no proof, but marks on the body had indicated that it might be the case. He knew that the leather straps found in the grave did not belong to Dobson, or at least no one had identified them as belonging to him. He stood and ceded his spot to Mr. Todhunter who was to confirm the identification he had made at the site.

Todhunter, blinking rapidly as if to stop tears, began by mentioning the watch and the Inverness cape, adding that he also recognized his brother-in-law's hands, teeth, hair, the shape of one leg, and a bone which projected from his thumb. When he finished, Mr. Russell stood to confirm his own identification.

Then it was the turn of Dr. Foppoly. Inspector James had already made notes from the autopsy while he drank his tea at the pie shop. He sat staring at the court, prepared to re-ask his question about acid or vitriol and waited. After he finally had the opportunity to ask Dr. Foppoly his question, and have it answered, a juror wanted to know if it was possible that the wounds were self-inflicted. The doctor replied, with an audible sigh, that it was not possible that they had been. His part was finished, and he left the stand. Mr. Revell pulled out his watch and suggested they adjourn until Tuesday. Witnesses were travelling from various places along the Arnold, from Maori Gulley, and from other places in the district and may need time to get to Greymouth.

Inspector James had one more request, and he stood to make it.

"I wish to charge James, Wilson—alias James Murray—with the willful murder of George Dobson, on the Grey and Arnold track, on or about the 28thof May last," he began. He noticed the reporter from the Grey River Argus start to scribble madly in his notebook. "The prisoner has been in custody in Hokitika on another charge," he continued, "but I now bring him up on the charge of murdering George Dobson." He outlined the circumstances of the murder, repeating what he had already said about finding the body, and concluded by asking for a remand. "There are other parties implicated in the murder." He would need Sullivan and his confession to convict Wilson, and getting the man from Nelson to Hokitika, where the supreme court trial would be held, would take time.

The magistrate granted the application and remanded Wilson to Hokitika until the following Monday. As Wilson was led away, he exchanged a frantic look with James. "It weren't me as did it," he said. "You know it weren't." James looked back at him coldly and did not reply. Perhaps there was not enough yet to prove Wilson's culpability, but there would be. He just needed to accumulate facts and eye witness accounts to make his case. A strong circumstantial case accompanied by Sullivan's confession should do it.

He sat for a while in the court room, thinking. The Rees inquest had been set for Monday and he was free until then, other than attending the Dobson funeral. Mr. Revell came down from the bench to talk to him.

"It's been a busy week," he said to the magistrate.

Mr. Revell nodded. "I had one of your fellows in here on Thursday. Did you hear about it? Up on larceny."

"One of my fellows?" asked James, surprised. He hadn't heard about any problems in his camp, and usually he would…although he had been up on the Arnold track most of the week.

"One of Inspector Broham's men, strictly speaking," said Revell. "Constable John Carr, from the police camp in Hokitika. The same Constable Carr who shot himself in the thigh with his own revolver during the New Year's Eve Irish riots down there. He was captured here by your men. I merely remanded him to Hokitika."

"I was told about Mr. Rees, the bank manager," said James, "but…"

"A busy week, as you said."

"What did Constable Carr steal?"

Mr. Revell marked the items off with his fingers. "Two pairs of riding pants, one cross-belt and pouch, one large sized Colt's revolver, one small sized Colt's revolver, two Dean and Adam's revolvers and cases—from the police camp in Hokitika."

Inspector James frowned. "Guns I can understand, but riding pants? Why would anyone want to steal a pair of riding pants?" He would have to go down to Hokitika and talk with Broham about this robbery. Apart from the fact that he reported to Broham and needed to keep him up to date on developments, the robbery could very well have some connection to his own case against Wilson, although how was unclear.

As he left the courthouse the reporter from the Argus accosted him. He was a small man, thin, with a suit that might have been passed down by an older brother and a greasy-looking bowler. He carried a notebook and a pencil in front of him, ready to write down anything Inspector James might say.

"Mr. James, Mr. James."

"I have nothing to say to the Argus."

"Could you tell our readers why you didn't arrest the gang, before they went to Nelson and…"

He shook his head firmly and walked on, ignoring the reporter's entreaties to let him have at least a word or two. What was the use? They were going to have his hide in the press anyway. They always did.

6

Greymouth, 1866: The Funeral

The rain was coming down in icy sheets as Inspector James left his house the next afternoon, a steady, cold rain that looked like it had set in for the day. He had his umbrella with him, and a good Inverness cape lined with India rubber that would keep him relatively dry and warm for George Dobson's funeral, taking place at the cemetery near South Beach.

It was Sunday, which he usually spent with his wife and children, but they were still in Hokitika. He expected them back later in the day, if the rain didn't strand them south of the Teremakau. The river, half way between Hokitika and Greymouth, would be in full spate, making a crossing difficult. A ferry punt had been swept off its ropes last year, and barely saved by a man holding his horse behind the ferry on a short rope; the horse had pulled the ferry punt with all the passengers to shore. And just a few weeks ago a young lad had been swept away and drowned while trying to ford the river on his horse.

He took Charlie with him, to give him a walk, which was usually Louisa's job.

Less than a fortnight ago, a two-day rainfall, coupled with unseasonably warm weather that melted snow up in the ranges, had filled the Grey until it burst its banks. Boundary Street, Gresson Street, and his street, Arney Street, were all several feet under water, and when townspeople began to use boats to navigate the streets some jokingly began to call the town Venice on the Grey. Mr. Revell had navigated his boat from the Court House down the Lagoon, around the outskirts of town, and moored it to the verandah of a store in Boundary street, much to the amusement of the storekeeper. He and Elizabeth and the children had passed an extremely difficult night sitting on the piano trying not to fall asleep, with water swirling around their feet, cold and hungry. The flood had taken them all by surprise, even Charlie, who had taken off somewhere, returning happily the next day, his coat damp, but otherwise no worse for wear. He was an expert swimmer and James suspected he had spent the time of the flood exploring the town.

He'd rubbed Charlie's neck and murmured, "You were supposed to keep us safe." The dog had favoured him with a wagging tail and a "woof," to show his appreciation of what he naturally assumed was a compliment.

As he walked along Mawhera Quay to his destination he could see a dozen vessels in port, all of them with ensigns lowered to half-mast. A sign of respect for George Dobson and his family, no doubt. It seemed most of Greymouth was set on attending the funeral. A throng of humanity was moving towards the Union Hotel, from where the funeral procession would proceed. Every class of person in town was represented: shopkeepers, businessmen, bankers, lawyers and men from the public service, many of whom had worked with George Dobson in Hokitika, even diggers. They moved forward in a stream of black umbrellas, dark suits, and tall hats, a few accompanied by wives and daughters in dark gowns and shawls.

He stayed back from the surging tide, which came to an abrupt halt as it neared the Union Hotel. Charlie was not fond of crowds and he tugged at his leash, wanting to return home. James put his hand down and stroked the animal's back, calming him. He'd trained the dog well, and he would attack anyone who threatened the family if his master said the word. But in a crowd like this he seemed cowed and uncertain of himself.

The body had been taken to the hotel after the autopsy, and would go from there in a funeral procession to Greymouth Cemetery, where the Lord Bishop of Christchurch was to perform a graveside service. At Edward Dobson's request, George Dobson was to be buried beside Mr. Whitmore and Mr. Townsend, two surveyors who had drowned during an expedition with Julius von Haast.

James stood by the steps of the Shotover Hotel and waited for the funeral procession to leave the Union. The hotel was for sale, he noticed. Perhaps he should leave the police and buy it. Being a hotel-keeper might be an interesting change, although owning one of the fifty-seven hotels in town might also be foolish: as he'd seen in Victoria, the halcyon days of a gold rush did not last forever and he'd be left with an empty hotel.

The crowd was noisy, almost festive, but when the double doors of the hotel opened a hush fell. The owner of the hotel and two members of his staff, all dressed in black, hats in hand, came out first and held the doors wide. Then came the Bishop, looking resplendent in his purple cassock and white surplice. A young boy walked beside him and quickly deployed an umbrella over the Bishop's head. Next came the coffin, placed on a stretcher, carried by four black-clad undertakers. A group of young men in suits and bowlers had been waiting on the verandah, and they sprang forward to take hold of the coffin; George Dobson's friends and workmates, by the look of them, as well as Mr. Rochfort, his supervisor. Behind the coffin came three men: Mr. Edward Dobson, and his two sons-in-law, Dr. Julius von Haast, the geologist, and Charles Todhunter. James wondered briefly if Arthur Dobson, George's closest brother in age, would be with them, but did not see him. Although Mr. Todhunter and Mr. Dobson were already in town, and had been for some time, he'd not seen Arthur at all. Not for the search, and now not for the funeral. Curious. The mother and sisters he could understand; the trip would be too grueling for them. But his brother, who had explored this district in the early days...?

GREYMOUTH, 1866: THE FUNERAL

The cortege walked down Mawhera and Richmond Quays and made its way to the bridge on Boundary Street. He could see a horse-drawn dray forcing its way through the water beside the Blaketown Bridge, which was large enough only for foot traffic or a small trap. A new bridge was to be built at the end of his own street, across the lagoon, which would mean that coaches travelling south to Hokitika wouldn't have to ford the lagoon and would reach Hokitika that much faster. With each improvement, the town became more accessible to the world, making it more comfortable to live there, but bringing in more and more of the sort he wanted to keep out.

They crossed the bridge, the rain still pouring down, and walked down the track through Blaketown to the beach. A dray pulled by two large black Percherons sat there waiting to convey the coffin along the sand to South Beach; but Dobson's workmates refused to give up their burden. They intended to carry it all the way to the cemetery, more than two miles along the beach from where the dray sat.

He cast a wistful look at the dray, which all the mourners now felt obliged to refuse. Walking on a wet beach at any time was difficult, and the rain was making things worse, although at least the gravel gave his boots some purchase. To make matters worse, the frequent holes made by diggers in search of gold in the black sand forced the procession to weave up and down the beach above the tide mark, the coffin bearers struggling bravely with determined looks on their faces. Every now and then a townsperson stepped forward to relieve one of the young men, but each one would return to his task as soon as he felt able.

Edward Dobson, Mr. Todhunter, and Dr. von Haast walked behind the coffin without umbrellas, hats in hand, heads high, shoulders squared. Behind them came Mr. Warden Revell, Mr. Warden Kynnersley of Cobden, and Commissioners Sale and Shearman. It was Shearman who had brought James to New Zealand, had hired him for the gold escort, and had given him his current assignment. Shearman fell into step with James, and said quietly, "Well done, finding the body."

"It took me some time," said James. "But now we must find and charge the culprits."

"I have complete trust in you, Inspector James," said Shearman. "This case could be the making of you, so give it your best. It will help wipe away the stain from Timaru as well. Inspector Broham will report to me on your findings."

The stain. Would he ever live it down, that momentary loss of control?

Finally, they reached the place where they would turn inland: a small creek that ran down from the cemetery to the beach.[ii] The track beside the creek was well-worn and muddy, and they were forced to climb over fallen logs on the way to the grave site. Dr. Harper led the way, holding his skirts aloft, the umbrella boy still at his side, until the mourners were clustered at the graveside. The rain was accumulating in the tarpaulin covering the grave and the men carrying the coffin put it down to shake off the water. The grave would be partially flooded as well, but they were used to that. This was Greymouth, the wettest town in the Middle Island. Large pools of stagnant water also surrounded the burial sites, most of which were nothing more than mounds of sand, some with crosses stuck into them.

When everyone had gathered, Dr. Harper began by offering a quick prayer, followed by the suggestion that they sing a hymn: *For the Beauty of the Earth*, most appropriately. He led off the singing, his deep voice firm and on key:

For the beauty of the earth,
  For the beauty of the skies,
  For the love which from our birth
  Over and around us lies,
  Lord of all, to thee we raise
  This our hymn of grateful praise.

GREYMOUTH, 1866: THE FUNERAL

For the beauty of each hour
Of the day and of the night,
Hill and vale, and tree and flow'r,
Sun and moon, and stars of light,
For the joy of human love,
Brother, sister, parent, child,
Friends on earth, and friends above,
For all gentle thoughts and mild,
Lord of all, to thee we raise
This our hymn of grateful praise.

The townsfolk joined in enthusiastically, their voices rising above the sound of the not-too-distant surf and the patter of rain on the mud. Edward Dobson, Dr. von Haast and Charles Todhunter added their voices as well; the two older men remained stoic, but Charles Todhunter had tears streaming down his cheeks, only partly disguised by the rain.

The Dobson crew were a tough lot, it seemed. Inspector James watched the three of them, as well as John Rochfort, who stood nearby, dressed in a flashy suit and bowler hat, a bit of a swell it seemed. Rochfort had been George Dobson's supervisor at the survey department, and was engaged to marry the sister of Arthur Dobson's fiancée. An interconnected group, not only by interest but by marriage. One of the larger mountains in the Southern Alps was named for Rochfort—by Dr. von Haast as it happened. Rochfort's role in finding gold and coal in the area had led to von Haast's geological survey. The extended Dobson family must feel that this was their town, their mountains, and their coastline, making it that much more difficult to accept the loss of the eldest son of the family patriarch.

As the ceremony continued, James looked around at the graveyard. It was not the kind of place he'd like as his final resting place. The town had set aside this piece of land in the bush, but miners were working nearby and threatening to spill into the area. Already it was covered with the tracks of men and cattle, some even crossing the sandy grave sites. James imagined that Edward Dobson would be horrified, seeing the place where his son was to lie for eternity. No doubt the family had a crypt in Christchurch, but taking the body back there from the west coast would be difficult, if not impossible, and there wasn't much purpose to it. The body would have turned to soup by the time it arrived.

The ceremony was over, the tarpaulin removed from the grave and the coffin lowered slowly, while the mourners watched solemnly. The rain had stopped falling and a fine sea mist hung in the air. The townspeople flocked towards the beach and James went with them. He'd intended to have another talk with Shearman, but could see him in the distance, striding purposefully towards town with Commissioner Sale. So instead he found an outcrop of rocks thrusting up from the sand and sat down to have a pipe and let Charlie run free for a few minutes. The tobacco was only slightly damp and after wasting three matches and sucking vigorously at the pipe he managed to get it started. Charlie took off towards the sea and plunged in joyously. James watched, and steeled himself for the shower of water he would endure when the dog returned. A man on a horse was riding along in the surf parallel to the beach, and the horse reared a little when the dog approached. Riding in the surf was a way to avoid being robbed. Robbers in general could not swim as well as Charlie, who could easily pull a man off his horse and bring him to shore.

As the last of the townspeople disappeared down the beach he heard a noise behind him. The four men, Dobson senior, von Haast, Rochfort, and Todhunter were coming from the grave site. Seemingly they had remained behind to share some final words or thoughts over the last resting place of George Dobson. Mr. Rochfort was holding forth on the loss they had suffered.

"I don't know how we will ever replace George," he said. "He was a good fellow, as honest as the day, always did his duty, first rate at marking a track…."

Edward Dobson nodded, looking at the ground as he walked, his face grim.

"Cut off in his prime by such wretches…"

"Has someone told Arthur?" he heard Todhunter say.

Most of the answer disappeared in the wind, but he heard the words, "No…Golden Bay…another month," from von Haast and a rumbled word from Edward Dobson: "Distraught."

He watched the four men walk briskly down the beach, a sense of power emanating from them. What would they do now? Would they leave him to do his work, or be on him at every move? He'd already interviewed Wilson in the presence of Edward Dobson and Charles Todhunter, and it had been difficult to stop them asking questions and uttering threats. Dobson senior had seemed barely able to stop himself from grabbing Wilson by the throat.

In front of him a group of three men were working a dig, a barrel of sea water beside them, bringing up the dark sand and sluicing it through a sieve. A dark line of seaweed separated them from the high tide mark and the water. The scene would make an interesting Indian ink sketch. He went over to watch them, but they looked at him suspiciously.

"Finding anything?" he asked.

"Nowt," replied one curtly. "Ready to give up. Nothing good here."

As he walked away, he saw the man digging frantically. A lot of effort for nowt. Diggers were notoriously protective of their claims and in constant fear that if they found the colour someone would be waiting to snatch away the winnings.

He whistled for the dog and it came galloping up from the water, its tongue hanging out. The walk along the beach back to town was bracing, and he arrived ready for a meal. If Elizabeth decided to return from Hokitika today, they would be on the late coach. He would have a steak and kidney pie and a pint at one of the hotels and stay around for their arrival. It wasn't possible to set your watch by the coach, but it usually arrived between five and six o'clock.

7

Greymouth, 1866: The Coach Returns

The road alongside the wharf was full of diggers walking along Mawhera Quay past the area rented out by the Maori landowners, looking for a cheap place to stay while they replenished their supplies and had their weekly debauch. Some of them had congregated outside a particularly run down hotel, leaning against the railing of the verandah, pulling on pipes. They did not look like men who had been laboring hard in the fresh forest and streams, but were mostly pale and wasted, the effect of living in shade during the day, and a foggy miasma at night, caused by the immense mass of damp and decaying matter. They would have looked more at home in the hospital ward than on the streets of Greymouth.

An old Maori woman with tattooed chin squatted nearby, pipe clenched between her teeth, on the lookout for marks willing to pay for a night's lodging with gold. The Maori had proved adaptable to the change they'd had to make when their pa had been plowed under to extend the wharf upriver, although many of them had moved grudgingly to Hokitika. Those who remained in Greymouth had taken up the search for gold, at which they had proven to be adept. It was unfortunate they had lost their village, but that was progress.

The thoroughfare alongside the Grey was narrow, and getting narrower by the day as the river ate away at the riverbank and came nearer to the shops clinging to the opposite side of the street. That

GREYMOUTH, 1866: THE COACH RETURNS

the town was prosperous could be seen at a glance, and Elizabeth and Louisa could have found anything they wanted here, but he was happy he'd sent them to Hokitika, nevertheless. Better that they were away from the town for a day or two. The inquest would have stirred up the criminal classes and he wasn't yet sure of the names of everyone connected to Burgess.

The coach pulled in, Louisa sitting up beside the coachman, looking pink and happy. He was annoyed with Elizabeth, who had placed Louisa in such a risky position, but he said nothing as he helped her down.

"I was riding up with the driver," she told him. She threw her arms around Charlie and began talking to him softly. The dog started to wag his tail, enjoying the attention.

"I saw," he said, but already she was ignoring him, her attention entirely on the dog.

Elizabeth climbed out of the door of the coach, trying not to step on the beach sand clinging to the step, looking apologetic. She had Harry, whom she had decided to take with her, clutched in one arm, and a parcel in the other. James took Harry from her and jiggled him, moving his head back and laughing as Harry grabbed at his mustache. His hand felt like ice.

"Are you cold, Harry?" asked James. He looked at him more closely. Perhaps it had not been a good idea to take him to Hokitika. His lips were almost blue. He was about to say something, but Elizabeth spoke first.

"I bought a christening gown for our new little girl," she said.

"Very good," he said. His son would just have to tolerate looking like a girl when he was christened. He wouldn't know any different, and perhaps it would make him more artistic when he was older. "Dr. Harper, who is here for the funeral, will be holding Divine service at the Greymouth Institute this evening. Would you like to attend?"

"I just want to go home," said Louisa, looking up from her post beside the dog. "I'm tired."

Elizabeth smiled apologetically. "We're all tired, especially Harry. "I suppose I should go, but…"

One of his constables walked by and touched his cap. James nodded back, thinking of the next few days, and how much he had to do. The Rees inquest. Then the continuation of the Dobson inquest on Tuesday.

"Excuse me, Mr. Inspector James."

James turned. "Yes?"

"The prisoner Wilson has requested that you come and see him. He's in a state of agitation, has been ever since he heard about the confession in court yesterday. Says he hears terrible things…"

"Could it wait until morning?"

"Sergeant Slattery is worried about the state of his mind. He thinks he might do himself some harm if you don't come as soon as you can."

Inspector James glanced at Elizabeth and Louisa, waiting for him.

"I'll be there within the hour," he said. "Just as soon as I accompany my wife and children home."

"I shall come home as soon as I can," he said to Louisa. "And we'll have some music." He knew she loved to sing, and sometimes he would accompany her on the piano. His piano was still drying out from the floods, but he would manage to squeeze a sound out of it. Charlie loped alongside them, happy to be going home.

"How was Mary Ann," he asked his wife quietly, as Louisa skipped ahead of them down Arney Street.

"Very sad," replied Elizabeth. "I don't know how she'll cope. But she says she will have more children. Many more children."

"Well, good luck to her," said Inspector James somberly, his arms tightening around Harry, who had his thumb stuck firmly in his mouth, his fair curls resting on his father's shoulder, fast asleep.

The home the force rented for him in Greymouth was a substantial two-storied house with a verandah. It had a tiled roof, rather than the commoner corrugated iron roof, a large window in the parlor that looked out over the verandah, and a brick fireplace with a tall chimney. He was pleased with it. Most of the houses in Greymouth were constructed of wood and calico, tinder boxes ready to burn in an instant. They were warmed by stoves with thin pipes that passed through the walls and ended just above the roofs, ready for a spark to jump out and set light to the walls. The waterfront, from where he had just come, was the scene of frequent drunkenness and at night men reeled down streets like his to collapse in a drunken stupor onto a cotton tick mattress with lit pipes still clenched between their teeth. He had set two large butts of water on either side of his front steps and insisted that they were always full; he could not help what his neighbours were doing, but he could take care of his own.

Before he went back to the lockup he made sure that Elizabeth and the children were safe inside and tied Charlie loosely to a post on the verandah. The dog would protect the three of them to the death. And if that was not enough, he'd placed an old Enfield rifled musket on a bracket on the wall of the kitchen close to the front door and had taught Elizabeth how to use it. She was reluctant, of course, but could at least point it at a villain if necessary. Greymouth was a hard town, with all the gold flooding the area. But they had both spent time in other hard towns – gold towns mostly – especially in Victoria. She did not expect him to stay by her side and keep her safe, although perhaps she should.

Wilson was pacing up and down inside his tiny cell, tearing at his hair. He lunged at the door of his cell when he saw James, a desperate look in his eyes.

"Mr. Inspector James," he said. "Thank God you've come. I can't be in this cell any longer, I…"

"We can hardly let you go free," said James. "You're facing a serious charge…"

"Not free," said Wilson. "Not free. Put someone in here with me. I hear things in the night. I hear such dreadful things."

"You're our only prisoner," said Sergeant Slattery, standing behind

James. "There's nothing for you to hear."

Wilson glanced at Slattery. "Not real things," he said. "I hear things in my head. It's driving me out of my mind. I'm afraid what I'm going to do to myself."

James turned away from the bars and said quietly to Slattery, "We could put Walsh in with him…"

A look of distaste flicked across Slattery's face. "He'd hurt the prisoner," he said. "Or want to join his gang."

James smiled. "Now, now Sergeant Slattery. What about McIlroy, then?"

"He's left the force," said Slattery.

A piercing scream came from the cell. "He's at it again," said Slattery. "He's been doing that for hours. I can go in and give him a whack with my stick if you like."

"As much as I'd like that, I don't think I can allow it." Especially not with Shearman in town. He'd used his stick on a prisoner back in Timaru and had almost been kicked off the force. But Shearman had come to his aid and hired him to lead the gold escort. No need to push his luck there. Shearman was a company man when it came down to it.

James turned and peered in through the gloom in the cell. Wilson had thrown himself to the floor and was pounding the ground as he screamed.

"Now then, Wilson," he said. "I'm afraid you've done a terrible thing, or at least you've been an accessory to a terrible thing, and you're going to have to pay for it. That's the law."

Wilson's lifted his head from the floor. "But you promised, Mr. Inspector James. You promised me that you would be lenient when I…"

"I did not," said James. "I promised you nothing. "We're remanding you to Hokitika tomorrow after the inquest, and I can do nothing more for you. You'll have plenty of company in the Logs in Hokitika. You can ask Inspector Broham for help." Broham would be most sympathetic, no doubt about that. Wilson would be lucky if Broham didn't make him live on bread and water until the trial.

Sergeant Slattery thrust forward a copy of an engraving offering a reward for information on the murder of George Dobson. "You could leave this with him."

James took it and threaded it between the bars of the cell.

"Read this, Wilson. I'll see you at the inquest tomorrow, and if you have anything to say to me you can say it then. Goodnight."

He left Wilson sobbing on the dirt floor of the lockup and went home to his family.

8

Greymouth, 1866: The Inquest: Day Two

The inquest resumed on Tuesday, and started with Dr. Strehz being called to the stand. He stood there, rigid, one thumb tucked into his vest, nervously answering the questions already answered satisfactorily by Dr. Foppoly. He was less used to the process than Foppoly. Eventually the examiner asked him what he considered to be the cause of death, and he answered more confidently that "he believed the cause of death to have been blows delivered on the top and sides of the head, and the pressure of a hand on the larynx of the deceased until suffocation ensued," adding, "if the pressure on the throat was made by a hand, it must have been the left hand."

The examiner asked if anything else could have caused the marks, and the doctor agreed that a handkerchief with a knot in it could account for the wound on the back of the neck, but not for the thumb print near the jugular. There would have had to have been a knot in a handkerchief at that exact place, which seemed unlikely to him. Wilson watched intently from his position at the side of the court, leaning forward and seeming to want to ask a question.

When Dr. Strehz was finished, William Anderson took the stand and testified that George Dobson had been at his store in Maori Gulley on a Sunday night near the end of May. He knew the victim well, had known him for several months, and knew that he was a surveyor. After breakfast the next day, he, George Dobson, and Mr. Fox had walked in to Arnold Township, arriving at about ten or eleven. He had talked to Mr. Dobson while Mr. Fox went into Duncan's store, and Mr. Dobson said he was going to walk to the Grey and on into Greymouth.

James leaned forward and took notice. Was this before or after he had warned Mr. Fox that the gang had planned to ambush and murder him? Perhaps the court did not realize the importance, but if it had happened after the warning, then there would still have been time to save George Dobson, if only he had managed to arrest the gang before they murdered the young man. Anderson continued, saying that he had suggested to Mr. Dobson that he join Mr. Fox and travel down by boat, but Dobson had refused, saying he wanted to examine the track he had built. A soft groan came from the townspeople in the court, and Mr. Todhunter, once more seated at the front of the court with Edward Dobson, gasped audibly. If only he had taken that boat with Mr. Fox.

One of the jurors asked if he knew what day that had been, and Anderson answered that he wasn't sure, but that it was a Monday around the end of May or beginning of June.

James stood and asked Anderson what George Dobson was wearing. The clothing had become a way of ensuring that it was George Dobson a witness had seen, especially the compass bag over his shoulder. The answer was inconclusive, but Anderson seemed to know Dobson.

"The deceased was dressed in dark colored clothes and wore black leather leggings. I'm not sure if he carried a loose cape or cloak with him. That I don't remember."

"And this pipe?" James asked, showing the pipe he had taken from George Dobson's pocket. It was wooden, with a rim of brass and copper around the top.

Anderson nodded.

"I smoked with him the night he arrived, the Sunday night, and that was the pipe he used."

"How long would it take him to walk to Greymouth?"

Anderson thought for a moment. "He was a good walker. He would have reached Greymouth by nightfall. Three or four hours to where the body was found, and perhaps an hour or two more to Greymouth. It's seven or eight miles from Arnold Township to where you found the body."

"He appeared to be in good health?"

"Yes. Very good I should say."

"And when was the last time you saw him?"

"When he had started, and was about two hundred yards down the track leading to Greymouth from the Arnold township. He was then alone, and I observed round his shoulders a leather belt, to which a compass hung."

James thanked Anderson, who sat down.

The next to speak was George Windover, a boatman on the Grey River, who remembered that he had been travelling on a Monday about a month previously and seen various people on the track. He described them laboriously. When he came to the description of men he had seen putting up a tent about a mile and a half from the coal pits, James listened intently. Here would be the crux of the matter. Had he seen the men, and had he seen George Dobson? If he could put them together close to each other the case would be half made. He would just need to discover which of them had done the evil deed.

"What can you tell us about the men you saw putting up the tent?" asked the examiner.

"I thought it was a queer time of the day to camp," answered Windover.

"What time was it?"

"This was about half-past one or two o'clock. They answered that they were not in a hurry and they did not want to get wet, as it was a little drizzling rain at the time. I afterwards remarked to my mate that the men were foolish to put a tent up there, as there was a good mi-mi close beside them, under which they might have put their tent."

And Dobson, wondered James, where was Dobson?

Windover continued, answering the unstated thought. "About a quarter of a mile further on we met a young man wearing a pair of glazed leggings. I noticed that he had a gold guard chain, and I asked him what time it was. I do not remember what he said, but I think it was somewhere about two o'clock. I asked him how far it was to the next shanty, and he told me it was a little over a mile."

"Would you know the men you saw putting up the tent if you saw them again?

Windover looked doubtful. "I don't think I would."

"Do you remember anything of how they looked?" asked a juror.

"They were both low-set men, one darker than the other."

"And the young man you met on the track?"

"He had a fair complexion, no hair on his face. About twenty-two I would say."

Another witness from Maori Gully gave his evidence, then it was the turn of David Duncan from Arnold Township. He had been driving cattle over the Grey River on Monday, May 28th and had seen a man he knew named DeLacey, on the river, and he could not recall seeing him other than that time. He also saw a couple named Mullins on the track. On Monday night, he had run into Mr. Fox at Arnold Township; Mr. Fox had told him that he had come up from Maori Gully that day and was staying for the night in the township. On Tuesday, he'd gone up the track looking for lost cattle and run into two men with swags heading down towards Greymouth he would recognize again if he saw them. James was about to ask him if he saw one of those men in court, when Duncan beat him to it.

"I believe the man standing there," pointing to Wilson, "to be one of them. They were carrying blankets but no tents."

"And could they have left Greymouth the same day and been returning when you saw them?"

"Yes, possibly, but…"

"But?"

"They would have had to have left Greymouth before daylight to have reached that far."

"Are you sure about the dates on which you saw these men?" asked the magistrate.

Daniel Duncan bristled. "I have the receipts from the cattle drive. I am sure."

Wilson leaned forward again.

"Could I ask the witness a question?"

The magistrate shook his head. "You are not on trial here, Mr. Wilson, and the jury has nothing to do with you. This inquest is simply to determine how, where, when, and by what means, the deceased came by his death."

That concluded the witnesses. The magistrate summed up, and sent the jury to deliberate. As they left the room, Wilson stood up and shouted after them: "You are swearing away an innocent man's blood, without giving him an opportunity to speak. If you allow me to say something I can tell where I slept on the night of the 28th."

The jury continued from the room, not paying attention, although a few of the men glanced in Wilson's direction looking somewhat sympathetic. Within a short time, they returned with the verdict.

"That the deceased George Dobson was wilfully murdered by some person or persons unknown, on the Grey and Arnold track, on the 28th of May last."

Wilson was upset again, assuming for some reason that he had been found guilty.

"I want to make a statement," he said. "A statement. Before I get sent to Hokitika."

James walked towards where Wilson stood between a constable and a sergeant.

"Sergeant Hickson can take your statement when you arrive in Hokitika," he said.

"I want you to take it," said Wilson stubbornly. "You've been in on this from the start. You know what I've done, and what I haven't done. Can't you take it now?"

James looked around the room. It was empty other than Wilson, himself, and the two policemen, who could act as witnesses. He made a quick decision.

"I'll take it now," he said. "But we'll need to be quick. The coach leaves in an hour." He turned to the constable. Go over to the Cobb's booking office at Johnston's Melbourne Hotel and reserve two seats on the Hokitika Coach."

Wilson looked relieved.

James gave the customary caution. "Remember, whatever you say will be taken down in writing and used against you in your trial."

Wilson nodded. "Yes, I know all of that." He started talking, and James followed along, writing as best he could in his notebook. When they were done, he had the sergeant sign his name on each page of his notebook, read back his statement to Wilson, and asked, "And do you have any more to tell me? The coach is leaving in twenty minutes."

Wilson added a few more interesting details which caused James and the sergeant to exchange glances. When he was done, the sergeant initialed the added page in the notebook, and James said quietly, "Couldn't remember where he slept on the night of the 27th because he was drunk. That's helpful. And he seems to think Dobson went missing on the 29th."

As he left the courthouse, one of his men, Sergeant Walsh, a big, barrel-chested Irishman, was waiting, walking up and down. He saw James and held up a bag.

"I was over at the hotel in Cobden, the one where Wilson was staying, and found these," he said. Cobden was on the other side of the Grey, and technically in Nelson, so Walsh should not have been there.

"Did you talk to Mr. Warden Kynnersley first?" Kynnersley was the magistrate in Cobden, on the Nelson side of the Grey.

Walsh shrugged, "Well, now then, not exactly, but…"

James felt a surge of annoyance. Walsh was a good sergeant, but not one to follow procedures. He'd get himself in trouble one of these days…

"What was it you found?" he asked.

Walsh dug his hand into the bag and let a stream of bullets run back into it.

"These," he said. "In Wilson's hotel room in Cobden. A bag of bullets."

"Give them to Sergeant Slattery," said James. "He'll know what to do with them." Not much, unfortunately. They would not be admissible as evidence.

9

Wanganui, 1888: The Boatman's Steps

"Mr. Inspector James," said Constable Crozier suddenly.

James was pulled from his reverie. For a moment he forgot that it was 1888, that the events in his mind had long disappeared from the public memory.

"You said you were on the gold escort, back in your old West Coast days."

They were on Taupo Quay and could see steamers coming from the Heads pushing in against the tide as it raced out to sea. A few ships were already moored and men were running backwards and forwards carrying bales of goods on their heads, or wheeling barrows holding steamer trunks. They stopped near the boatman's steps and leaned on the parapet, looking down at the eddies of water swirling around the dock.

"I was, but only for one trip," said James. Hadn't he mentioned that in his speech?

"Why was that?"

Was the man trying to make conversation with him, or did he care? "It was a very dangerous trip, across the mountains," James said.

Crozier moved the framed testimonial, balancing it on the sea wall. "Were there *Hauhau* waiting to attack you?"

James started to smile, but stopped himself. "No, indeed not. No *Hauhau*. Not in the South Island. The Hauhau were heading this way around that time, I believe, or soon after. Titokowaru came out of Taranaki in the late sixties and swept down the coast to Wanganui, I remember. But nothing like that in Greymouth, just…"

"I was in Wanganui then," said Crozier. "In late '68. I'd just joined the force a couple of years before. We were terrified. We thought we were all going to be captured and eaten. Decapitated first. They burned Wanganui."

"There was some decapitation where I was," said James. "I found a body without…"

"Not Hauhau though," said Crozier.

"Not Hauhau. Bushrangers, in my case I believed, an especially vicious group of them. I mentioned them earlier, the Burgess gang. But it was the threat of bushrangers that stopped us continuing the gold escort. Bushrangers and the government not insuring the gold, and the diggers who sent the gold directly to Melbourne by sea. Many reasons."

"And you stayed in Greymouth after that?" asked Crozier. "After the gold escort was done?"

James nodded. Those had been the days. Back then he'd lived an exciting and dangerous life. Not like now, when arresting a twelve-year-old boy for robbing an orchard seemed to be the extent of his peril. Poor Joshua Bason with his incorrigible father, what a waste it was when a boy like that, able to bring down a rabbit at a hundred yards with his rifle, was not able to make good in life and had to be sent to the industrial school. His father was the one who deserved to be sent away…

"Do you have children?" he asked, thinking of fathers and sons.

Crozier blushed. "I have two boys. I wed two years ago for the first time, a farmer's daughter, a young woman twenty years my junior. She's changed my life, she and the boys."

James looked at the constable with new-found respect. In his forties, and married to a farmer's daughter in her twenties - one with prospects as well, no doubt. Crozier was not as stupid as he looked.

"Two boys. Well done."

Crozier's face reddened even more, if that was possible. "We named the younger one William, after you…"

James was amused. "Why thank you, I'm honoured." Why had nobody mentioned this to him? He should probably have given the boy a christening gift. What did one give in that situation? A beer stein? A silver spoon perhaps? Although he had already been born with a silver spoon, considering his grandfather was a landowner.

"William Alexander Jubilee Crozier," said Crozier. "Alexander for me, and Jubilee, for, well, you know…"

James did. Many children had been named Jubilee last year, in honour of the old Queen, who had celebrated her Golden Jubilee in '87. He'd read that in London alone over three hundred children had been baptized with that middle name last year, often with the first name Victoria or Albert. What names to saddle children with…not that he hadn't chosen the occasional odd name himself…

"You have a son, sir? An architect I heard."

"I do, Thomas, born in Greymouth not long after I started at the police camp. We're very proud of him, my wife and I."

"Just the one son?"

"Yes." Said James. He was feeling uncomfortable. "And two daughters… grandchildren as well. My daughter Louisa has three boys: Stanley, Cyril and Erima. She married a newspaper man, the owner of the Hokitika paper." The irony of it, he'd thought at the time. His Louisa marrying a newspaperman, after all the battles he'd had with editors and reporters.

"Life on the West Coast must have been exciting," said Crozier. "With the gold rush and all. An uncle of a friend of mine was there about the same time, Albert Smith?"

James shook his head to show he had not met the man.

"He used to talk about those murders, the ones down in Nelson. Five men, or more, I think he said? That would have been about your time, wouldn't it?"

"The Maungatapu murders? Yes, I was involved in those - in catching the ruffians. I knew them even before the murders, unfortunately."

They had reached the end of the quay, and stopped to look out at the water, which churned past them as the tide ran out to sea. This river was not like the rivers on the west coast, which were broad and flat, with channels running between islands of gravel, even after rain. The Whanganui was water from one bank to the other with no breaks or places to cross. James stared into the depths, half expecting to see a body. He had seen so many bodies in Greymouth, men who had drowned in the river and been swept out to sea, only to wash up again on the beach. Mr. Fox, the gold trader, had perished that way, a few years after George Dobson's murder, still a young man of forty-seven. Fox's broad Scots brogue echoed in James' head for a minute, telling him he would nae be intimidated by yon bushrangers.

"How was it that you were involved in murders that happened in Nelson?" asked Crozier. "When you were down in Greymouth."

"The first murder was in Greymouth," said James. "George Dobson, a young surveyor. I was already familiar with the gang before the murders, and one of them, a man named James Wilson, came to see me around the time of the murders. He was a bell-ringer in Nelson. The curly-headed bellman, the papers called him, almost as if he was some kind of play actor."

He stared into the black depths of the water, thinking he could almost see all of them in it, floating just below the surface, the five men murdered on the Maungatapu Track, George Dobson; Burgess, Kelly, and Levy; and Wilson, the scoundrel, who had misled him from the start. His mind drifted back again.

10

Greymouth, 1866: The Suspect

Before the Disappearance of George Dobson

One night late in May of '66, weeks before he knew anything about George Dobson's disappearance, James was awoken by the sound of a board creaking on the verandah, and sat up, alert suddenly. Someone was out there. Steps shuffled towards the door, paused, retreated, then came to the door again. Whoever was on his verandah was not trying to disguise his presence, but seemed to be deciding what to do. James swung his legs from the bed and tiptoed down the stairs to the kitchen, where the Enfield hung on the wall, taking it down as quietly as he could. His cartouche filled with ammunition was on the floor beneath it; he scooped it up, and climbed back upstairs to the bedroom. The children were asleep in the other bedroom and he was careful not to wake them.

"Elizabeth." He lay his hand on her shoulder.

She was awake instantly, the whites of her eyes glinting in the darkness, not moving or making a sound.

"Someone is on the verandah. Load the Enfield and be ready to shoot."

She sat up and took the gun and the cartouche box.

He slipped on his coat and trousers, checked to make sure his

Beaumont and Adams was still in the pocket, and went towards the door, crouching low and staying away from the parlour window. He was almost there when the footsteps came again, followed by a thunderous knocking. Peering through the tiny peephole he'd drilled into the door, he saw a dark shape on his front verandah, outlined in the moonlight. Charlie, roused from his sleep on the kitchen floor, padded to his side, growling softly, his hackles up.

"Stay, Charlie," he said softly, his hand on the dog's neck. He heard Elizabeth tear open the packet of powder and plunge the rod into the barrel, forcing the bullet and paper wadding into place. She was an expert loader, could load in the dark with the best of them, but had never had to shoot at anything more animated than a pumpkin; she could hit one of those without difficulty, but firing at a human being was something different, he knew that.

"Who's there?"

The shadowy figure moved forward, peering at the peephole. "I have something of great importance to communicate to you, Mr. Inspector James."

The voice sounded familiar. He could make out a man wearing a black waterproof coat with a comforter around his neck, and a dark slouched hat, rain dripping from its brim. His shoulders were hunched around his ears, his face in darkness.

"Elizabeth, lock the door after me and hold Charlie," he said.

He stepped out onto the verandah staying near the door, his hand resting lightly on the revolver in his jacket pocket. Jamie Wilson stood there staring back at him, looking much smaller and less-threatening than he had seemed through the peephole.

"I've been walking up and down all night," said Wilson, "trying to make up my mind to talk to you. Two hours it's been. I need to make a statement before a magistrate." Wilson's pale face was twitching, his eyes unfocused and wild. "About Hill and Harmon."

"You mean Burgess and Kelly?" James was used to the aliases criminals used.

"Yes, yes," Wilson said. He took off his hat and flicked it, sending a cascade of water downwards. "And I need a guarantee of forgiveness from the magistrate, and some ready to leave the province." He looked around nervously, as if Burgess and Kelly might jump at him from the bushes. "If they find out I talked to you they'll kill me, Inspector James, I swear they will."

"I'll take you to see Mr. Revell," said James. "He'll be at home at the courthouse. He can take your statement there."

"Right, then," said Wilson. "But you go on ahead. I don't want anyone to see me walking with a peeler. It'd get back to them…"

James fetched his coat, put Charlie on a leash, and set out in front of Wilson across the bridge to Mr. Warden Revell's house in Blaketown, near the courthouse, to make a statement. Before he left he checked on Elizabeth. She was propped up in bed, the Enfield across her lap, sound asleep. He lifted her hand from the stock, took the gun gently from her hands, removed the cartridge, and returned the gun to the wall in the kitchen.

Mr. Revell was not at home. After Wilson once more threatened to walk up and down all night if he could not see the warden and make a statement, James left him at the courthouse, little more than a one-roomed shack with a table fronting rows of benches, and went to find the magistrate. It was well after midnight when they returned.

A sleepy constable was holding the fort, a loaded stick resting across his knees; Wilson was sitting on one of the benches, watched by Charlie. The dog eased himself lazily to his feet, licked James' hand, and flopped back on the floor, his eyes still on Wilson.

"Mr. Warden Revell sir," said Wilson, standing up quickly. "I need a guarantee of forgiveness and money to leave the province, and then I'll give a…"

Revell shrugged off his dripping coat and threw it across the chair, stared at Wilson coldly and shook his head. "No." He paused for a minute, and then added, "But I'll do my utmost with the government to get you money or a slighter punishment for anything you tell me that results in an arrest. What do you have to tell me?"

Wilson sat, slumped down in the bench. "I'm a thief, I admit I am," he said. "I 'ave been for some time. But I ain't a murderer. I want you to know that."

Mr. Revell nodded slowly. "Who is it that you ain't…I mean who you aren't going to murder?"

"Mr. Fox," said Wilson

"Mr. Fox the gold buyer?" asked James, exchanging glances with the magistrate.

Wilson nodded. "They stole a shovel, said they were going to use it to catch him out, hit him from behind when he weren't looking. He carries a gun in his hand all the time, Mr. Fox does, and he'd be hard to catch out with…I want no part of that. I'm a thief, but I ain't…"

"A murderer, I know," said Revell. "Who stole the shovel?"

"Hill and…Burgess and Kelly, I mean. And that's why I need to get out of the country, with some ready…"

"When is this attack to take place?" asked James.

"DeLacy will give them, Burgess and Kelly, the heads up when Mr. Fox leaves Greymouth, and they'll wait for him on the track."

"DeLacey, the stable man?" asked James. Wilson nodded, avoiding their eyes.

"And do you know when and where this is to take place?"

"We're s'posed to go out tomorrow, me and Burgess and Kelly, and Levy as well, to the usual place. The iron store, up towards the coal pits."

"Are they armed in any way, other than the shovel?" asked Revell.

"They had some firearms they got in Hokitika," said Wilson. "Stolen, they were, but they destroyed most of those. They still have some tools, but those are square. Two guns and a revolver."

"And are you sure they intended to kill Mr. Fox?" asked Revell.

"Sure as anything," said Wilson. "I made some masks, so as we wouldn't be recognized. But they said they didn't need masks as they were going to burke anyone they stopped…"

"Strangle, you mean," said James. He had heard the term before, referring to the two killers Burke and Hare, the Scottish murderers who murdered to provide bodies for a doctor to use in his anatomy lectures.

"Right, strangle," said Wilson. "And I was afraid to say anything. I thought they might kill me too."

"Will you repeat this in court?" asked Revell. He was taking notes with a pencil.

Wilson shook his head vigorously. "I don't want anyone to know, and I don't want it in the paper. They'll kill me. I just want some ready so I can get out of the province. You can stop them killing Mr. Fox…"

Mr. Revell sighed and stood up. "Is there anything else you'd like to tell us?"

Wilson shook his head. "I just want to make sure I get the ready…"

"If possible," snapped the magistrate. "But don't rely on it. Now, make sure you go back to your lodgings and stay out of trouble. Don't leave Greymouth. I'll put out a warrant on you if you do."

James clicked his tongue at Charlie, and the dog lumbered to its feet, ready to accompany his master home. He waited outside in the shadows until Wilson followed them dejectedly outside. Once out of sight of the magistrate he drew Wilson aside. "Listen, go out on the track with the others tomorrow as planned. I'll have a word with Mr. Fox to persuade him to go a day later."

Wilson nodded nervously. "I won't let them know he's going later, I swear I won't, Mr. Inspector James." He started to walk away, then stopped. "Do you know anything that would make powder incombustible?"

"I don't," said James. "Why would you ask?"

"I don't wish to assist Burgess and Kelly in murdering Mr. Fox," said Wilson.

They did have guns then. He would send armed men to arrest the gang the next day, and persuade Mr. Fox to delay his trip.

After Wilson had come to see him on that Wednesday night at the end of May, he had gone to see Mr. Fox, the Scottish gold buyer and storekeeper, to warn him that there was a plot afoot to steal the money he'd received for the gold he had brought with him to Greymouth from the Maori Gully diggings, and sold at the Bank of New Zealand.

Mr. Fox, a tall thin, stooped Scot who reminded James somewhat of the recently murdered President Lincoln, listened to James and shook his head in contempt.

"Away wi ye," he said. "I dinna think those idiots will tak' me by surprise. I carry a revolver in my hand, ready tae shoot at th' scoondrels."

"Apparently they intend to get behind you with a shovel and knock you out," said James.

Mr. Fox rubbed his sparse beard. "Weel then," he said. "If I hud a companion…"

"I'll accompany you with some men," said James. "I'll have them wear plain clothes and follow behind, as if they're another party. You can handle an attack, no doubt?"

"Oh aye," said Fox. "Nae doot at all. How did they ken I was leaving the day?"

"They have a spy in town. I'm not sure who it is - probably DeLacey."

"Oh aye," said Fox. "He provides mah horses for mah trips. Guides me as well. Nae any more though. And come tae think on it, he asked me to tak a letter for him this morning…wanted tae find out when I was going, nae doubt."

James assigned two constables in plain clothes to go up the track ahead of them, and with a sergeant and two constables followed Mr. Fox up the Arnold Track as far as the Twelve Mile, having a difficult time keeping up with the gold buyer's long loping stride. He stayed back thirty or forty yards from Fox, with his men further behind. Along the way, a horseman passed them at a gallop.

The sergeant caught up to him. "That was DeLacey."

"We'll catch up to Mr. Fox," said James. "I'll walk with him and you keep behind where you are."

A short time later they heard a horseman approaching fast down the track.

"If they see a large party with you they won't attack," he said to Fox. "We'll hide until he passes."

From their ambuscade in the bush they watched as DeLacey galloped by once more. James walked with Mr. Fox for several miles after that, with the sergeant and constables behind them but within gunshot distance. Both he and Fox had their revolvers drawn, but no attack came.

For two days, he wondered what had gone wrong. Then on Friday he received a letter by post from Wilson, asking to meet him at the Grey Hotel near the Blaketown bridge at five o'clock. The letter was signed "Incognito" but it was clear who had written it. In his letter, Wilson requested that James walk into the hotel as if he was not meeting anyone, and to contrive to meet with him accidentally.

Wilson was waiting in the parlor of the hotel. James bought himself a beer at the bar and took it into the parlor, pretending to be surprised to see Wilson already there, but sure they were fooling no one. He sat down across from him and said abruptly, "Well, what is it you want to tell me?"

As before, Wilson was jumpy, looking around the room and through the parlor window nervously, as if Burgess or Kelly might suddenly appear on the verandah.

"You received my letter then?"

James sipped his beer, wiped the froth from his lips, then replied, "Of course."

Wilson leaned forwardly and said quietly, "I went up the track and met Burgess at the iron store, but we came back down to town after seeing your party pass by." He stopped and peered out the window again. "See, things were badly arranged on your side and we knew something had gone wrong. And I didn't say anything, but Burgess was suspicious. We saw two men looking like constables on the road, going by their dress. They were loitering in the scrub and we went deeper into the bush and hid. Then we saw your party pass by and…"

James took another sip of beer to hide his consternation. Damn. They had been that close then. He'd known they would be on the lookout for Mr. Fox again, having missed him on Tuesday when he came down from the Arnold by boat a day later than expected.

"We have a lot of ways of getting information," Wilson continued. "And we heard that Mr. Fox knew he was going to be stuck up as someone who always goes with him had turned around and was not going."

He was going to have to arrest Wilson, that was clear, before Wilson spilled everything to the gang, as well as to keep him safe from them. And DeLacey as well, so it seemed. DeLacey, whom Wilson had already named as a spy for the group, usually accompanied Mr. Fox on his bi-weekly trips to and from Maori Gulley. Wilson was not being straight with him.

Wilson saw things differently. "You can hardly have acted on your promise to me," he complained, "bringing that group up to catch us. I hope none of the other details leak out—don't tell anyone on the force."

"Why…" James started to say, but stopped himself. Could there be a spy on the force? An inside man? Not just DeLacey who was keeping them informed? Wilson had said they had many sources of information. Who would it be keeping them informed?

"And whatever you do, take precautions to stop anything getting into the newspapers," said Wilson. "Nothing about the wanted party. They'll take extra precautions if the force speaks to the newspapers about my having been seen on the raid in their company."

"I won't," said James. "I'm the only one who speaks to the newspapers, I can assure you. And I have very little to say to them."

"Let the common constables have a slight down upon me in the matter," suggested Wilson. He leaned forward and spoke in a whisper, glancing around as he did so. "The party gets information through so many channels that even what the police talk confidentially about is liable to reach their ears."

He had said more than he realized, and Inspector James had taken note. An inside man, as he suspected.

"I'll pass on that suggestion to Sergeant Slattery," he said.

"Good. Try and throw some suspicion on me," suggested Wilson. "Although not too much, just enough to…"

"If I can," said James. "Now, what transpired that day, the day you met Burgess and the others at the iron store?"

"Burgess, Kelly, Sullivan, and me, we were up the track that day, lying in ambush, and DeLacey rode up and told us that Fox had left Greymouth, but he thought he saw two constables in disguise following him."

"You could tell they were constables?" They had been in plain clothes, but it was hard to disguise people on the job. He had frequently been recognized as police himself, even when he first arrived from Australia and no one knew him. Something about the posture and the confidence, perhaps.

Wilson nodded. "We went further into the bush, as I said, and then you passed, you and your party. We watched you pass. We thought of attacking you, but our lookout had seen other parties following Fox and didn't want to start an attack."

James sighed and stared into his beer, saying nothing. He was no longer thirsty.

"I don't suppose you have some ready you could give me Inspector?" Wilson asked. "I'm hard up…"

James reached into his pocket and came up with five shillings. "This will get you supper and breakfast," he said. "That's all I can give you."

"What about the government money? Could you advance…"

James shook his head firmly but said nothing. He was hardly going to recommend a government reward for Wilson for the slight information he had given. And he was clearly fully involved in the attempted stick up, even though he had confessed in advance.

"Can you tell me where Burgess and Kelly are staying?" he asked. He was waiting for warrants for their arrest for conspiracy to commit robbery against Mr. Fox.

"At the Provincial Hotel on Richmond Quay," said Wilson. The hotel was up for auction, the proprietor having failed to make a go of it, what with the regular clientele not being the crème de la crème of the town and there being so much competition amongst hotel keepers. He would go there and arrest Burgess and Kelly as soon as he got the warrant. In the meantime, he would seek them out and give them a warning. If they left town, he wouldn't have to worry about them. The warrants were for conspiring to rob Mr. Fox, and he'd have a hard time making that case, with Wilson as his main witness. Best if they left town and were no longer his problem…let Broham or Shallcrass deal with them.

11

Greymouth, 1866: The Warning

With Mr. Fox safely on his way back to Maori Gully, James went looking for Burgess and his crew at the Provincial Hotel. He enlisted the help of Sergeant Walsh, who was handy with a loaded stick, even if he didn't always follow procedures. They stopped first at the Police Camp to collect a gun from the armory. If he drew his weapon it had to be one he had signed out from the armory, not his own personal revolver, which he left at his house.

A different uniformed constable stood on guard outside the armory hut, his rifle at the ready to fend off thieves; he'd stood there immobile for hours, and was happy for the chance to move. He unlocked the door to the armory hut and ushered them inside.

"There you go sir," he said, pointing at the two walls of weapons. "Rifles and carbines on the left, side arms on the right, ammo in the large cartouche boxes at the far end."

James thanked him solemnly. He'd set up the armory himself, and they both knew it.

The rifles were used mostly for guard duty and organized attacks, while the shorter-barreled carbines were used by mounted constables in saddle holsters for fast extraction. James ignored those, and selected a Dean and Adams, his personal favourite, from the side-arms wall. Sergeant Walsh followed him in and picked up one of the newer large Colts.

"You should give this a try," he said, handing it to James. "It comes with a very nice belted holster and feels good in your fist. Weighty. Easy to get at as well."

James took it from him. "Heavy bugger, isn't it? But I heard the cylinders tend to rupture after firing."

"Not if they're kept clean," said Walsh. "You need to keep the powder from the mouth of the chamber. I like to put a bit of lard in the mouth of the cylinder as well, just to be on the safe side." He took the Colt back from James and sighted down the barrel at the guard standing at the door. "They're good out to a hundred yards, and pack a wallop. Blow a fist-sized hole in the back of anyone running from us."

"I think I'll go with the Dean and Adams," said James. "I doubt I'll need to fire - I just want to put a scare into them. Force them off my patch. I can't very well shoot them in the back if they run off. You'll do better with your stick."

Walsh patted the loaded stick that hung from his belt loop. "I can bring down a man at twenty yards, needs be."

The Provincial Hotel was on Richmond Quay, not far from the police reserve. The quay was busy, as always, but the crowds parted before them, many making a point of not looking at what they recognized as police on a mission. Benjamin Barnard, the proprietor of the hotel, was standing in the doorway of his business soliciting customers. He saw them coming from a hundred yards away, turned and ran back inside the hotel.

"They're in there and he's going to warn them," said James, breaking into a run. "Go down the alley and come in through the back. Make sure no one leaves."

Walsh pulled out his stick and ran towards the alley. James gave him a couple of beats to get into place, then burst in through the bar parlor door. Barnard was standing in the hallway looking around wildly like a cornered rat wondering which way he should run. Several doors led from either side of the hallway; a larger door to what appeared to be the rear exit was partly open at the end of the hallway. As Barnard came to a decision and took a step in that direction, Walsh rushed through the rear door. "Just a small yard back there with nowhere to hide," he said. "The only exit is down the alley. If he warned them they would have run into me."

"Where are they?" said James to Barnard.

"Who?"

"You damn well know who, Barnard," said James. "Burgess and his crew."

Barnard shifted his eyes away from James and shrugged. "They was here this morning. Must've left while I was out getting the post," he said. "They're not here now."

"How do you know that?" asked James.

"What do you mean? They're not here…"

"You said you were out getting the post. We saw you come in just now. Did you check all the rooms when you came in?"

Barnard started to shake his head, then realized his quandary.

"I can't hear them anywhere," he said. "They must've gone."

"They're still here," said James. "Aren't they?"

He patted his pocket and found his box of Bryant and May's. "Keep an eye on him," he said to Walsh. I'm going to check these rooms." He struck the match against his trouser leg, then remembered it was one of the new safety type that lit only on the box. It took him a couple of tries using the box, but the match lit up. He carried it carefully to the first door and pushed open with his elbow. The flickering light showed four mattress pallets on a rough wooden frame. No room for anyone in there. Holding his palm around the lit match to protect the flame, he pushed open the second door and saw a table and four chairs. A deck of cards lay at one end of the table. The match was almost burned down, but he still had time to look in one more room. He pushed the third door open, expecting once more to see nothing, not wanting to waste a match and felt the flame bite at his thumb. He cursed and dropped the match. He was going to have a blister.

The room was lit up by the falling match, then engulfed in darkness, blinding him briefly. But in the last flicker he had seen three dark furtive shapes, arms raised against the light, squatting against the far wall. Rats. Human rats.

He slammed the door shut and leaned against it, squeezing his thumb to dull the pain of the burn. "They're in there. Three of them. Take Barnard to the kitchen and bring back a candle."

Walsh grabbed Barnard by the scruff of his neck and marched him away. He returned alone holding a lit candle propped inside a glass bottle with a wire handle.

"He's sitting at the kitchen table," he said. "I told him if he ran for it you'd blow his head off. Told him you were a crack shot and would love the chance to pop one into the back of his skull."

James smiled grimly and pulled out his gun. "Stand behind me with the candle so I can see inside. I'm going to open the door. Let's hope they're unarmed."

He took a stance, both hands on the gun, and nudged the door open with his foot.

"I know you're in there, Burgess. Come on out with your hands above your head."

Behind him, Walsh raised the candle. "I can't see—yes I can. Over to the left. Careful."

James moved to the right of the doorway and peered into the darkness on his left. The candlelight showed three figures once more. They had moved since he first saw them in the match light, had crawled over into the corner and were hunkered down low, with grey coats dragging on the floor. Two were barely visible, but one face he could see, and recognized.

"Joseph Thomas Sullivan," said James. "We meet again. You can come out first." He had met Sullivan years ago, when they were both in Victoria. The man was a villain, no doubt about it, but he was also a coward. He would be the easiest to handle.

A fair-complexioned man of about forty came slowly forward on all fours, looking up at James through heavy eyebrows. He reached the door and used the handle to pull himself up, straining with the effort. He was almost the height of James, but stouter, with broad shoulders, an overly large face, and dark whiskers along his jawline.

"Sullivan," said James. "Not the first time we've met. But this time you'll be staying around, not running off and leaving me to fight off your attackers."

"I didn't run off," said Sullivan. "I was just going to get help, and…"

Walsh put down the candle in the doorway and grabbed Sullivan roughly by the shoulders. "Against the wall."

Holding Sullivan's hands on the wall with his loaded stick, he ran his free hand down either side of Sullivan's body to check for weapons. He removed a set of brass knuckles and slipped them into his own pocket. "You know this one?"

"Knew him in Victoria," said James. "Up near Wedderburn. Biggest coward I ever met. Saved his life from some Germans who were about to stab him and he left me with them, took off into the bush. Used to hang around with Black Douglas and Gypsy Smith. Probably killed a few people up there as well, although…"

"I was never convicted of anything," said Sullivan defensively.

"I was about to say that," said James. "You were charged, however. You were lucky to get off." He contemplated the room again. "The next man can come out."

The second man crawled forward and rose to his feet slowly, staring at James contemptuously as he did so, his lips pulled back in a sneer. He was a brutish looking fellow of the criminal type, short with a small head, a sallow complexion and deep-set eyes. A heavy moustache met up with full whiskers, so that his eyes seemed to look out at the world through a pelt. His rolled-up shirt sleeves revealed well-muscled forearms with tattoos of mermaids and sailors. The top of a crucifix tattoo showed above his shirt collar at the neck. Above his shirt collar on his chest. Where Sullivan had been nervous and obedient, this man was a surly and belligerent. Not as intelligent as Sullivan, James thought, and likely to be his own worst enemy.

"Sullivan," said James. "Tell me this man's name."

"Say nothing, Jack," said a soft voice from inside the room.

Walsh gave Sullivan an encouraging tap on the head with his loaded stick.

"He's Kelly," said Sullivan, rubbing his head. "Tommy Kelly. Sorry master, I…"

Kelly made a lunge for Sullivan and got his left hand briefly onto Sullivan's throat. Walsh grabbed Kelly and slammed him face forward against the wall, putting his stick against Kelly's temple. "Keep still now or I'll give ye a good kick up the arse." Kelly raised his bent arm and smacked Walsh's nose with his elbow.

"Hell's bells," said Walsh, doubling over and pinching his nose to stem the flow of blood. "You little bastard, I'll…"

Sullivan took advantage of the distraction and lurched in the direction of the bar parlour door. He was almost there, gathering speed, when Walsh stood up, elbowed Kelly in the solar plexus, raised the loaded stick and sent it spinning towards Sullivan's calves. Sullivan fell heavily to the floor with the stick tangled between his knees. Walsh strode over to retrieve it.

"Stay there Sullivan or I'll clout you good and proper with my stick," he said. "And you, Kelly. Get down on the floor beside him." He watched as Kelly obeyed him, glaring at him through narrowed eyes, and lying on the floor face down, his whiskers brushing the filthy carpet. Walsh stood over them and nodded to James. "Over to you again."

"Thank you," said James. "Well done with the stick."

"Ah, she's me old shillelagh," said Walsh, patting the stick as he slipped it back into his belt. "Couldn't do without her." He placed his boot toes against the top of the two prisoners' heads, giving each of them a quick kick as he did so. Sullivan protested loudly, but Kelly took it without a murmur.

James was grateful to Walsh, doing what he himself could not, but he knew the worst ruffian was still in the room. In the flickering light of the candle he could see the third man crouching against the wall. He took a stance with both hands on his revolver and said sharply, "Now you, Burgess. Out you come. One wrong move and I'll shoot you right between the eyes. I won't miss from this distance."

The third man rose from his corner and sauntered forward smiling; he was short, with a strong body that exuded power. Despite his diminutive stature, he was clearly the leader of the three, heavily bearded, like Kelly, but with a receding hairline. He walked straight at James and stopped inches away, so that the barrel of the revolver almost touched his face.

"Good morning, sir." he said. "Who do I have the pleasure of addressing?" His smile did not extend to his eyes, which were deep set and as black as two lumps of coal.

James stared along the barrel of his Dean and Adams at the eyes; despite his calmness and his smile, this was a man who didn't care if he lived or died, a man with no soul who would kill a man as easily as he would swat a biting sand fly.

"It's Mr. Inspector James, master," said Sullivan, lifting his face from the floor. "From the police." Burgess eyes flickered briefly in Sullivan's direction and back to James.

"I'm here to warn you off, Burgess," said James. "Or are you going by Hill these days?"

"Warn me off?" said Burgess, his tone light and curious. "Warn me off what precisely? What bloody crimes do you suppose I have done that you must warn me off?"

The sibilant similarity between the v and the w and the missing aitches, pointing to a cockney heritage, confirmed this man's identity for James. He knew something of Burgess' early years. Like James, Burgess was a Londoner, but one forged in the muck and depravity of the rookeries, where he ran with a gang of Street Arabs. He'd been sentenced to transportation for the theft of a handkerchief at seventeen. He'd been sent to await transportation in Pentonville, the new model prison, where mental and physical isolation were the preferred methods of punishment: prisoners wore masks when they were out of their cells, and exercised in silent, shuffling rows before returning to solitary cells.

Shortly after his eighteenth birthday, as was the law, he was transported to Australia with a conditional release, meaning he could not return home; by then he was a hardened criminal and Australia did nothing to change that. Within a few years, he was sentenced to the floating hell of the prison hulks in Melbourne, brutalized by regular floggings. Released early on a ticket of leave, he'd met Kelly in the gold fields of Victoria, and together with a third man—Levy—the gang had followed the gold to Otago, then to the West Coast.

"I know your history," said James. "You're a violent felon from the goldfields of Victoria who washed up in this country when the gold ran out; you were run out of Otago by the force after time in gaol for attempted murder of a police officer; since you arrived on this coast the police have had eyes on you in Hokitika. Broham warned me about you."

"Broham?" Burgess said, chuckling. "Oh, you mean Inspector Broham." He jerked his head sideways at Walsh, his eyes still holding James' eyes steadily. "One of his people, isn't he? A vile Irish…"

Walsh leaned forward and gave Burgess a sharp smack on the back of his head with his loaded stick. Burgess's eyes flickered, but he did not move and his eyes held James's.

"We don't need your type here," said James. His right hand had begun to tremble, and he tightened his grip so as not to reveal himself to Burgess. How could a man who smiled at him exude such malevolence? "I want to see you gone from my district by tomorrow."

"Or you'll do what? Put me in gaol?" He sighed and shook his head. "Ah, God assist me in my hour of need. Gaol? I spent six years in the convict hulks in chains and the Lord taught me many things…to endure many things."

"I'll have the Argus publish a warning about you," said James. He lowered his revolver and stepped back, but kept it at the ready. "Stop you from doing anything in this town, from buying anything, from staying anywhere. And I'll have a man on you at all times."

Burgess was half a head shorter than James, but had positioned his head so he could look along his nose at him; he stared at James with hooded eyes, like a cobra about to strike.

"Inspector James, never would a greater wrong be enacted towards one fellow against another. But the Lord will forgive you. I give you his blessing." he said.

James pulled himself up so the four of five-inch height difference between him and Burgess was amplified, stepped forward and pushed the gun barrel hard against Burgess' temple. Their noses were just inches apart.

"People you work with, perhaps not. But none of the merchants will sell you anything and you won't be able to travel anywhere except by foot. And if I see you around after tomorrow I'll arrest you on suspicion of robbery in Hokitika. Broham knows you were up to something down there. He'll get a warrant if I ask him for it." No need to reveal Wilson's role by mentioning the conspiracy to murder Mr. Fox. That warrant was already on its way.

He saw a quick flash of something in Burgess' eyes—amusement he thought. He'd already done something, and James was wide of the mark talking about a robbery in Hokitika.

Burgess stared at him for several minutes without speaking, the smile fading from his eyes but lingering on his lips. Why did he seem to be amused that he was merely being accused of robbery? What else had he done?

"We're leaving, Mr. Inspector James," said Sullivan, breaking the silence. "We've got…"

"You must not speak, Joseph," said Burgess. He spat on the floor next to Sullivan's head without looking at him. "You must say nothing to this copper."

Sullivan raised his face from the ground and looked up at Burgess.

"I didn't mean nothing, master," he said. Burgess turned slowly in his direction, causing Sullivan to flinch visibly and drop his head.

James put one hand on Burgess' shoulder and propelled him towards the door. "If I see you again in Greymouth I'll arrest you…have you doing hard labour on the roads."

Burgess shrugged, took a couple of steps towards the door, then stopped and looked back at James, smiling as if he had just remembered something.

"Oh, Inspector James," he said. "I believe I know your wife. I've seen her at the opera house…"

James leapt forward and caught him by the throat.

"Anything happens to my wife, you're a dead man," he said. "Law be damned. I'll cut out your guts and throw them to the gulls. Then I'll kill you." Burgess let him squeeze his throat and said nothing, still smiling slightly. When he finally removed his hand, there was a red mark on Burgess's throat, which Burgess ignored. James could feel his heart pounding and breathed slowly to calm himself. He couldn't let this bastard bring him down.

He nodded at Walsh to let the other two men go; Walsh pulled them up roughly by the arms and stood with James at the door of the hotel as the three trudged off along the quay. Barnard came out from the kitchen wringing his hands, his eyes darting from James to the retreating backs, clearly wondering who was the greater threat.

"Maybe we should have put them in the lockup," said Walsh. "Charged them with something. Use of abusive language would hold them."

"Not for long," said James. "And the trial could take weeks—months even—leaving them free to do whatever they liked in this district. I want them gone. Come back here tomorrow and make sure they haven't returned. But I have the feeling they were leaving town anyway. Did you hear what Sullivan started to say?"

He picked up the candle and went into the room where the three men had been hiding. Their bed rolls were piled in one corner, and dirty tin plates and mugs had been flung carelessly on the floor. The room smelled of unwashed bodies. On a table in the corner flies hovered around a loaf of bread, a hardening wedge of cheese, and a tin of jam.

"If they come back for their bedrolls, let them have them," he said to Barnard. "But if you allow them stay you're going to gaol. Sergeant Walsh here will be around to check on you. Did you know them before they paid you to lodge here?"

Barnard shook his head, avoiding James' eyes. "Not exactly. One of them said he'd seen me when I was on the Kanieri, at the diggings, but I don't remember him."

"Do you have any idea where'll they'll go now"

"They spoke of going back to…to…Hokitika," said Barnard.

"Charge him with harbouring bad characters," James said to Walsh as they left.[iii]"We'll check here again tomorrow with the conspiracy warrant for Burgess, Kelly and Sullivan. It should be on the mail coach tonight."

"It's to be hoped they'll leave," said Walsh. "Go back to Hokitika where Broham can deal with them again."

"I'll believe that when I see them gone," said James sourly. "Barnard is no more honest than any of them. They'll either find another place to hide, or catch a steamer north somewhere. Wilson wants to leave the country. I hope that's their plan as well. Australia can take them back. They'll fit in there." He was feeling uneasy. What was it that Burgess had done, that he, James, did not know about? Had the gang been up to something in Greymouth he didn't know about? He shook away his misgivings. Whatever it was Burgess had done it was better that he and his crew left town.

He returned his weapon to the armory, once again to the relief of the constable on guard. As he was leaving, Sergeant Slattery came huffing out of the station holding a letter. "Inspector Broham sent this," he said. "Wanted to let you know that the Bank of New Zealand in Okarita was robbed last week—on Tuesday. He's requesting you to be on the *qui vive* for anyone attempting to sell a large amount of gold."

"How much did they get?"

"Six hundred ounces," said Slattery.

Sergeant Walsh whistled. "Almost a thousand-quid's worth. Not bad for a day's work."

"Oh, and we've got a missing man," said Slattery, not looking at Walsh, his disapproval evident. "One of Mr. Rochfort's survey boys."

"What does Mr. Rochfort think happened to him?" asked James. He was not particularly alarmed. Men were always going missing around here. Sooner or later they turned up, or their bodies did. Mostly it was drink that did them in.

"He went up through Maori Gulley from Hokitika to check the tracks, and was coming back along the Arnold. Mr. Fox came in and said he expected to meet him in Greymouth. He said he'd been talking to you but forgot to mention it. They met on the Arnold, and Fox saw him head in this direction a few days ago. He should've been here by now."

"Maybe he made camp somewhere," said James.

Slattery shook his head. "He had no blankets or supplies with him—Mr. Fox wondered if he fell down a gully and broke his leg. He was apparently an excellent bush man and not likely to get lost. A good swimmer as well, by all accounts."

"Have you sent a search party out to look for him?"

"We did. With a group of Maori trackers—the best trackers they could muster. They just returned and found no sign of him."

"Give him a couple of days to find his way home, then send out another party," said James. He started to leave, then turned. "What did you say his name was, this missing boy?"

"Dobson," said Sergeant Slattery. "George Dobson."

12

Greymouth, 1866: The Arrest

James went back to the Provincial Hotel the following day, this time with a warrant for the arrest of Burgess, Kelly and Sullivan, but they had gone, or so Barnard said. He had asked Mr. Revell to include James Wilson, also known as James Murray, on the warrant, and before he went looking for Burgess again he left a letter at the Criterion Hotel suggesting that Wilson meet him at the post office. Wilson replied saying he would be there the following day.

He was starting to wonder about the missing boy. Mr. Fox had unexpectedly decided to stop overnight in Arnold Township before proceeding to Greymouth. He had watched Dobson leave along the Twelve Mile after suggesting he stay the night in Arnold Township and take a boat down the Grey. If Dobson had been on the track at the time Mr. Fox was expected, could Burgess and his crew have attempted to rob him, thinking he was Mr. Fox? Could they have killed him because he wasn't? It was possible the boy had not met with foul play, had fallen and broken his leg after straying from the track. But why would searchers not have found him in that case? Have heard him calling out? He could be dead, buried, murdered by Burgess and Kelly. Was that what Burgess was hiding with his smile, when James told him to leave town or he'd have him arrested for burglary?

On the 5th. of June, at nine o'clock at night, he was waiting at the window of the post office, talking to Mr. Stevenson, the postmaster, when Wilson arrived. Wilson was dressed in a grubby white pea jacket, a red muffler, and the same black felt hat he had worn when he came to James' home earlier in the week. Seeing James, he took of his hat and twisted it in his hands.

"You wanted to talk to me, Mr. Inspector James?"

"When did Burgess and Kelly leave?"

Wilson avoided his eyes. "Dunno. Yesterday? A couple of days ago?"

"And where did they go?"

"Up north, I think."

"To Nelson?"

Wilson nodded. "Or south to Hokitika, one or the other." He stared out the door for a minute, then added, "I saw in the paper there's a surveyor missing on the Twelve Mile."

"George Dobson," said James. "What do you know about that?"

Wilson kept his gaze on the doorway. "When was 'e last seen, this Dobson?"

"Why do you ask?"

"Was it between the Arnold and Twelve Mile, or Twelve Mile and Greymouth? The paper said at the Arnold. On May 29th."

"He was last seen at the Arnold and Twelve Mile, on May 29th," said James. "Should that make a difference?"

"If it was between the Twelve Mile and Greymouth, then no doubt Kelly and Sullivan put him away," said Wilson.

James felt the hairs on the back of his neck stand up. "You think Burgess and Sullivan killed - murdered him?"

"I thought Burgess and Kelly went up to the Buller," said Wilson, ignoring James' question. "But I went up the Arnold Track as far as the iron shanty with Burgess on the 28thand we met Kelly and Sullivan there, at about nine in the morning. We had a cup of hot tea, then we went up the track to find a place to amb—to wait for Mr. Fox."

"Did you see Dobson pass by?" asked James.

"We only stayed there an hour, and it came on to rain," said Wilson. "So we went back to the iron store. Sullivan and Kelly stayed at the iron store to dry their clothes, and I came back to Greymouth. Burgess too." He looked directly at James for the first time. "I slept that night at the Criterion Hotel. You can ask them there if…and I slept in late. I went into the main street in the morning and met Tommy—Kelly I mean—and he asked me where Dick was. He gave me a swag, which I took to Coburn, George Coburn."

"What was in this swag that you took to Coburn?"

"Guns," said Wilson. "There was guns in the swag."

James sighed. That was it then. They'd murdered Dobson and were trying to hide the evidence, he was sure of it. Wilson had come to him just days after the murder with the story about the plot against Mr. Fox because he was afraid of being implicated in the murder, a murder that had already happened, not because he wanted to stop the robbery and possible murder of Mr. Fox.

"James Wilson, also known as James Murray," he said. "I am arresting you for…" He saw Wilson's eyes widen in fear. "For the conspiracy to commit murder of Mr. Fox, the gold buyer from Maori Gulley." Wilson relaxed perceptibly. He wouldn't swing for conspiracy to commit. James cautioned him and took out his cuffs. "Come on then, we're going to the station."

"I told you before anything happened," protested Wilson. He was looking past James at the postmaster's window. "I swore out a statement to Mr. Warden Revell. He said…"

"He promised you nothing," said James. "And neither did I."

At the station, he searched Wilson in the presence of Sergeant Slattery, discovering three one pound notes and two shillings and three pence in silver in Wilson's pockets. More than he'd expected from someone who'd recently had to borrow five shillings from him.

"I'm not divulging nothing more," said Wilson as he watched the money disappear into a cash box. "Nothing. I don't trust you no more Mr. Inspector James."

The following day Mr. Edward Dobson arrived from Christchurch on the Cobb's Coach and began organizing a hunt for his son, still with the faint hope that his son was alive somewhere near the track. James met him at his hotel and told him bluntly of his fears.

Dobson said nothing for several minutes, then sighed. "He's a first-rate bushman," he said. "I can't imagine that he would lose himself. Drown, perhaps, even fall down a ravine or into an old mining shaft. But murder…"

"Nothing is certain," said James. "It's no more than a suspicion at the moment…"

"His mother will be upset," said Dobson, running his hands through his thick grey hair. "I have to let her believe for a little longer that George is merely lost; however, I believe you are correct in thinking he's been murdered." He gave a deep sigh. "Thank you for being honest with me."

James went to the lockup to persuade Wilson to give the Dobson family some relief by telling him where the body was buried, but Wilson refused.

"I swear, Mr. Inspector James, I don't know nothing about where the young man might be."

James placed the government reward poster beside him on the bench. Wilson glanced at it and looked away, then stared straight ahead for a long time. Finally, he said, "I took some old clothes up to the track. For them to disguise themselves when they jumped Mr. Fox."

"Clothes? Why would clothes disguise them?"

"I shaped out four cloth masks. I used a waistcoat for that. I planted them up between the iron shanty and Alabaster's. You can probably still find them there. I don't think…"

"You don't think Burgess and Kelly used them? Was it too late for them?"

"I don't remember," said Wilson. He looked sullen. "I don't know what they did with the stuff. But if it's still there you can find it behind that big rock, the one with the red stripe down its side. About halfway between the shanty and Alabaster's. You can't miss it. I stuffed it under a log behind the rock."

James left the reward poster in Wilson's cell and went outside. His neighbour Mr. Bain, the government surveyor, and one of his assistants was talking to Sergeant Slattery on the steps.

"He's told me where he left some clothing they were going to use as disguises," he said. "And some masks he made for them. I'll ride out tomorrow and check it out. He won't tell me anything about what happened to Dobson or where he might be buried."

"You think George Dobson is dead?" asked Bain, looking startled.

James nodded. "I'm afraid so. It's starting to look as if he may have fallen victim to Burgess and his crew."

"I'll ride out with you," said Bain. He gestured to the man beside him. "And George here as well. George Sayle. He's my articled assistant. We can keep an eye open for a possible burial…" he stopped, as if realizing what he had just said. He'd worked with George Dobson and knew him well. Now, less than two weeks after the young man had disappeared he understood that a murder could very well have taken place.

They rode out along the Twelve Mile the next morning, and soon found the place Wilson had described. While Bain and his assistant scoured the area looking for signs of a burial, James searched for the log. He found it quickly, a fallen totara tree, partly rotted and crawling with slimy white huhu grubs the size of pencils stubs. He brushed them aside and knelt behind the log. The clothing had not been well hidden, and he pulled outtwo pairs of old trousers, a woolen jumper, and four pieces of cloth which he assumed were the masks Wilson had mentioned.

"No sign of digging, or anything untoward," said Bain, coming back along the track. "We should search more in this area. Perhaps you should drag the bed of the river."

"Good idea," said James. "I'll get that underway in a day or two."

Bain stood for a moment, staring at the log. "I hope you find him soon," he said. "He was one of the most promising young men to work for me for a long time. He worked on some of the largest engineering undertakings on the west coast, and explored the west coast road. He delighted in his work. A good colonial man…it would be such a waste if…"

James nodded. "I understand. But if I find him, he won't be alive you know Bain."

"That's the tragedy, Inspector James," said Bain. "The tragedy and the enormous waste."

13

Greymouth, 1866: The Reporter

Inspector James was lunching at Jack's Nonpareil Pie Shop on Mawhera Quay, and watching anxiously as boats rode higher in the Grey, hinting at flooding upstream, when the reporter from the *Argus* sat down across from him. He placed both hands on the table between them and leaned forward with a knowing look.

"So you 'ave Jamie Murray in the lockup, then?"

"If you're talking about James Wilson, then yes, I have," said James.

"Saying anything, is he?"

James shook his head.

"E's connected to that Burgess character, don't you know?"

James ignored him and kept eating his pie, a pork pie, which reminded him that John Heron, the proprietor of Jack's, kept his pigs - illegally - within the town limits.

"There's been four serious robberies on the West Coast recently, ain't there?"

James pushed aside his plate and wiped his lips with the table napkin. "Four? Can you enumerate them for me?"

"Well, there's the robbery of Mr. Walmsley," said the reporter. "He was the agent of the Bank of New South Wales sent up country to purchase gold…"

"That was last year," said James. "Before my time." The Walmsley robbery was partly responsible for the establishment of the gold escort that had brought him to this district; the case had been used to put pressure on the Canterbury government. The *West Coast Times* had railed about it at the time, painting a picture of a single bank agent who traversed countryside ideal for bushranging, "his horse sinking nearly to its girths in the mud, or stumbling over the stumps of trees hidden far below the slimy surface, with dense bush on either side, offering alike excellent cover for the lurking thief and a secure hiding place when the crime is committed."

"The second one was the abstraction of the gold from the escort," said the reporter, counting off on his fingers. That was the escort from the southern gold fields up to Hokitika, James remembered.

"And…?"

"The robbery of the Ross mailman. That's three." The reporter raised all four fingers and leaned in triumphantly. "And the robbery of the Bank of New Zealand at Okarita."

"Inspector Broham is looking after that," said James.

"Last, but not least," said the reporter, leaving his four fingers in place although he was now up to five events, "Is the disappearance of Mr. Dobson under circumstances that lead to the opinion that he has been foully robbed and murdered. Is that not the case?"

"We have no way of knowing that," said James, rising from his seat. "We have no body, as yet…"

He could feel the reporter's eyes on his back as he left the pie shop, and wondered what was in store for him in the next day's paper.

The following day the Argus arrived at his office featuring a long article calling for an increased police presence on the West Coast, especially in the up-country districts, to "discover and punish the lawless scoundrels who have been let loose on society." He had already considered sending the resourceful Sergeant Walsh up country, and decided he should give it more thought when he had the time. Walsh excelled in his handling of rough characters, partly because he was somewhat rough around the edges himself. Perhaps he could take a constable or two with him as well, establish a camp of his own in one of the gold mining areas. As evidence of the need for more police, the paper mentioned two men who had recently been released from gaol in Otago after serving time for robbery under arms and were now charged with stealing revolvers from the police camp in Hokitika. Revolver cases had been found on one of the suspects but the magistrate had released him after a witness had sworn he had seen the suspect pick the cases up in the street. According to the paper, however, the witness was not of sufficient character to justify releasing the suspect.

James read the rest of the article with sinking heart. Could it be Burgess who had supposedly found the revolver cases? No names were mentioned, but he knew Burgess and Kelly had been in gaol in Otago. To make matters worse, the paper went on to say that the two men in question had moved on to Greymouth where "the first thing they did was to concoct an elaborate plan for waylaying and murdering one of the Arnold gold buyers, and they were only defeated in their plans by the accidental discovery of their intentions."

He should have realized…the reporter had known about Burgess and Kelly and their possible connection to the disappearance to George Dobson before he accosted him in the pie shop, and had been looking for a good quote. Thank God he had not said anything untoward.

As to the words accidental discovery, that was outrageous. Wilson had come to him in the middle of the night because he knew that if he didn't, and James discovered what he had done, he would come after him. There was nothing accidental about it. It was the natural result of months of good police work, and the reputation that followed that work.

The reporter went on to say that although the men could not have been arrested merely because they were known to be thieves, the English Vagrancy Act could have been used, or at least attempted, to arrest them before they left the area. But no attempt had been made. No attempt! He had waited for a warrant from Hokitika, and by the time he had received it the men had gone. And yet here he was, implicitly blamed for failing to arrest Burgess and Kelly when he'd had the chance. And now, the paper said, these ruffians, meaning Burgess and Kelly, were suspects in the mysterious disappearance of George Dobson.

"Got the Argus, I see." Sergeant Slattery appeared at the door to his office.

"Can't you see the steam coming out of my ears?" asked James, slapping the back of his hand on the offending article.

"They say it's our fault because we think our job is detecting not preventing," said Slattery, who had not detected anything for years. "They say we would rather catch the criminals at it, instead of stopping them before they commit a crime."

James did not reply. Sergeant Slattery would understand that James was being blamed for not arresting the men when he had the chance, thereby preventing the murder of George Dobson. But was that the case? He believed now that George Dobson was already dead when Wilson came to see him, raising questions about his honesty and intentions, not to mention his motives.

"I have some more information on the robbery of the Bank of New Zealand at Okarita," said Slattery. "Inspector Broham has sent a warrant for the arrest of Mr. Henry Jones, proprietor of the Manuherikia store. He thinks he may be in Greymouth. Jones purchased some gold from a man named Richard Banner and Broham thinks it's part of the Okarita robbery. He's sending a report on the gold tomorrow, as soon as he receives it from the bank. The bank claims it's been identified as coming from them."

"Send someone to arrest..."

"You may want to arrest him yourself," said Slattery. "There were three men involved in the sale. Richard Banner was one, and a second was named Sullivan..."

"Richard B...," said James. "And Sullivan. You're right. I will arrest him myself."

Henry Jones was enjoying a fine breakfast of bacon, eggs, fried bread and blood sausage - washed down with a pint of ale - at the Union Hotel when James arrived to arrest him. He was a portly man with large whiskers who obviously relished the repast in front of him. He looked questioningly at James when he sat down across the table from him but continued eating.

"Good morning," said James. He leaned forward and added quietly. "Henry Jones, I arrest you for the felonious receipt of a portion of the gold stolen from the Bank of New Zealand in Okarita on the 22nd of May, of this year, 1866. I must caution you that anything you say may be taken down and used against you in the event of a trial."

"I didn't..." began Jones; he belched loudly as he pushed away his unfinished plate of food.

"The courts will go easier on you if you can give me information pertaining to the robbery."

Jones wiped his lips with a napkin, blinking nervously. "I had no idea...robbery you say? I'll give you all the information I can...I don't wish to keep anything secret..."

James pulled out his notebook and pencil. "Can you tell me when you received the gold?"

Jones muffled another belch with the napkin. "Sometime between May 29th and June 2nd."

Right before James had told Burgess and his gang to get out of town then - and after the murder of George Dobson. James noted the dates in his notebook, and asked, "And from whom did you purchase the gold?"

"He said his name was Sullivan," said Jones. "There were three of them, but the one who sold me the gold was Sullivan."

"And the names of the others?"

"One of them was Richard Banner. The other I'm not sure."

"Can you describe them for me?"

"Sullivan was above average in height, about your height I would say, brown hair and fair complexion," said Jones. The other two I don't remember as well. But both short men. Darker than Sullivan and less…less pleasant to look at."

Burgess and Kelly, thought James. Or possibly Burgess and Levy, as Levy was the money man. "How much did you purchase?"

Jones scratched his chin and looked thoughtful. "Eighty ounces," he said. "At a cost of three pounds and fifteen shillings per ounce."

"Did you not wonder where they found the gold?" asked James.

Jones shook his head firmly. "No. They told me they found it at Saltwater Creek. I had no reason to doubt…"

"And was the gold in the form of dust or nuggets?"

Jones leaned back and looked at the ceiling. "I also purchased some from Sullivan later, and that was in the form of amalgam." Amalgam was formed during the process of finding gold. Miners placed mercury in the riffles of the sluices and when it connected with small particles of gold the two formed an alloy. Later the mercury could be separated out and reused. It did point to gold that had come directly from a mine, rather than from the bank, but he would have to await the report from the bank before he could be sure.

"You gave them a rather large sum of money," he said.

"No," said Jones. "It wasn't all in the form of money. I gave Banner some of his in goods. A bag of flour and a side of bacon."

James pushed himself from the table and rose to his feet. "I'm going to need to search you," he said. "Would you prefer it at the station, or will you allow me to search you here?"

Jones opted to be searched at the hotel rather than at the station, and James took him outside to the lean-to beside the kitchen.

"Banner told me he'd supply me regularly with parcels of gold," said Jones, as James searched him. "He said he'd have some for me every week. But I told him I was unable to purchase any more. I told him to see Mr. Broadbent."

"You were suspicious, then," said James. He pulled a pocketbook from Jones' vest pocket, opened it and found a large wad of cash. "I'm going to count this and I'll have to take it into custody. But you can sign for it and you'll get it back…in due course."

"There's almost eight hundred pounds there," said Jones. He narrowed his eyes. "Or shall we say, seven hundred pounds…"

"No, we shall not," said James. "If you're trying to bribe me it won't work. No officer of my force would take a bribe."

"It works sometimes," said Jones, looking unhappy. "Oh well."

James wrote the exact amount in his notebook—788 pounds—and had Jones sign his notebook on the same page. "I'm afraid I'm going to have to cuff you," he said.

Jones put his hands out and sighed heavily as James locked the cuffs.

"Could I carry my coat over the cuffs?"

James walked with him to the station, holding Jones by the elbow, the coat draped casually over the cuffs. We probably look like two old friends out for a stroll, he thought.

The reporter was lurking on Gresson Street, just outside the station. "'Ullo Mr. Inspector James," he said. "Who's this then?"

"Mr. Jones is helping us with our enquiries," said James.

"Can I sit in?" asked the reporter. "With the enquiries, I mean."

"I'm off to Stillwater today," said James. "Perhaps when I return." Or when hell froze over. It was drizzling rain as he accompanied Jones into the station, but he smiled to himself anyway.

14

Greymouth, 1866: The Interview

It had been several days since Inspector James had been to Stillwater looking for the masks; heavy rain and snowmelt in the mountains had swollen the river. After he left Henry Jones at the station with Sergeant Slattery he gathered a team and took them up the river in a flat boat loaded with all the equipment they would need to pull up a body.

James and his team dragged the Arnold and all the creeks in the vicinity. The heavy flooding upstream had not reached Greymouth when they left, and the search was more difficult than he had expected. As well, while he was searching a heavy storm hit. The Arnold rose six feet and began to run so rapidly it was difficult to sink the drags. He spent several days looking before he gave up.

He returned to news that four men were missing in the Nelson area. Dudley, Kempthorne, de Pontius, and Mathieu were friends and businessmen who were moving all their gold and money down to the Bank of New Zealand in Nelson, possibly as much as a thousand pounds' in cash and gold. A friend had planned to meet the group in Canvastown and travel with them for the last forty miles into town, and when they had not appeared after several days he alerted the police. In Nelson, people worried, but in Greymouth everyone's minds flew immediately to George Dobson, making a connection between his disappearance and that of the four men in Nelson.

Rumours began to circulate that a gang was on the rampage and that as many as twenty or thirty men had been robbed and murdered on the coast road between Hokitika and Greymouth and buried in the sand. The passage of gold between the diggings and the banks dropped to a trickle.

James went to talk to Wilson in the lockup at the police camp. He was slumped on a bench in his cell, staring blankly at the opposite wall, chewing his nails. His curly hair was standing up on end, giving him an annoying air of youthful innocence. James had had hair like that once.

The poster James had left lay in the corner, crumpled in a ball, but he had another one with him; he thrust it through the bars.

"Wilson, I want you to look at this reward poster."

Wilson turned towards him with a vacant stare. "Poster?"

"Two hundred and fifty pounds," said James. "It's a lot of money Wilson. Think about it. If you could just tell me…"

"You never gave it to me before, when you could have, the reward," said Wilson. He rose and came towards the door, clutching at the bars. "If you don't find them it's your fault, not mine."

"You mean you knew all along where…wait a minute. Find them? What do you mean them? Who else have Burgess and his crew murdered in this area?"

Wilson shook the bars of his cell. He was becoming agitated. "I don't know if anyone was murdered. But it stands to reason, doesn't it? If they killed one man and didn't get anything, wouldn't they kill again?"

James put his face close to the bars and said urgently, "Wilson, his family must know what has become of him. Think of that. Just give me a hint, like you did with the clothing, and I'll do the rest."

Wilson returned to his bench and leaned against the wall, his eyes closed. Clearly nothing more was to be got from him.

As James left the lockup, Slattery, the Sergeant of the Watch, came out of the station with two men. James recognized them both: Charles Todhunter, who had been in Greymouth searching for his brother-in-law for most of June, and Edward Dobson, George Dobson's father, to whom he had already spoken. Sergeant Slattery introduced the men, and James shook their hands, offering his sympathy.

"Mr. Inspector James," said Dobson. "You have no more information for us? Anything more on George's fate?" Edward Dobson, the provincial engineer, was a tall, hawk-faced man with intense blue eyes with a frown line between them, gingery side-whiskers and a firm mouth. In normal circumstances James knew Dobson would be the kind of man who would expect any order he gave to be followed to the letter. But these weren't normal circumstances, and Mr. Dobson seemed at a loss for ideas.

"Mr. Dobson," said James. "Mr. Todhunter." He gestured towards the door of the lockup. "I've been talking to Wilson, trying to get something out of him, but he refuses to say any more than he has."

"You offered him the reward?" asked Todhunter. Mr. Dobson made a noise that sounded like a tsk.

"I have no intention of giving him the reward," said James, more for Dobson's sake than Todhunter's. "But I've implied that I would."

"Could we speak with him?" said Todhunter.

James glanced at Dobson. "Would you wish to?" Dobson nodded.

"Give me your stick," said James to the guard standing nearby. "We'll go into his cell, the three of us. We may have more luck that way."

Wilson was huddled under a grey blanket, and jumped to his feet when he saw them, looking at Dobson with a panicked expression. James wondered how much the younger Mr. Dobson resembled his father. Edward Dobson's face was closed, expressionless, and he moved away from Wilson and stood behind James and Todhunter.

"What are you going to do?" asked Wilson. He stared at the stick in James' hand.

James tapped it lightly against the side of his leg. "Nothing. Why do you ask?"

GREYMOUTH, 1866: THE INTERVIEW

"And who are these toffs?"

"My name is Charles Todhunter," said Todhunter. He moved forward as if he intended to shake Wilson's hand, then thought better of it. "I've been in town assisting the search for George…for Mr. Dobson, the young surveyor who has gone missing."

"Don't know nothing about him," said Wilson. "I told that to Mr. Inspector James." He sat back down on the bench and folded his arms dismissively.

"You were in the area, however," said Todhunter. "At about the time he went missing, or shortly before. We just wanted to know if you had seen anything, or heard anything, anything, that would help us find his bo…to find him."

Wilson looked up at him suspiciously through narrowed eyes and said nothing. Todhunter moved forward and squatted in front of him, his hands held forward, almost as if he were praying. "You see, Mr. Wilson, he's a much-loved young man, and his family would very much like to…"

"For Christ's sake, Charles," said Edward Dobson suddenly. He took three steps in the direction of Wilson. His whole body was tense, vibrating with rage, and his face had turned a dark wine colour. "For Christ's sake. Don't speak to this less-than-human piece of filth in that way. Don't treat him as if he were…as if he were an equal." He spat the last word out contemptuously.

Todhunter stood up abruptly; Wilson turned sideways and drew his legs up onto the bench, putting one arm over his face. "You can't talk to me like that," he said. "Mr. Inspector James, he can't speak to me like that."

"Like what?" asked James. "I don't see anything wrong with the way he's speaking. He's the model of politeness."

"Dobson," said Todhunter. "Let me continue, please. The important thing is that we find out…"

Dobson strode to the other side of the cell and slapped his hand against the wall. "Speak to him how you damn well like." He remained standing with his back to Wilson, his chest heaving with rage.

"Now Mr. Wilson," said Todhunter, resuming his squatting position. "As you know, the government has offered a substantial reward…"

Edward Dobson made a sound that was half way between a growl and a laugh.

"A substantial reward," Todhunter repeated, "and I'm sure there would be some kind of consideration if you gave us any useful information…" He stopped and looked at James, who gave a curt nod. "We need information, and we are certain you have it. Surely you can tell us something, anything…"

Burgess and Kelly done it," said Wilson. "That's all I can say. If anything has happened to your man, then Burgess and Kelly done it. I don't know for positive, but if anything happened to him, they done it."

James stepped forward. "That's good Wilson. That's what we think already, but that's good. Now if you can just tell us where…"

Wilson set his mouth in a thin line and shook his head firmly. "I told you before, and I'm telling you now, I don't know nothing."

"Nothing?" said Todhunter. "Surely…"

James sighed and looked at Todhunter. "We're not getting any more out of him," he said. He reached over and picked up the grey blanket, now lying beside Wilson in a dirty heap. "This looks like it needs a wash. I'll take it to the laundry. Wouldn't want you to catch an infection from it."

"But I'll freeze without it," objected Wilson.

"It will be washed and back to you in a day or so," said James. "Three days, at most." He stepped towards the door, and the other two men followed him. "If you have anything to tell me, just let the guard know, and I'll come immediately. With the blanket of course…"

Outside, Edward Dobson managed to calm himself enough to talk.

"Thank you for your efforts, Inspector James," he said. "I'm not sure there's anything more I can do here. I think I may have to return to Christchurch. Mr. Todhunter will remain, however, and will offer any assistance you may need."

"He's just a bloody waste of space, Wilson is," said James. "I wish I could strangle him with his own…"

Sergeant Slattery was hurrying towards them waving something in his hand. "Mr. Inspector James," he said. "Cobb's Coach just arrived from Westport with this telegram for you." A telegraph office had not yet been opened in Greymouth, although one was expected within the month. The line was being built alongside the road from Hokitika, the road that George Dobson and his men had helped build.

James snatched the telegram from Slattery and scanned it.

"What does it say?" asked Edward Dobson. "Is it something about…?"

James looked up from his reading. "Those Nelson men who were missing on the Maungatapu Track," he said. "There are no bodies yet, but they've just arrested four men for murder." He paused, almost hating to say the names. "Levy, Kelly, Sullivan, and…and…Burgess."

Edward Dobson's head dropped into his hands and he rubbed his eyes. "He's gone," he said. "They killed my son."

"Have they…" said Todhunter, his voice husky. He tried again. "Have they found any trace of the bodies? Or their equipment?"

James nodded. "Unfortunately, yes. They've found the pack horse belonging to the missing men in a gorge near Franklyn's Flat, still wearing the pack saddle and the swags attached to it. It was dead, shot in the head. It's just a matter of time before they find the bodies. They have no doubt that they're victims of Burgess and his crew. They're all in custody, the four of them. They're setting up a committee to search for the bodies."

Edward Dobson did not respond, but stared ahead, his face drawn and tired, with a hint of sadness in his eyes. Charles Todhunter took him by the elbow and said, "Come along Dobson. Let's see if we can still buy a ticket to Christchurch on Cobb's Coach for you. I'll stay here and take care of things. I'll let you know the minute there's news."

James watched them go then turned to Slattery. "The horse had been backed to the edge of the gorge, and shot in the temple so it fell down into the gorge. The police believe the men were led into the bush with pistols to their heads and shot some distance away—possibly strangled to make sure they were dead. They're brutal men, Slattery. Brutal. I hold out little hope for Dobson at this point."

Later, James wondered why Edward Dobson would not to want to stay and continue the search for his son, now that it seemed the search was showing signs of progress; could it be that he did not wish to be present when the body was discovered? He seemed to be made of sterner stuff than that. His question was answered by Charles Todhunter, whom he encountered in Jack's Nonpareil Pie Shop the next day.

"Mr. Dobson got away safely, I hope?" he said.

Todhunter was sipping a cup of coffee and reading the Argus. "Thank you, yes. He would have preferred to stay, but his wife, George's mother, is upset - understandably - and he felt he should return to Christchurch to comfort her."

"Ah," said James. That made sense to him. "And there are other children? George was…is not his only child. I know of Arthur, of course, but…"

Todhunter nodded. "Arthur, yes…" he stared out the window, something obviously on his mind. "Arthur is two years younger than George…he worships him. And then Caroline, my wife, is the next eldest. The Dobson's have ten children in all."

"A large family," said James.

"He has a brother in Nelson, as well." Todhunter added. "Mr. Edward Dobson, I mean. Arthur, like his nephew. The boys stayed with him for a time after they returned from Tasmania." He took a sip of his coffee, looking thoughtful. "Mr. Dobson came to Canterbury with the two boys, George and Arthur, in 1850, on one of the first four ships to the colony. His wife and several more children followed a year later. But the two boys were somewhat difficult to manage, and he sent them to Tasmania to another brother, the Reverend Charles Dobson, and they stayed there for three years. Of course, their high spirits were a sign of their intelligence and persistence, as is often the case with boys."

"They must be very close," said James. "George and Arthur."

Todhunter put his coffee down, wiped his lips with a handkerchief and pulled a watch from his vest. "Goodness, look at the time. I'd best be going." Clearly he did not intend to answer James' question. He started towards the door, then turned back and said, "Mr. Dobson and I would like to start a fund for the search for the men missing up on the Maungatapu track. Perhaps your sergeant would like to collect the funds and see them forwarded to Nelson."

15

Greymouth, 1866: The Body

As things transpired, it took some time to find the bodies of the men missing in Nelson, despite the large number of volunteers joining the search. News of the search filtered down to Greymouth by mail, steamer and travelers. Rain initially caused delays, and when the search party did go out they returned with nothing, frustrated by their lack of success. Finding the horse had led them to believe that it would be a simple matter to find the bodies of the four men...or what they believed would be four men.

One group of searchers arrived back in Nelson and requested permission from the search committee to take Phil Levy to the site with a rope around his neck to force him to show them where the bodies were. He was universally seen as the most likely to talk, as well as the most likely to be innocent—or at least less guilty than the other three. But the search committee refused to comply with the request. Some members of the Hebrew faith sent a rabbi into the gaol to talk with Levy because it was assumed he was the one who had been sent off to shoot the horse; everyone knew it was an historical and statistical fact that Jews were averse to the shedding of men's blood, although strangulation was apparently still an option, if it was done cleanly. Levy swore a sacred oath on the bodies of his parents that he had not shed the blood of any kind of beast at all.

Mr. Kempthorne's brother published an offer in the Nelson paper of a two-hundred-pound reward for information about his brother's whereabouts; the government also offered a reward for information, adding that anyone not directly involved with the murders but with knowledge of it would receive a pardon for other crimes. The searchers would find the bodies and be given the reward, but it would not go to any of the murderers—at least that was what everyone hoped.

In Greymouth, it was widely assumed that the gang who had killed the four men had also killed George Dobson, and the Argus openly speculated not only that Dobson had been murdered, but also that he had been murdered by the Burgess gang. Commissioner Shearman posted a notice in the Grey River Argus offering a reward and a free pardon for any information pertaining to the disappearance of George Dobson, which James attached to the wall above the Davenport in his study. Perhaps the notice would bring someone forward - one of the many hangers-on and confederates. If not, perhaps one of the gang members would confess.

It came as a surprise to everyone when that someone was Joseph Thomas Sullivan.

James and Elizabeth were spending a rare night out together at the Kilgour Theatre to watch a play: *The Octoroon*, which had been much celebrated in America and played successfully around the country. The story of the doomed love affair between the heir to a plantation and the daughter of the plantation owner and one of his slaves (the said daughter being the titular octoroon) did not end happily; the young woman, Zoe, took poison and died in the arms of her lover just as he was about to learn that he had inherited the plantation, preventing her sale into slavery. The women of Greymouth, including Elizabeth, left the theatre at the end of the evening with tears streaming down their faces, causing some men to comment that the town was in danger of flooding yet again.

The reporter from the Argus was standing outside shivering, his collar turned up and his overly-large bowler hat pulled down below his ears.

"Mr. Inspector James," he called, as they left the theatre. "They're saying that Wilson has confessed and has told you where Dobson's body is buried, even though he wasn't there at the time."

James had been about to walk on and ignore him, but instead asked, "Confessed? Wilson? Who is saying that?"

"The Nelson Examiner," said the reporter, holding out a newspaper. "The Argus wondered if you'd had a confession because you went up to drag the river…"

James took the paper, skimmed through it quickly, then returned it to the reporter.

"All they say is there was a rumour - a rumour mind you - that they were unable to substantiate," he said. "Something said to have come over the telegraphic wires from Picton, which were shown to have been disrupted at the time, so therefore the story could not be true."

"Is it true, as they say, that Wilson told you the gang had dug a grave in advance?"

"No, it certainly is not true," said James sharply. "And neither is it true that they mistook him for Mr....."

He stopped, but the reporter was onto him immediately.

"You don't think he was mistaken for Mr. Fox? Why not. Everyone is saying that."

"Everyone is wrong," said James. He had just realized that himself. He turned to Elizabeth, who was standing beside him wrapped in a shawl, her face pale and blotchy from the crying bout she had just suffered. "My wife is feeling unwell, I'm sorry. We have to leave."

"I'm not feeling unwell," said Elizabeth, holding tight to his arm as they marched off through the mud towards Arney Street. "Actually, I feel better than I have for ages. A good cry is a wonderful way to cheer a person up."

"Why have they not published the numbers and marks on the bank notes," the reporter called after them. "Surely that would connect them to some of the crimes…"

"He got that one from the Examiner," muttered James as they continued walking.

A dark shadow was waiting for them on the verandah of their home, and for a minute James thought it was Wilson, come from the lockup in ghostly form to beg for his freedom. But the shadow stepped forward and revealed itself to be Sergeant Walsh.

"I've been waiting here for some time, walking up and down," he said, unintentionally echoing the words spoken by Wilson. "I'm just back from Hokitika. Inspector Broham has received a telegram and he wanted me to bring it to you immediately."

James took the telegram from Walsh.

"Thank you. Would you like to come in for a warm drink?"

Walsh shook his head, obviously not tempted by the offer of a "warm" drink, as James had known he would not be…a strong drink perhaps…and left in the direction of the Quay, probably with the intention of finding some other source of warmth.

James opened the telegram.

"What does he say?" asked Elizabeth.

"Sullivan has told them where George Dobson's body is buried," he said. He folded the paper and put it into his pocket. "I'll get a search party tomorrow and we'll go out and fetch him home."

Elizabeth clasped her hands together. "At last," she said. "His mother will be so relieved."

But of course, it did not prove as easy as they assumed.

First, Inspector Broham arrived from Hokitika in the wake of his telegram determined to lead the search. He was a young man, a good dozen-years younger than James, with a tall healthy physique, dark, curly red-hair and red whiskers around his jaw that had the effect of masking a slightly receding chin. He'd been known to ride over a hundred miles in one day and was famous for his strength and resolve, as well as for his tightly controlled discipline. He always made a point of arriving first at a new rush, so that any miners who arrived subsequently would see him there and understand that they should be on their best behaviour. James found him most annoying.

Broham arrived early in the morning the day after his telegram, having left Hokitika before dawn. He was already at the station when James arrived, and looked askance at James, making a show of pulling out his watch and checking the hour.

"Good morning James," he said. "Have you gathered a search party yet?"

James was forced to acknowledge that he hadn't; there was no point in mentioning that he hadn't received Broham's message until late the previous evening. Broham was his superior officer and was therefore always right.

Sergeant Slattery came to his rescue. "I have the list of names here, Inspector James. If you remember, you mentioned to me a few days ago that it would be wise to have some names ready in the event…"

"Of course," said James. "Thank you for reminding me, Sergeant. Inspector Broham, perhaps you could walk down to the Quay and find a breakfast somewhere while we gather the team."

"Now then," he said, as Broham left, walking briskly off along Gresson Street. "Whom do we have available?"

Slattery handed him the duty list. "Three of the constables are available today," he said. "They're going on street duty but they're still in the mess hall I believe. Also, Mr. Todhunter and Mr. Bain are keen to direct another search, and the lads from the survey department want to participate—only they couldn't be here for a couple of days."

"Hmm," said James. "Send word to Mr. Todhunter telling him we have a possible burial site and asking him to gather a group. Let him know about Bain. I'll take the three constables and head out this morning. No doubt Inspector Broham will want to be along when we find the body…I'll tell you what. I'll head out while he's having breakfast and when he returns tell him to ride up after us."

He was boarding a flat boat on Mawhera Quay with his three

constables when Broham tracked him down, apparently after having eaten his breakfast at a rapid speed. He climbed into the boat and began issuing orders to the boatmen, who exchanged glances. The Grey ran in two directions—up-stream and down-stream—and they thought they knew enough to tell which direction they were supposed to take.

The boatmen began pushing on their poles, moving the flat boat upstream. To distract Broham from telling them more about how they should proceed, James said, "It's a pity we weren't able to warn the Nelson force in time for them to stop the murders." The thought had been weighing on his mind for some time.

Broham stared at him, his pale blue eyes bulging. "I sent officers with warrants in plenty of time - on the Kennedy. But the Kennedy was delayed by bad weather, else the gang would have been stopped and arrested sooner."

"You told them of my suspicions…"

"Your suspicions? Oh, you mean that they may have murdered Mr. Dobson? No. The warrants were for robbery. I'd heard from one of my sources that they intended to rob a bank in Collingwood, up in Golden Bay. As they had possibly already robbed the Bank of New Zealand in Okarita on May 22nd it seemed likely to be true. In fact, they were heading for Collingwood when they were apprehended."

"Yes. I arrested Henry Jones for feloniously receiving some of the gold from that robbery…you heard about that? He said two men named Sullivan and Banner sold him the gold…"

Broham nodded, his eyes narrowed as he watched the boatmen maneuver their way around a rocky island in the middle of the river, ready to advise them if he thought they weren't doing it correctly. "I suspected it was them from the start, but now Sullivan has confessed to it. Or at least, confessed on behalf of the other desperadoes. We have the porter of the bank up on charges, thanks to Sullivan. He also said they had a confederate in the police, which would be Carr, of course." He leaned forward and spoke to the lead boatman. "You'll be stopping about a mile and a half below the coal pits."

"Constable Carr?" asked James. "The constable who stole the guns from your camp?"

"Exactly. And we knew he was connected to Burgess, because…hey there, mind the rocks. Time for a couple of you to hop out and pull." Two of the boatmen, who had been about to do that exact thing, jumped from the boat into the shallow water holding ropes, and began to pull it into deeper water.

James was confused. There was too much to absorb. Why had he not been told about Carr earlier? And why had Broham not mentioned before that he believed Sullivan and Burgess were involved in the bank robbery? He said nothing, watching the boatmen silently until in due course they pulled the flat boat up on a sandy beach on the Canterbury side of the river. He jumped out onto the sand, and said, "Three of you come with me. The other two can stay here with the boat until we return." The three jumped out onto the sand, while the other two lounged in the boat and lit up their clay pipes, watching Inspector Broham with amused expressions, as if waiting for another irrelevant command. Broham contented himself with repeating James' instruction for the constable and the three boatmen to go with him.

By mid-afternoon James, his three constables, the boatmen and Broham were on the track below the coal pits ready to search. They headed away from the pits towards Greymouth, looking for markers mentioned by Sullivan. After searching carefully in every gully and creek for a half mile down the track, Broham ordered them to head back towards the coal pits. "We're too far west," he said, and James concurred. He was standing not far from a high terrace, studying the area around it, seeing very little, and gestured for the constables to follow him. They had trodden down some of the fern by the look of it, but obviously not found anything. As they moved towards the coal pits he had a stronger and stronger feeling that the body was close by. He could feel it in his bones. The track was narrow and shaded by trees, and there were several possible places he could imagine Burgess, Kelly and Wilson sitting in wait for Mr. Fox, pretending to put up a canvas shanty.

Unfortunately, the light began to fail. It was not much past the shortest day of the year and sun started to set soon after the search began. A fine mist had fallen on the river and it was impossible for a searcher to see more than a few feet ahead. They walked in a line, each man guided by the back of the man in front. Little could be seen on either side of the track. James sent the boatmen back to the boat and carried on, without much hope of finding anything.

"We'd best be getting on to the coal pits, find a place for the night," James said eventually, when it was clear that Inspector Broham was not going to be the one to suggest that they give up the search. Broham agreed readily enough, but it was another hour before they reached the ferry across to the coal pits, an hour of slogging their way over ground that was worse than a swamp. This was the stretch of track that George Dobson was intending to check when he left Mr. Fox, and James could see why. It was in a terrible state, thick with mud interspersed with stumps of trees and huge boulders, and all of them, except for Broham, had at least one fall and were covered in mud and scratches by the time they arrived at the ferry landing. When the ferry loomed out of the dusk, candles flickering, they were all relieved. They could find shelter at the coal pits for the night and start anew the next day.

The next morning, at first light, they were on the search again, but with no more luck.

And on the third day, special constable O'Brian arrived from Nelson on the S.S. Claud Hamilton with a tracing done by one of the Nelson surveyors based on Sullivan's instructions. Yet again they searched and found nothing.

Inspector Broham headed back downstream to Greymouth, but James determined to give it one more day. The shelter he and his constables found at the coal pits that night was abysmal. The small cottage and the tents at the coal pits were occupied, and they lay on the ground outside, warmed by a small coal fire. Without the opportunity to change his clothes, and with the sandflies assaulting him, he awoke on the fourth day with a throbbing head and a stiff body. But he also woke with a vision: the report from the couple who had passed the ruffians on the track, and who said they arrived at the coal pits in the dark. He decided to search further down-stream, below the rocky island, around where they had turned back on the first day of the search.

And there it was. The toe.

16

Wanganui, 1888: The Maungatapu Murders

James was exhausted. The walk and the reminiscing had leeched the energy from him and he could feel pains shooting down his calves. Perhaps it had been time for him to retire.

"Would you like to stop for refreshments?" he asked Crozier. "My shout, only I'm feeling weary and need a pick-me-up." He wished he'd thought of food earlier; he could have stopped at the pie shop on Ridgeway Street. He'd always been fond of pie shops.

"I could hop back up to Woolley's on the Avenue and fetch a couple of a coconut ices," said Crozier. "My wife and I are very partial to Woolley's ices. You sit on the bench over there and I'll go fetch them."

James sat down on the bench overlooking the river and felt the ache in his calves abate. He would have to see a doctor about the pain. He'd felt it for the first time a few months ago and it was coming regularly now. "An excellent suggestion, Crozier," he said. He held out a pound note. "Take this. I'll have a cheese and onion sandwich, if you don't mind, rather than an ice. I find they hurt my teeth. And bring a ginger beer for me. You have one of their ices if you wish—or whatever you would like. On me."

Crozier returned a twenty minutes later holding a lemon ice, a cheese and onion sandwich and a bottle of ginger beer. "It's been some time since I had a ginger beer," he said as he handed it to James. "My mother used to make it, but my wife never learned how. Her mother gave her ginger beer plants many times, but she…"

James untwisted the wire, pulled out the cork from the bottle and held it up. "Do you remember how there used to be competitions for tying these?"

Crozier looked at him blankly.

"Perhaps you don't," said James. "Before your time. Two or more men would compete to see who could tie the most ginger beer corks into bottles within a specified time - usually an hour. Watchers would make bets on their favourite man. A wonderful thing to watch. You could hardly see their hands moving."

"How many could a man tie in an hour?" asked Crozier, scooping out a spoonful of his ice from the fold of greased paper. "As many as a hundred, perhaps?"

"A hundred?" said James. "More like a thousand. I recollect a contest in Greymouth between two fellows where they each tied close to a thousand—an average of seventeen bottles per minute, I seem to remember—and that included tying each cork properly, with the ends of the twine cut off neatly…" January 1867, that contest had been held, during the trial. The month that had seared itself into his memory.

"And there was gambling on the winner?" asked Crozier. His tone indicated he did not approve of gambling. He should have been in Greymouth in the old days…

"Some," admitted James.

"Gambling leads to crime," said Crozier. "In my experience. About those murders you mentioned…"

"By the Burgess gang?"

"Did they catch all of them, the men who did the murders? The Burgess gang?"

"They did, and they were all tried…"

"How many people did they kill?" asked Crozier.

"Four in Nelson and George Dobson in Greymouth, possibly a few more," said James, shifting uncomfortably on the bench. "At the time, everyone thought they'd killed dozens. Sullivan even said that he'd heard Burgess say he'd killed dozens, but we never found more than a few bodies—oh, and I forgot about Old Jamie, so that would be five in Nelson, or just outside Nelson on the Maungatapu trail between Canvastown and Nelson."

Old Jamie. Funny thing that. At the time he'd thought it reasonable that the prospector who had been found first should always be known as Old Jamie. Later he'd discovered that Jamie Battle had been fifty-two; in retrospect that seemed like the age of a man in his prime, not an old man. And what a fighter he'd been. He wasn't a wealthy man, but had been working at an accommodation house cutting flax near Canvastown. He'd left the job to move on, and been paid a little more than three pounds for his efforts. He'd been found not far from the other bodies, face-down, partially buried under a pile of leaves and dirt, his body in a terrible condition. There were signs that he had fought back against his attackers, and Sullivan and Burgess confirmed that he had.

When Battle encountered the gang, Burgess said later in his deathbed confession, he looked more like a man who needed a good loaf of bread than someone who had gold in his pocket, but they killed him anyway after Burgess saw him move his knife around in his pocket, looking as though he suspected them of something. Burgess held a gun to his head and demanded any money he might be hiding in his poke, and Old Jamie pulled out the knife and attempted to defend himself.

After wrestling with him to take the knife away, they dragged him into the bush under the pretense they were going to tie him up and leave him. Then they strangled him. Burgess complained of the difficulty, saying Battle's breathe kept bubbling up when he took his hands away. Sullivan had to push on Battle's stomach to finish the job. They buried him using his own shovel. Afterwards, Sullivan had remarked that it was a nasty job for so little. Of course, the confession was all part of Burgess' attempt to implicate Sullivan more directly in the murders after Sullivan had turned Queen's evidence against the gang, but it rang true in the details at least.

"My uncle's friend said Nelson was in a state of excitement when the men were missing," said Crozier. "The four businessmen. Hundreds of men went searching for them, and when the bodies were brought down the whole town gathered…"

"Much the same in Greymouth," said James. "The whole town was waiting when I brought the body down the river. And most of them attended Dobson's…"

"And the funerals," said Crozier. "He went to the funerals, or funeral, I should say. They were all buried at once. Thousands of people accompanied the cortège. It made quite a strong impression on him. The bodies were taken up to the Nelson cemetery in two carriages, with all kinds of dignitaries in more carriages, and horsemen following those, and a police escort, and…who was the man in charge of the police in Nelson back then?"

"Sergeant-Major Shallcrass," said James. He'd spoken to Shallcrass at some point; he couldn't remember when. He'd asked him about giving immunity to Sullivan. Why had he done that when Sullivan was clearly guilty? And Shallcrass had said he was aiming to get Levy, the Jew, to confess, had in fact separated him from the others for that purpose, but Sullivan had got in first. That was how it was done back then. Find the weak link, get him to confess, send him off on a ship to Australia or England, and then hang the rest. As it turned out, Sullivan was the better witness; everything he said that could be confirmed had proven to be accurate. He'd told Shallcrass where a gun had been hidden, for example.

"That's right. Shallcrass," said Crozier. "He was there as well. He was given the task of searching for the bodies. Like yourself in Greymouth, I suppose."

James nodded. Broham had been technically in charge, but he'd given up too soon, allowing James to claim success – which hadn't sat well with Broham later.

"You weren't in Nelson for the search, then," said Crozier. "Or the trial. Do you know how they died? The victims? My uncle's friend didn't know about that. He wasn't a very good reader, and…"

James nodded again. They'd done the same thing to the four men as they had to old Jamie Battle; told them they were just going to tie them up and leave them in the bush, away from the track, to give themselves a head start. The men were not armed and had no means of protecting themselves, probably thinking there was safety in numbers. But three were strangled and one was shot when strangulation didn't kill him.

When they returned from the murders, they went through the swags attached to the horse's saddle, then tried to lead it down a gully, but it fell and got stuck, so Sullivan shot it right in the white blaze between its eyes. Fortunate, really, as they'd been able to match the bullet to one of the guns when they dug it out of the horse. Sullivan claimed he had been left to watch the track; he'd asked Burgess if he could be one of the men to go into the bush, but Burgess refused his request, saying they should all keep their stations. It was as if they were all clerks at the Bank of New Zealand, with assigned positions and levels of authority, and Burgess was the manager.

"It wasn't pretty," said James. "What they did to those men. They were hiding along the track, with two of them, Sullivan and Levy, behind a big rock - it's been called Murderers' Rock ever since - and they stepped out in front of the victims and said 'Stand. Bail up,' meaning get together in a group. The victims threw their hands up in alarm. Kelly and Burgess then came down the track each holding a gun and a knife…"

"Those poor men," said Crozier. "How dreadful it must be, knowing you're going to die…"

"At least three of them knew they were going to die," said James grimly. "Once they'd killed the first one…"

"It's like something from a dime novel," said Crozier. "Only without a hero to save them…"

That felt a little too close to the truth for James. He stood up and placed his ginger beer bottle on the bench. "Let's continue on. Elizabeth will be wondering…"

Crozier had finished his ice, and tossed the container into the river. He picked up the framed testimonial and rested it awkwardly on his hip. "Let's carry on then," he said. "Can't keep Mrs. James waiting." He started to walk and then stopped. "You mentioned Kelly, Inspector James. Does that Kelly have any connection to the outlaw Kelly, the Australian one?"

"Not that I know of," said James. "A common enough name I believe. Although I did know that other Kelly, Ned Kelly, in a manner of speaking. I was sent to Mitchell in 1860 to be the Clerk of Court, and his family lived in the district, in a town called Beveridge. He would have been just a lad at the time. I remember when he was presented with the sash, after he saved a boy from drowning. Probably the only decent thing he did in his entire life. His father's fault, no doubt. He was a thieving bast…devil. I met them once, his parents. They came in to complain about the police, said we were persecuting them. And, of course, Ned died in a shootout with police."

"The people must have been relieved," said Crozier. "Glad he was gone from their lives."

"Strangely enough, they weren't," said James. "He was very popular. They saw him as a kind of hero, almost like Robin Hood." Now that he thought of it, Wilson had been seen in a somewhat similar way by the general populace, as a likeable person, because he was too young and innocent-looking to have killed anyone, with his small stature and his fair curls. What was it about people that they could not see through someone like that, understand the depths of evil that rested inside them. Like Kelly the outlaw, Wilson had deceived many who should have known better.

17

Greymouth, 1866: Neither Man Nor Boy

Building the Case Against Jamie Wilson

Thinking back to that time, James remembered spending months tracking down the actions of Jamie Wilson, finding out what the gang had done to George Dobson, and making a case against his murderer.

With the body found, the inquests and the funeral over, and the trial to prepare for, he had settled down to the hard slog of tying down the evidence for what he was sure had happened. He began by reading Sullivan's confession. He'd learned more about the gang since the Dobson inquest: in his gaol cell in Nelson, Burgess was boasting he was not afraid of death, convinced he would meet a better life on the other side, as unlikely as that seemed. James had a rather good idea where Burgess might be heading and it wasn't towards the pearly gates. And Levy, who was known as a "putter upper," or crime planner, and was therefore considered less vicious and more likely not to have been involved in the dirty work, had in fact kept a sly grog shanty on the road to the goldfields in Otago near the Molyneux River from where many diggers had gone missing or been found dead in the river. Burgess and Kelly had been in gaol in Otago for sticking up and shooting at the police in Wetherstones; Sullivan had also been involved but had been given a lighter sentence, afterwards leaving for New South Wales. The Otago police had been surprised to learn that he was back in New Zealand.

Minutes into Sullivan's confession he realized that Wilson, or Murray as Sullivan called him, had been left in Greymouth to keep an eye on James while the gang planned the murder of Mr. Fox. That explained why Wilson was staying at the Criterion Hotel, which was on the corner of Gresson and Arney Streets, and fifty yards from James' own house, rather than in the Provincial Hotel with Burgess and Levy. Strange that he hadn't seen…more importantly, Sullivan had placed Wilson on the scene of the murder of George Dobson, not just as a hanger-on, but as a central participant. Luckily, Wilson was in custody and going nowhere until the trial, and there was plenty of time to make a case. According to Sullivan, not only had they murdered Dobson in his district, but they had also murdered a storekeeper at the Grey, and an accomplice whom they considered too weak for what they wanted to do.

He read through the confession carefully, starting with the deaths on the Maungatapu, noting the methods of the murderers, looking for similarities to Dobson's murder. The men on the Maungatapu had been strangled and shot, and one, Pontius, had been stoned—when he refused to die, the villains picked up rocks and smashed them on his head until he succumbed. One method was not enough for any single victim, as with Dobson, who had been hit on the head and then strangled.

Three of the bodies were buried in shallow graves under dirt and leaves, but the killers spent considerable time burying the fourth body under rocks. Sullivan explained that Burgess and Kelly thought that when three men were found and the fourth was seen to be missing, everyone would assume the missing man had killed his mates and sloped off with the gold and money. Clearly Burgess and Kelly did not understand that some men, especially those they had killed on the Maungatapu track, were known to be decent men and would not therefore be suspected of such a heinous crime. Old Jamie had been murdered because he had seen the gang, and Levy had decreed that no man should pass along the road alive. He too had been buried in a shallow grave and covered with dirt and leaves. The rule seemed to be that anyone who could identify them had to die.

And as if strangling, shooting or stoning victims was not enough, the gang had, Sullivan said, also obtained strychnine with which to poison unsuspecting victims after they had befriended them. James knew that ingesting strychnine was one of the most painful ways to die; anyone swallowing it would die in convulsions. The gang's scheme was to share a campfire with their would-be victims, partake in a pannikin of tea and a drop of grog laced with the poison, and when the victims died, to throw them in the river to be "found drowned," be swept out to sea, or left to rot at the bottom of the river to provide food for eels.

Sullivan noted that Wilson had known Burgess for some time, but had never been in on a big robbery and was keen to try. Kelly introduced him to Sullivan, telling him that Wilson was a clever pickpocket who survived by pretending to sell newspapers. He'd been a bellman at a hotel in Nelson, a bell-ringer some called it, but was convicted of petty theft and gaoled for six months, after which he'd moved to Hokitika. He'd begged Burgess to be allowed to accompany the gang on the stick-up of Mr. Fox, and Burgess had given it some thought before he agreed. Reading this, James was struck once more with the way Burgess managed and manipulated the men. They seemed to consider it an honour to work with him. What did they see in him?

On Monday the 28th of May, the day Dobson was murdered, Sullivan claimed that he, Kelly and Wilson had been sent up the Twelve Mile to look out for Mr. Fox. Burgess had remained at the Provincial Hotel to await Levy, who was coming up from Hokitika—he couldn't accompany the others as his boots were wet and he couldn't get them on. But if they saw Mr. Fox coming by boat they were to send a message to Burgess by DeLacey.

Interestingly, Sullivan claimed DeLacey had told them to be careful as there were plain-clothed policeman playing about on the track. He reread the date: if Sullivan was talking about the plain clothes men James had sent out, then the date was wrong. The constables had gone out after the date of the murder - after he had spoken to Wilson on May 30th, in fact. The murder date was firmly established in James' mind as May 28th because David Duncan, who had given evidence at the inquest, was so sure of the day and had presented a dated receipt to prove he had been there. Sullivan said he had seen Duncan herding cattle on the day of the murder, and could not therefore have also have been expecting to see the plain clothes constables on the same day. The puzzle of the dates did not prove that Sullivan was lying, however. In fact, most of his information rang true. The question was, did he not remember the correct date, or was he trying to sew confusion about the dates without seeming to lie? Perhaps he was trying to develop an alibi after the fact. Of course, in a town like Greymouth dates and days of the week often meant nothing to people. They lived by the weather and the light.

Kelly and Wilson had donned masks and waited for Mr. Fox, hiding inside a tent that was "stretched out" to make it look as though they were putting it up. Sullivan, who was not known to Mr. Fox, was sent up the track to engage him in conversation. Mr. Fox was described to him as "a tall, round-shouldered man with a long stride." Sullivan had waited, but Mr. Fox had not come. Instead, a young surveyor, described later by Kelly as "neither man nor boy," with his whole life still before him, came down the track and spoke to Sullivan. Sullivan described the encounter:

"I met a young man and asked him how far it was to the shanty; he replied about half-a-mile. This was about 2 o'clock. I should think it was about half-a-mile from the bridge where I met him. There was no other tent between that spot and the iron store but ours. The young man had on

dark clothes, and had what appeared to be a top coat suspended across his shoulder by a strap. I do not recollect whether he had a cap or hat. He had leggings or boots on. He had an albert guard. I think I would know it again ... It is what I call a snake guard. I continued my way, and the man went on towards Greymouth." Grey River Argus, 6 December 1866

The next time Sullivan saw Dobson, a half hour later, he was leaning slumped against a tree with his tongue sticking out grotesquely, dead. Kelly and Wilson told him, unconvincingly, that the young man had died of fright. Sullivan thought they shouldn't leave the body where it was, and waited while the other two - Kelly and Wilson - buried him under a layer of dirt and leaves, which they then stamped down, much in the way the gang had later stamped down on the graves of the five men on the Maungatapu. They buried the watch and chain with the body, he said, but he had burned a deposit receipt worth forty-two pounds.

Dobson was murdered because the gang had been unable to rob Mr. Fox, and were annoyed. They knew who they were killing, and had not killed him in mistake for Mr. Fox, as the papers had speculated; after all, either Wilson or Kelly had described Mr. Fox to Sullivan, and Dobson in no way matched that description. The brutes may have mistaken him for someone who carried cash - a bank agent like Mr. Walmsley, perhaps - but they would soon have realized he was merely a surveyor checking a recently-built road who would not carry a large sum of money on his person. But once they had stuck him up he had seen them and had to die.

With blood on their hands, Burgess, Kelly, Levy and Sullivan had left Greymouth when James had told them to leave, and gone on to Nelson, apparently with the idea of robbing a bank there; soon after, five more men had been killed.

Wilson had come to him two days after the murder of George Dobson, more afraid of Burgess and Kelly than he was of the police, to confess to a future crime knowing he had already been present and assisted at a murder himself. He must have hoped that Dobson's body would remain missing; he had underestimated James' persistence.

He stopped reading, thinking hard, drumming on the table with his fingers. The facts were there. Everyone agreed that the murder had taken place on May 28th; but Wilson had come to see James at his home on May 30th– he had the date in his notebook – and Mr. Warden Revell would confirm it. Wilson's "confession" was intended to cover his own tracks, and use the police to save himself from Burgess. It was a sleight of hand. Confess to being involved in a conspiracy to rob and throw suspicion away from a murder he had already committed - or at least been present at.

After James had warned the gang off, they had boarded the S.S. Wallaby and gone to Nelson, where they had continued their murderous rampage. He would need to find more out about how they had gone north, and when; he would talk to the captain of the S.S. Wallaby when he had an opportunity. He skimmed through the rest of the confession, noting that Sullivan had described how they had killed a storekeeper on the Grey. They had gone into his store and demanded money. When he had refused to give them any they had "half strangled him." They had promised to let him live if he told them where the money was, and when he had done so they finished strangling him and threw his body in the river. As usual, they had left no witnesses.

He put down the confession and rubbed his eyes with the flat of his hand. Never had a murder affected him the way this one had. George Dobson had been an able, popular young man who had died before he'd had a chance to fulfill his promise after encountering the most brutal gang of men New Zealand had ever seen. Jamie Wilson had not been part of that gang until a few weeks before the murder, but he had wanted to belong, had gone along with them willingly on what he may or may not have thought was a merely a robbery. He had been present when the murder was committed, and had done nothing to stop it – had at the very least helped bury the body. Men had hung for much less. Why should a man like Wilson, with no value to the community, not pay for what he had taken from that community?

James knew he could not save George Dobson, but he would at least see justice done for the young man and his family. If he didn't he would never forgive himself. He sat and thought about it for a long time.

18

The Arnold Track, 1866: More Bodies

He arrived at his office the next morning to find the police camp abuzz with news that another body had been found on the Arnold track about four miles from Greymouth. The corpse had two broken legs and was missing its head, which was nowhere to be found.

"Does anyone know who it is?" James asked Sergeant Slattery.

"Hard to tell," said Slattery wryly. "Dressed in the usual clothes, boots, whatever, can't recognize his face because…"

"He hasn't got one?"

"S'right. Could be the other storekeeper"

"Other storekeeper? Which other storekeeper?"

"The other storekeeper that Sullivan mentioned."

"I assumed the storekeepers were Mr. Fox, the gold buyer, and Mr. Watts from the iron shack," said James. "Although Mr. Watts was found back in March…"

"When Burgess was still in Hokitika," said Slattery. "Although it does sound like murder. He was naked, and face down in a shallow puddle behind his shack. Hard to commit suicide that way…"

"What did Dr. Foppoly have to say about it? Any bruising?"

"There wasn't an inquest," said the sergeant. "We didn't think it necessary at the time. And he's in the ground now. Could be drink of course. And then there was Mr. Gregory, the storekeeper from Noble's Gully. He drowned as well."

"When was that?" asked James. There seemed to be a surfeit of shopkeepers who could qualify for Sullivan's murdered, river-tossed storekeeper.

"In April, but not a suspicious death. He was taking a flat boat up the river to Twelve Mile, amidst a freshet - he insisted on going, even though he was told it was unsafe—and four men drowned because of that decision. They were swept down the river to the wharf at Cobden, four of them clinging to the boat. A Mr. Jackson managed to swim ashore, and he saw two of the others disappear beneath the surface and not come up. Mr. Gregory was still clinging to an oar wedged in the boat, and Mr. Jackson called to him to keep hold. Two men rowed out to save him, but he let go of the boat and was clutching onto a gin case, which kept him afloat for a few minutes. But then he disappeared beneath the waves just as help arrived. We found him on North Beach wearing nothing but trousers, as per usual."

James head was starting to spin with all the unnecessary information. "Not a possibility for the headless body, then," he said.

Slattery was not done. "In late June, a storekeeper named Mr. McCormack from Old Moonlight drowned. He was with another man, on the same horse, and the horse missed its footing and threw them into the river. The other man swam to safety but Mr. McCormick was washed away. He's still missing, so…"

"He could be our headless body," said James.

Slattery nodded. "Quite possibly," he said.

James sighed. "And now there's another dead storekeeper out there somewhere?"

"Just a dead body," said Slattery. "And we don't know who he is because…well, you know why not."

"Yes. Well, keep me informed," said James.

Slattery nodded and was about to leave, but remembered something. "Mr. Watts," he said. "He was still wearing a ring with his initials, but missing some money; people who knew him said he should have had about thirty pounds on him."

James looked at him and waited.

"And that seems to be what Burgess and his crew do. They leave something valuable so it looks like the person died natural like...and wasn't robbed."

"Very good sergeant," said James. "It's possible they were up in Greymouth earlier and returned to Hokitika, and in that case we would know who the storekeeper is that Sullivan..."

The sergeant wasn't finished. "No," he said stubbornly. "I'm having second thoughts about that. Sullivan said they killed a storekeeper and threw his body in the river—the puddle wouldn't count as a river, would it? And he also said they killed one of their own to keep him quiet. More'n likely Mr. Watts was one of their own. So the body without the head, that might be the mysterious storekeeper."

"Worth checking into at any rate," said James. "I think I'd better get up to the Arnold and check on all known and unidentified bodies. I'll take my swag with me—I'd best take a revolver as well. Send someone to tell Mrs. James I may not be home for a few nights."

"We have a list," said Slattery. "A list of missing people. It's quite long..."

"Could you give me a couple of names?" asked James patiently.

"There's a baker," said Slattery. "He disappeared while baking bread. Left a batch sitting beside the oven. Then there's Mr. Tapperell, Mr. Montgomery's storekeeper, who's been missing for a while. I'm not sure..."

"A boatman from the Grey was missing as well, wasn't he?" asked James.

"Joseph Meirnick," said Slattery. He was found. He was swept out to sea with those floods and then washed up on the beach a few miles north. He was six feet from the water's edge and had no marks on him, well just on his face - eels got him in the river, more'n likely - but he was otherwise fresh. Naked but for a pair of high boots and his navy duck trousers, which happens when they're swept out to sea. There was an inquest on him when..."

"When I was searching for Dobson," said James. "Right. Put something in the *Argus*. Ask the public for names of anyone else who might be missing. Be sure to tell the paper to mention Mr. Tapperell specifically, even though he's been missing for several months. Say that any information relative to him will be received with thanks."

"Oh, and I forgot Cook…"

"A cook and a baker are both missing?" asked James. "Is there a kidnapper hoping to set up his own hotel, do you think?"

Slattery shook his head and looked serious, obviously not getting the joke. "No, it's Mr. Cook. Employed by the Card brothers, down in Saltwater Creek. And there's Mr. Jolly's store man, from his branch on the old Totara goldfield. The gold was taken from the store, but he—the store man—left money in the bank when he disappeared. Inspector Broham thought he might be another victim of Burgess…but the general opinion seems to be that he wandered off into the bush in a state of incipient madness, from…"

James completed his sentence. "From drink," he said. "That seems to be a common reason for disappearances in these parts."

He walked along Mawhera Quay to where several flat boats, manned by eager boatmen, were tied to tree stumps out in the water. He picked one who had a team of five sturdy fellows with him and beckoned them over. They pulled the boat up onto the sand and he stepped in.

"I need to stop about four miles up, wherever you can find a landing. And a second time across from the coal pits. Then you can put me off at Stillwater Creek," he said. The creek was about half a mile below the junction of the Arnold and the Grey, where the rivers converged into a narrow gorge with a fast-moving current.

The trip up the Grey was slow and difficult. The owner of the boat sat at the stern holding the rudder, while the crew divided into pairs, two pulling on oars, two using poles to keep in the deeper parts of the river. The river flowed initially though a narrow channel and other than the current, the boatmen had an easy pull upstream; after rounding a huge bend the river changed; wide swathes of gravel slowed them down, and the pole men were kept busy keeping the boat in the narrow channels between the sandy areas. When the water became too shallow, most of the men hopped into the water and took hold of ropes to pull the boat. James watched them labouring in the freezing water, sometimes chest-deep. It seemed like a dreadful job, but the men were well paid and happy to do the work, even though they knew the work would shorten their lives.

At the four-mile mark, with the two islands below which George Dobson's body had been found just starting to become visible, the boatmen pulled over to a large sandy area. He could see an iron hut not far away, and asked the boatmen to wait for him while he walked to it.

An old man was sitting outside having a pipe. He nodded at James but said nothing.

James got right to the point. "Did you know William Watt?" he asked. "The former owner of this…"

The old man took the pipe from his mouth and spat on the ground. "He's dead," he said. "Murdered. Not that the police seem to care."

"What makes you think he was murdered?"

"You think he'd take all'n his clothes off, and lie down and drown hisself in a puddle?" The old man's voice was heavy with sarcasm.

James smiled. "I'm sure you're right. But why would anyone want to drown him?"

"Had some cash hid away," said the old man. "Thirty quid, maybe. I'd say that would be enough for someone to kill another human being."

"You've heard of the murder of Mr. Dobson, I presume?"

The old man recommenced smoking his pipe and nodded slowly.

"And you know the police have a gang of men in gaol up in Nelson for his murder, as well as several more?"

The old man anticipated his next question. "Didn't see them round here back then," he said. "Though I did see that Sullivan hanging around up here a couple of days before the Dobson murder. Had a fowling piece, he did. Said he was shooting birds."

"Was Mr. Watt acquainted with Burgess do you think?"

"Maybe," said the old man. "I did see Sullivan hanging around here, as I said. And Mr. Watt, he wasn't above a bit of malarkey. But did you check their thumbs, the blokes who murdered Mr. Dobson?"

"Thumbs?"

"I didn't hear tell that any of them had bite marks," said the old man. "Someone stuck up Johnson, the storekeeper, two men I heard. They took four-pound weight of gold from him. Says he put up a good fight, and bit one of them on the thumb very hard."

"Yes, I know of that robbery," said James. "But I believe Mr. Johnson said there were two men who spoke with strong German accents. And one of the robbers later drowned." And is still missing, he thought. Yet another possibility for the headless body. The waters of the Grey must be awash in corpses. "We'll catch him soon," he said. "The robber who didn't drown."

He disembarked from the flat boat a second time at the ferry dock opposite the coal pits and walked up to a shanty nestled in the cliffs. The owner came out from his shanty to meet him, a short sturdy man with a grizzled but cheerful face. He doubled as a ferryman and a publican, although illegally in the latter case as his shanty was unlicensed to serve alcohol. James would have to charge him with sly grogging at some point, but now wasn't the time.

"Morning Alabaster," he said.

"Morning Mr. Inspector James," he said. "Come to see the corpse, 'ave you?"

The smell in the shed was strong, pervading the air within twenty feet of the shed—the same sickening smell that had led him to George Dobson's body. The body had been sewn into a canvas bag, and Alabaster pulled out a bowie knife and slashed it open. James took hold of the two separated sides of the tear and pulled them carefully apart.

At first it was hard to tell that a human being lay inside. He could see what looked like rotting meat with a large bloody slash at the top. Then he realized he was looking at the headless shoulders of a man.

"He's missing his head," said Alabaster, in case James hadn't noticed.

James nodded. "I can see that," he said. "Where was he found?"

"My ferry pulled him up," said Alabaster. "He was bobbing around on the edge of the river - he must have reached here from upstream."

"Not on the track then?" asked James. That was what he had been told. "Any idea where he might have come from?"

Alabaster did have an idea. "See this cut?" He pointed to the place where the head had been. "Looks to me like he got caught in machinery. I'll bet he was a miner upriver - up by Twelve Mile or Red Jacks, somewhere like that - and he fell and got caught up in the waterwheel that feeds the water race, left his head behind and came down the river. The fall could have broken his arms as well, or that could have been done by my ferry..."

James looked. The head had been torn off—cut half way across then pulled off the rest of the way. If he'd been alive when he fell he'd have gone through hell before he died. It was to be hoped that he was dead before his head was torn from his body. "I can see what you mean," he said. "Although I can't tell whether the injuries are post mortem. Maybe your ferry tore off his head and broke his arms, after he'd been in the river a while."

Alabaster seemed unperturbed by that possibility. "Could have been murdered, couldn't he? Been pushed in by someone who knew he would drown. And then got caught in something that took off his head..."

"Hard to prove that," said James. He bent over the corpse again. "Any identifying marks on him?"

Alabaster leaned forward to take a closer look. "He's dressed like a miner," he said. "Now if it was Mr. Tapperell..."

"You know about him?" asked James.

"Of course. I believe he may have been heading - coming - this way, but dressed in his Sunday best, and this man clearly is not…"

"Ahoy there," said a voice in the distance. The two men stood up. A man in a high bowler and long top coat, holding a crook in his hand, was hailing them from the other side. When he had Alabaster's attention he made a drinking gesture at him, which Inspector James pretended not to notice. He would definitely send a sergeant up to make a sweep of the sly grog shanties at some point.

"I'll be right over," Alabaster called to him. To James he said, "What would you like to do with him? Should the coroner see him?"

James shook his head. "Can you find a place back in the bush to bury him? I don't think there's anything here that makes me suspect foul play. It looks too much like an accident." He turned to go, then stopped. "But if his head turns up, let me know."

After the corpse was wrapped up again, he went back to the flatboat to continue towards where the Grey met the Stillwater. The river was flowing fast downstream and it took all the strength of the boatmen to get him that last half mile. He would walk up to the Arnold from there, easier now that a bridge spanned the Stillwater Creek. Curtis and Co. had done a good job on that one, although with the Stillwater living up to its name the bridge was probably safe for many years. He paid the boatmen and sent them back down the Grey. Once up at the Arnold he could walk along the track to Arnold Township and on to the lake, where he'd find a room for the night.

He crossed the Stillwater bridge to the Arnold track, which ran from the Arnold-Grey junction down to Greymouth in one direction, and to Brunner Lake in the other. Above the junction, the Grey basin spread out into a wide valley where every ravine and creek was proving to be rich with gold, and therefore equally replete with miners. From the Arnold Valley east to the mountains, dozens of mining operations, both big and small, had sprung up, hampered only by the bush, the mud, and the lack of good pack roads. It was the condition of these roads that George Dobson had wanted to investigate, as he walked up from Maori Gully to Arnold Township, and down towards

Greymouth.

James wasn't finding much evidence related to the Burgess gang, however, and doubted they'd been in this area.

The walk along the Arnold was arduous. The recent rains and high winds had washed away the banks and fallen trees lay across the track. Every hundred yards or so he was forced to climb over tree trunks and newly-formed streams. Finally, at Arnold Township - not much more than a collection of shacks - he came upon a ferryman sitting on a log enjoying a pipe. His ferry, a small punt capable of carrying two or three people, was secured by a rope to a stump sticking out of the water.

The Arnold River was narrow in places with frequent muddy shoals, and difficult to navigate. Passengers would often be forced to disembark ashore while the ferryman dragged his craft through rapids. In December, at the same time Mr. Tapperell had disappeared, a flat boat loaded with supplies had pulled from its moorings and been swept away. The owner, a Greek, had been saved, just barely, after a period of insensibility; two other men were swept away and drowned. Their bodies had not been recovered and were probably out to sea by now as they hadn't washed up on the beach.

Few other options were available for travel: just the track and the ferry. There'd been talk of constructing a better bridle path beside the river so a horse-drawn boat could be put to work, but nothing had come of it so far.

"Good day. I'm investigating missing men in the area…."

"Ah, Mr. Dobson, no doubt," said the ferryman. He knocked the ash from his pipe on the bottom of his shoe, and stamped out the resulting spurt of flame in the dry grass at his feet. "I 'eard he'd been found. You'd be the copper who found 'im then?"

"Yes," agreed James. "But we seem to have several more missing men, and we've had a confession from a member of the gang who murdered Mr. Dobson. He says they murdered a storekeeper. I'm interested in knowing if…"

"Mr. Tapperell, he were a storekeeper."

"He was one of the men I wanted to know more about," said James. "Can you give me any information? You were acquainted with Mr. Tapperell?"

"He were right here on this boat," said the ferryman, pointing to the seat in the rear, as if he expected James to be able to see the man still seated there. James waited. "Took him down to the Brunner, I did. Let him off there. And he says," the ferryman paused for dramatic effect, stabbing his finger at the seat where the presence of Tapperell still sat, "He says, Joe…that's my name, Joe. He says, Joe, I'll be back later today." He shook his head. "But he weren't. He ain't been seen since."

"And a search has been made…?"

"Mr. Montgomery, the owner of the store where he worked, and his friend Mr. Leith, they searched the river on both sides, thinking he decided to walk back and got lost. But nothing. Neither hide nor hair of him."

"Did he say where he were…was going?" asked James. "Whom he intended to visit?"

The ferryman shrugged. "Didn't ask, and he didn't say…"

"When was this?" asked James. He seemed to remember it had been several months ago.

"Afore Christmas," said the ferryman. "Mid December, as I recall. If he were in the river he'd be down the Grey and out to sea by now I 'spect, after all that rain we've had."

So he'd disappeared several months before Burgess and his crew had arrived on the West Coast. James would have to say something to quash all those stories back in Greymouth about Mr. Tapperell being a possible early victim of Burgess and Kelly. He would get Slattery to place an announcement in the Argus when he got back to the station.

"How was he dressed?" asked James, remembering the headless body he'd just seen.

"His Sunday best," said the ferryman. "Intending to meet someone, all dressed up that way. Not a woman though."

"What makes you say that?" asked James, interested.

"He were already three sheets to the wind," said the ferryman. "Four sheets even. He could hardly stand straight. Last time I saw 'im he were tottering off towards the public house down by the lake."

James sighed and mentally crossed Mr. Tapperell off his list of victims. Yet another victim lost in the bush or the rivers of the district while in a state of inebriation. "Not the victim of a crime then," he said.

The ferryman stared at the river for a few minutes. "Not a victim, no…" he said.

"You know something more about him?" asked James.

"He were from Australia," said the ferryman. "Sent there, if you know what I mean…"

"Transported?" asked James, surprised.

The ferryman nodded. "He didn't say that to me, but some things he said, about Australia and the like…he were, well, he were transported, I could tell. Said he arrived in Van Diemen's Land in '53, for one thing. So that would mean he were a crook."

"Trying to remake his life in New Zealand," said James. "He wasn't up to anything nefarious here, was he, working at a store…"

The ferryman nodded his agreement. "Came here to get away from two women," he said. "Had a son back in Tasmania by another woman. S'why lots of us are here…"

He left the ferryman and continued his walk. Not all men were lucky enough to have a woman like Elizabeth who would stick by his side whatever happened. Not that he would ever be unfaithful to her…

The waters of Lake Brunner came into view, with the ranges in the distance. Another, larger, camp abutted the water, with more stores and shanties and tracks radiating into the bush. The same thing, all over the district. He walked down into the shanty town slowly, thinking. The headless body was not the victim of a crime, and Mr. Tapperell had most likely died entirely by his own actions. He was sure to discover other such stories in the town he was approaching. What he really wanted to know - needed to know - was more about what had happened to George Dobson. He would take the road to Maori Gully and talk to Mr. Anderson, the man who had seen him there. Then he would walk towards the coast in the direction from which Dobson had come, and find out everything he could about the young man's journey.

19

Maori Gully, 1866: George Dobson's Last Walk

At Maori Gully he headed for the Shamrock Hotel, gathering place for local merchants and businessmen. One of them would give him further insight into George Dobson's walk and help him establish exact times and dates.

He'd been thinking of establishing a small police force in the area. He'd start with that, and lead slowly into his questions about Dobson to avoid encouraging the frauds who liked telling stories; he'd find himself an honest talker. Several of the residents of Maori Gully, including Mr. Fox, had asked for a station, saying two constables could keep the peace and also act as a gold escort between the township and Greymouth now that so much gold was coming down from the district.

There'd been robberies, of course. Only to be expected. But most robbers took their ill-gotten gains and ran, sometimes not bothering to tie up their victims, or even take their horses. Burgess and his gang were the first group he knew of who left no witnesses, killing them in such a brutal manner. George Dobson must have assumed he was about to suffer the usual type of robbery; he would lose the little money he carried with him, but he would live to talk about it with his mates at the survey department.

He found a group of men huddled around a table in the bar of the Shamrock talking animatedly. One of the men greeted him and made room for him at the table.

"What brings you to the district, Inspector James?"

"Various things," he replied, raising his finger to summon the publican. "Checking on your policing needs, and following up on some missing persons…"

A tall, dark-haired man leaned forward in his chair. "You thinking of setting up a police station up here? We need a gold escort…"

"Costigan's right," said another. "We have to worry about being robbed every time we take our gold down to Greymouth, and Mr. Fox won't take it all. But we need a medical man here as well. Perhaps you have some influence with that? All those winds we had last month." He looked around the group. "Right men? A doctor? Think about those two blokes who died then. They would have lived for certain if we just had a doctor here…" He turned back to James. "A tree fell on their tent in the wind and crushed them. One broke his leg and died of gangrene before we would get him to the hospital in Greymouth. Just faded away into sleep, but talking up 'til then." He stopped and took a swig of his beer, to wet his whistle so he could continue his tale. "The other man was bending over his bed and the tree fell on his back. Course he only lived a few hours and didn't speak…he was insensible…but at least his suffering could have been relieved. And others lived by sheer luck with all the trees coming down. One tree landed on a stump and turned sideways, else four…"

"They should pay attention to what they're told, and cut the trees down around their dwellings," said Costigan. "We need police, and we need a surveyor to tell us where the gold…"

"A post office," said another man standing at the bar, putting his mug down firmly to emphasize his point. "What we need is a post office and a road for the mail and goods. Ten or twelve days it takes to get a letter from Greymouth. We had a meeting last month and nothing came of it. Take that message back to Greymouth, Mr. Inspector James. Two thousand pounds for a road eight miles long, good enough for pack horses, and we could…"

James' beer arrived and he took a long sip. There was no way he would be able to steer the conversation around this table. It was like a careening coach with no coachman. He may as well just get straight to the point.

"I heard young Mr. Dobson passed through here on the way to…"

"That he did," said Costigan, an Irishman by the sound of him. "Stayed the night and went off with Mr. Fox the next morning. Mr. Fox is a neighbour of mine…"

"And you saw him…spoke to him?" asked James.

"I had a pipe with him," said Costigan. "Lovely young fellow, he was. Very friendly, no side to him at all. Said he was worried about the condition of the road from the Arnold to Greymouth and wanted to look for himself. Would have been easy for him to turn around and go back to Hokitika, but he was a conscientious chap. The survey department sent him up here to look at putting in a more direct road to Greymouth, through No Town and down to the Saltwater, not to check on his own track…terrible how it all turned out for him…"

"Terrible," agreed James. He had found his honest talker - or at least a talker.

"I met the Kelly gang, you understand," said Costigan. "At Jimmy Pots' shanty at Omotomutu."

"And Burgess?" asked James. He considered Burgess the leader, not Tom Kelly, who clearly provided the brute strength – the emphasis being on brute.

"Him too," said Costigan. "I knew Levy personally, as well. Knew him in Queenstown. He kept a small shop there. They invited me for a cup of tea…"

"You didn't accept, I hope," said James, thinking of the strychnine.

"No, I was on my way somewhere," said Costigan. "In a hurry. But I met Kelly and Burgess once or twice on the Maori Gully road. They asked me how the diggings were going."

A seemingly innocent question, of course. "And you told them?"

Costigan nodded. "As I said, Mr. Fox was my neighbour, and he was the main gold buyer from the district, so I always knew how much gold was going down to Greymouth."

"Did they ask you when Mr. Fox was likely to be going down to Greymouth?"

Costigan's face expressed shock as he took in the implications of what James had just asked. "I didn't, I never…"

The door to the Shamrock opened and Mr. Fox blew in, his coat flying, as if the mention of his name had invoked his presence.

"Gude day to you, Inspector James," he said. "What brings you here?"

"Just passing through," said James. He had already spoken to Mr. Fox extensively about what had happened the day he parted from George Dobson. "I was thinking about setting up a police station here…"

"Gude idea, gude idea," said Fox. "And while you're on it, could you nae speak to someone about the water race? We've formed a company…The Brunner Lake Grand Trunk Water Race…if we could just see that built we'd be able to take much more gold from the district and not have to rely on this rain we've had recently for the sluicing…"

He left the Shamrock and went in search of William Anderson's store. Maori Gully was not a small, contained township, but spread out through a large valley with diggings and tents dotted throughout and raised terraces on either side. A wooden flume ran down from one of the terraces with long toms thrusting out at irregular intervals; the long toms were used to flush the wash dirt over the riffles and separate gold from rocks and sand. He could see shacks, calico tents set up as permanent living quarters, in amongst the trees and too close to them, many with smoke rising from tin chimneys. A cluster of stores and rooming houses sat in a single row adjacent to the Shamrock, connected by logs laid on the mud but already sinking into it.

Anderson was in his store, huddled beside a hot stove, working on his accounts. He was a tall lean Swede with light eyes and a ruddy complexion. He put down his pencil and stood up to greet James.

"Good evening Mr. Inspector James. You look for a place to sleep tonight?"

James had his swag on his back, so the question made sense. He'd been going to spend the night at the Shamrock, but he could just as well stay here, where it was quiet. At the Shamrock, he'd share a room with several other men, here he'd be alone. "I am looking for a place to stay," he said. "And a good breakfast in the morning, which I know you supply."

Anderson nodded. "Ya, sixpence for sleep and breakfast - better than the Shamrock. Make yourself a spot on de floor. Would you like a slice of bread and butter before…?"

James tossed his swag on the floor and spread out his bedroll. "I'd be most grateful, if you'd be so kind. Also, I wanted to ask you something…Mr. Dobson stopped here on the way up to the Arnold," he said. "Or so you said in your evidence at the inquest."

"Ya, he did," said Anderson. "And I walk up to Arnold Township the next morning with him and Mr. Fox. About three and a half miles. We arrive at half past ten. Mr. Fox goes into Duncan's store, and Mr. Dobson and me, we go into Murphy's. While we are there, I tell him to take de boat with Mr. Fox - I worry about bushrangers, but he says, no I want to check my track. He's very…how would you say…"

"Conscientious?" said James.

"Yes. Conscientious. A good word. He's like his father in this way."

Anderson cut a slab of bread off a loaf with a serrated knife, opened a jar and added a generous helping of butter to the bread. James ate it hungrily. He had some hard tack with him in his swag, but it was as digestible as a lump of coal unless dipped in coffee. The bread and butter was much more agreeable.

"Did Dobson appear to be in good health?" he asked, after he'd finished his feast.

"He did," said Anderson. "Very good health, not exhausted at all.

But he said he was tired after walking from the New River. That's why he wanted to stay the night at my store."

"Was anyone else staying here that night?" Anderson had been somewhat unsure of the dates at the inquest, so another witness was always helpful. The dates would be important at Wilson's trial.

"Mr. Gardener," said Anderson. "Mr. Edward Gardener."

James jotted the name in his notebook.

"We had a pipe together," said Anderson. "Outside the store, the three of us."

"Was Mr. Costigan here as well?" asked James.

Anderson looked surprised. "Costigan? No, I think he was not...now wait a minte. I remember he walked past us, as we had our pipe. Mr. Dobson was smoking the pipe you showed me at the inquest..."

The next morning, after a breakfast of bread and butter and herrings, and a large mug of good strong tea, Inspector James set off towards the place where George Dobson had been before he arrived in Maori Gully: one of the Card Brothers' two stores on the New River, between Saltwater and the Teremakau, known as the Tower Store. The brothers had another store several miles inland known as the Upper Store and were well known in the district. They'd cut the pack road from the Teremakau to the New River themselves, but were constantly pushing for more roads and a more direct route for their goods, which cost as much as fifty pounds per ton for carriage; goods had to be brought up the river and then carried by pack horse on the Card Brothers' track. Robert Card had met Dobson at Saltwater and walked with him up to the Tower Store in New River on the Friday before the murder. Mr. Card was also missing an employee: William Cook, who was believed to have drowned in a waterhole.

He found Card outside his store unloading a string of pack horses. Men with backboards lined up as Card removed goods from the horses and loaded them onto the men's backs to be carried into his store. Card was looking pleased with himself. The goods had come up the Teremakau on horse-drawn barges and had arrived intact. Men with long poles could push the barges in the deeper water, but in places where the river was too deep for the horses they would be taken on board until they were needed again. However, in deep water after a freshet the risk of overturning increased and many loads of goods had been lost when the water was high and fast and the horses forced to stand unsteadily on the barge.

"Ah, Inspector James," said Card. "Out for a stroll, are you?"

James smiled and shook Card's hand. "I'm making enquiries into men who have gone missing in the area, making sure they were not victims of Richard Burgess and his crew. Sullivan has claimed that the gang killed several men in the district. I believe you're missing a store man…"

"Mr. Cook," said Card. "Yes, I did report him missing. He was a packer at my Liverpool Gully store. He was heading here with another packer and got left behind in the dark. We went out the next morning and found his hat beside a waterhole. We searched the waterhole in canoes, but didn't find him immediately. But we found him a few days ago."

"And had he drowned?" asked James.

"He had," said Card. "He was in the waterhole. His body floated up…"

"I'll send up a constable to investigate the circumstances," said James. "I also wanted to talk to you about Dobson. I'm retracing his journey, but backwards."

"Well then, you're in the right place. We walked together from Saltwater to here on Friday 25th, three days before he was so cruelly murdered."

"A long walk?" said James.

Card shrugged. "Eleven, twelve miles. Not exceptionally long. He stopped the night at my store and went on to Maori Gully - I expect you've just come from there if you're following his tracks in reverse. Will you walk to Saltwater today yourself? You're welcome to stay the night."

It was not much past noon, and James was sure he could make Saltwater by evening. "Thank you for the offer," he said. "But I think I'd best continue." He looked back the way he had just come. "The last time you saw Mr. Dobson he was walking that way? Towards Maori Gully?"

"Yes." Card shook his head, looking sorrowful. "I walked a little way along the track with him, talking. Then he went off walking briskly with his case slung over his shoulder - a compass case it looked like - and I never saw him again. Hard to believe…"

"And he said he was sent up to look out a horse track?"

"Indeed," said Card. He had said the same thing at the inquest. "What a loss he has been. So much that needs to be done in these parts if we are to make a go of the gold fields, and now one of our most accomplished young surveyors has gone."

"And that was Saturday morning, the 26th of May," said James. "You have no doubt about that?" He had seen the flaws in Sullivan's testimony regarding the time and he wanted to be certain when the murder had taken place. So far, all the testimony fit perfectly, and an upright citizen like Robert Card would be a convincing witness.

Card pulled out a notebook from his trouser pocket. "Yes. Saturday morning, May 26th. I note here that I was in Saltwater that morning and I walked up with Mr. Dobson." He closed the notebook and tucked it back into his pocket. "I keep good records and I'm sure the date is correct."

He left Mr. Card and took the road towards Rutherglen, a new town that had sprung up as a centre for some of the gold diggings. He reached Rutherglen in just over an hour. A recent article in the Argus had described Rutherglen as "A collection of dwellings of wood, calico and iron, put together without much, if any, regard for architectural or picturesque effect." In other words, a place much like all the other impromptu towns that had sprung up around the West Coast. Like Maori Gully, Rutherglen was situated in a long valley between high terraces and the whole area had been torn up by tunnels and diggings in a tireless search for gold. From Rutherglen, he would walk down to Saltwater, along a swampy flat and from there, if he was so inclined, take the tram to Greymouth. He was almost home and starting to think of the warm room and the good meal that would be waiting for him when he arrived.

He picked his way through the muddy streets of Rutherglen and on down to Saltwater. It was getting dark by the time he arrived, and the tram was sitting at its stop, about to leave. He hopped aboard and sat back for the relatively luxurious journey home in a tram pulled along a rail track by a team of horses. That was more like it. If only there were trams like this throughout the district, everyone would be happy.

Greymouth felt like the finest town in the colony when he arrived home. His trousers were covered in mud to mid-thigh, the soles of his filthy boots were almost worn through, and his back was aching from carrying his swag for three days, but the streets of the town, although muddy, were bordered by shops, restaurants and hotels, and he could see the trappings of civilization everywhere he looked: the police camp, the warden's office, the council chambers, the opera house, even the newspaper office for god's sake.

He trudged down Boundary and along Gresson to his home on Arney Street and found Elizabeth sitting in the kitchen unpicking the hem of Louisa's frock, which Louisa was still wearing. Louisa, who kept growing out of her clothes, was seated patiently on a footstool watching her mother work on the hem. She held a book in her hands, a reader intended for children much younger than she.

"Louisa has been reading to me," said Elizabeth through a mouthful of pins. "My goodness. Look how filthy you are. Did you have a difficult walk?"

"I was hoping to wash myself," he said. He patted Louisa on the head. "How is your schoolwork progressing?"

"I don't like it very much," said Louisa. "Miss Heaphy isn't very kind and the other children know nothing. I wish I could go to the other school. It's much closer, and…"

"It's only Mackay Street," said James. "Barely two hundred yards away. When I was your age I walked…"

"But St. Patrick's School is right across the road on Arney Street, and they learn Geography and History and the pianoforte, and…"

"It's a boys' school," said James. "And besides, it's Catholic." The Church of England had held a meeting soon after he first arrived in Greymouth and decided that a schoolhouse could be erected and used for church services on Sundays. A committee was formed to move that idea forward, but so far nothing had happened.

"Nothing is wrong with Miss Heaphy's school," said James. "You can learn everything you need there. Your mother can teach you to sew, and I can teach you to play the pianoforte…"

Louisa took the pins from her mouth one at a time and pushed them carefully into a pincushion. "St. Patrick's school has protestant children attending," she said. "They send them away during religious instruction. Mr. Harrison told me it's an excellent school, and there's no reason a girl couldn't attend."

"It would cost two and six a week," said James. "The other school is in the Misses Heaphy's home and they are paid by the town. I'm sorry, Louisa, but I'm afraid you must continue to attend the Mackay Street school."

He saw mother and daughter exchange a glance. They had discussed this question before, thereby undermining his authority. "I'd like to wash myself in some hot water, if that's possible," he said, knowing it was. "Where's the girl?"

"Upstairs with Harry," said Elizabeth. "He was feeling poorly and she's helping him get to sleep. Poor dear…he seems to need so much sleep."

"Louisa, go upstairs and tell the girl I would like her to fetch some water from the cistern," said James.

"I have some hot water ready," said Elizabeth. "I was making tea. But send the girl for some more. Louisa, make sure you're very quiet when you talk to her and don't wake Harry."

"On second thoughts," he said. "Perhaps I'll go down to the camp first and have a word with Sergeant Slattery. Then I can stop off at the hairdressing saloon and have a hot shower. He's open until ten o'clock." Perhaps also have some tea…a pie, or…

"Why not go and talk to Sergeant Slattery and then come home for a sponge bath?" said Elizabeth. "Why waste three shillings? The girl will have the sponging bath ready by the time you return. I have some tea for you as well. Some leftover mutton chops, and some boiled onions and potatoes."

"Contact Mr. Ross at the Argus," he told Sergeant Slattery twenty minutes later. "And tell him to put out the story that Inspector James has returned from his trip and believes that Mr. Tapperell has not fallen prey to villains."

"Yes sir," said Slattery. "And what do you think has become of Mr. Tapperell?"

"Same story as usual," said James. "He wandered off into the bush in a state of inebriation."

"And what about the body without the head?" asked Slattery.

"No need to mention that one," said James. "I'm fairly certain that it was an accident of some kind. He wasn't a victim of foul play; just one of the countless, nameless men who've been lost in the bush through an accident. He and Mr. Tapperell, victims of their circumstances."

"There's far too much drinking in these parts," said Slattery. "I wish we could do something to quell it."

"Not much chance of that," said James. "Wherever there's a large body of men gathered in one place, they'll fall to drinking and gambling. That will never change."

Sergeant Slattery pursed his lips, as if he disagreed, but said nothing.

20

Greymouth, 1866: The Skittle Alley

He arrived home from the police camp the following day to find Elizabeth sitting on the verandah, a copy of the newspaper on her lap, rocking furiously back and forward, Harry asleep on her lap and a drowsy Charlie flopped at her side. He was glad to see she was looking spirited again, even if the spirit evinced was anger.

"Something has upset you." He sat on the step below her and massaged his aching calves, which the shower at the barbershop the night before had done little to improve.

She moved Harry against her shoulder and opened the paper to the letters page.

"You remember that horrible leader the Argus had about you last week before you left?"

He did, and had tried to put it from his mind.

"Someone has written a letter…listen to this. 'Had there been a vagrancy act, Mr. James could have…wait a minute…you must be aware that Mr. James is not like the Argus of old, possessed of a hundred eyes…what does he mean by Argus? Is he talking about the newspaper?'"

"It's a reference to a Greek myth," said James. "Argus was a giant with a hundred eyes. I find two are enough, myself. How has this story made you angry?"

She turned to an earlier page "The letter was very kind, but listen to what the fools at the *Argus* had to say in response—in another leader." She spoke in a different voice, putting on a Scottish accent, pretending she was the editor of the *Argus*, Mr. James Kerr. "We are perhaps better able than '*Scrutator*'– that's the *nom de plume* of the letter writer—to form an opinion of the zeal and industry of the police department stationed in this district, and we gladly subscribe to the opinion that Mr. Inspector James has, since his arrival here, been indefatigable in his exertion to prevent and detect crime—exertions entailing a vast amount of hard work and anxiety. Nor would we for a moment exclude the subordinate members of the force…"

"I'm happy to hear that this rag is complimenting my subordinates…"

Elizabeth raised her finger, "No, but William, listen to this. They say, 'When we, as we think correctly, expressed the opinion that the police authorities were not free from blame respecting the non-arrest of Burgess, Kelly, and Co., we include the whole department, which is responsible for the preservation of society from such scoundrels as the men who are now charged with such terrible crimes…'"

"I do feel that to be the case, somewhat," said James. "Although I wouldn't admit it in court. And anyway, *Scrutator* is the bane of Mr. Kerr…I almost feel pity for the man. He has to respond somehow."

"Here's what else they say. 'We do not for one moment doubt that Inspector James acted according to the best of his knowledge and ability to stay the career of these men when they were here; but the question is - was that sufficient for the intended purpose?'" She raised her eyes from the paper briefly to look at him angrily. "And here's the bit that troubles me. 'We say not, and we believe we are expressing the general opinion of the public in saying so. In fact, the further the inquiry is pushed the stronger are the reasons for thinking that much more might have been done than was done.' The gall of this newspaper…"

"I'd like to know what they think I should have done," he said. "You know that I've hardly been home for the past few weeks…"

She smiled, folded the newspaper, and threw it at him. "And I've missed you, you great dobick," she said. "Now go and put this newspaper in the privy, where we can put it to better use than reading."

After tea - mutton stew again - he took Charlie out for a walk, heading down to Mawhera Quay, thinking he might find the Wallaby docked there. Businesses had closed for the day, and the drunkards had not yet settled in for their evening of carousing, but men were wandering up and down seeking tonics against the tediousness of their lives.

He could see several ships, both screw and paddle steamers, grounded in the river, waiting for the tide to refloat them. A notice posted outside the shipping office reported that the Wallaby was late coming from Nelson, delayed by bad weather. The seas from Nelson and down the West Coast were treacherous and even after making it safely down the coast, boats often had to wait out in the roads for the tides to float them in. The *Lioness* had grounded on the bar in January, run up on the beach while attempting to free herself and been dragged in by tug. And the schooner Northern Light had gone aground in June while being towed across the bar and sat stranded at the mouth of the lagoon for days while the paddle ship Woodpecker brought its cargo up to the wharf.

A steamer bobbed out in the roads, probably the Wallaby. In the meantime, Jack's Nonpareil Pie House and his "always ready" coffees called to him like a Siren. He preferred tea, but coffee was better for energizing his brain. John Heron would be waiting for the *Wallaby* to deliver the fresh eggs he advertised, and would alert James when the boat arrived.

Passing Tait Brothers' Photographic shop he noticed a photograph on display; a panorama of Greymouth taken from the South Spit showing the town, the river, and the wharf. It made a pretty picture. He would purchase one for Elizabeth for her birthday. The photographs they could take these days were astounding, almost as true to life as paintings. He thought he might just be able to see the roof of his own house in the photograph.

A smaller photograph to one side showed two children seated beside each other on a settee. He leaned forward to take a better look, then recoiled in revulsion. One of the children, a boy of perhaps nine or ten, was obviously dead, his eyes flat, his head flopped slightly to one side. His left hand had been placed limply on the shoulder of his sister, who sat beside him looking stunned - but alive. Memento mori: he'd heard of those, portraits taken after children had died to capture an image of the child for eternity. Mostly the children were arranged in a seated position on the floor, their lifeless heads resting on their mothers' laps. He walked away quickly towards the government shipping office, trying not to imagine how the photograph had been accomplished. He could tolerate the sight of deceased adults, but bodies of children disturbed him.

At the shipping office, a tall, thin serious-faced man sitting at a desk on one side of the room asked if he could help. A sign on the front of his desk, had his name painted onto a piece of polished wood: H. Smith, Clerk of Shipping.

"I have a question about last month's sailing of the Wallaby," said James.

"Early June, it went," said the clerk. He consulted a large register sitting on a podium to one side of his desk. "Here we are, leaving June 3rd and arriving in Nelson on June 6th. Then on up to Wanganui and Taranaki. Carried a large load of coal, from the Buller, up to the North Island. Then back in Nelson July 12th and returning here soon. I received a telegram when it left, but no sign of it yet. Are you awaiting something?"

James shook his head. "No. I'm an inspector with the police." He took out his warrant card and showed the clerk.

"Ah," said the clerk. "You'll be looking for information about Burgess and his crew no doubt. They went off on the *S.S. Walla*by on that trip. Pity they weren't stopped before they…"

"Yes, yes. A great pity. Is there something you can tell me about them? How much they paid for the trip…"

"You should talk to the Greek boatman. I heard they got some money off him. He's that mad now because he's not going to get it back, especially if they hang. A few quid it was, too."

"Where would I find this Greek boatman? And does he have a name?"

"He's the Greek boatman," said the clerk, looking mystified at the question. "You'll probably find him at the skittle alley. The one at the Alabama Hotel, down on Richmond Quay. Spends a lot of time there, he does."

"What about the Wallaby? Is that her sitting out on the roads?" He could wait for her at Jack's and go to the Alabama Hotel later, when things were more likely to be heating up there.

"Could be," said Smith helpfully. "The Wallaby is due soon. If it's her, she'll come across at high tide, in an hour or two."

Dr. Foppoly was sitting in Jack's having a thick black coffee and reading the *Grey River Argus*. Inspector James fetched himself a strong coffee heavily diluted with warm milk and doused with sugar and pulled up a chair at the doctor's table.

"I see you're reading our magnificent local rag."

Dr. Foppoly smiled. "The editor is not fond of you apparently."

"It would seem not."

"Don't let yourself become upset about what they write," said Dr. Foppoly. "Anyone close to the investigation, as I am for example, knows you've done all you possibly could."

"Thank you."

"I've become somewhat tired of the local politics," said the doctor. "Especially regarding the hospital. The board is reluctant to take my advice, and I can't make the improvements I would like. They refuse to believe in the need for cleanliness during surgery, for example. I'm thinking of leaving Greymouth soon—in fact I've decided to leave. I'll be returning to Italy."

"You'll be missed," said James, carefully sipping his coffee and thinking about Elizabeth's accouchement. "Who'll be taking over your women's surgery? Specifically, with childbirth?"

"Dr. Strehz is an outstanding doctor," said Dr. Foppoly. "Why do you…"

"My wife," said James. Perhaps they should just find a woman with experience, as Elizabeth wished. Elizabeth didn't want to go to the lying-in hospital anyway.

"Although I've never met him, Dr. Jackson has an excellent reputation as well," said Dr. Foppoly. He took one last sip of coffee, scooped out the dregs with his finger and licked it, then set the cup on the table. "He's coming to us from the Dunstan District Hospital and is a Licentiate of Midwifery in Edinburgh and the Rotunda Lying-in Hospital in Dublin…"

Dr. Foppoly returned to reading his paper, and Inspector James sat thinking about his case against Wilson. What was Wilson's level of importance within the gang? Generally, the press talked about the Burgess gang as consisting of four men: Burgess, Kelly, Levy and Sullivan. But there seemed to be several hangers on—DeLacey for example, who kept stables in Greymouth and across the river in Cobden and frequently escorted the gold buyers for whom he supplied horses; and the unknown connection or connections within the police. Of course, that could very well turn out to be Carr, the constable from Hokitika who had been arrested for stealing guns and trousers, although that sounded more like a theft of convenience. Trousers? Why trousers? He would have to talk to Broham in Hokitika about the robbery, when he got a chance to ride down there.

Dusk had fallen when the S.S. Wallaby finally crossed the bar; he left Jack's to return to Mawhera Quay. The steamer was pulling alongside of the wharf as he arrived, and sailors were leaping from the gunwale and to secure the mooring. As soon as the gangplank was dropped he boarded the vessel and went to find the captain. Captain Palmer was at the bridge, watching his crew perform their duties. He greeted Inspector James with a brief nod.

"You need to speak with me?"

"I'd like to know anything you can tell me about Burgess and his gang. I heard they went up to Nelson on your…"

"If I had known they were on their way to commit murder and mayhem in Nelson, I would never have let them…"

"Of course not," said Inspector James. "As would not I, in hindsight, have let them leave the district. But now with everything we know it's important that we try these scoundrels and…"

"Hang them," interrupted Captain Palmer. "Hang all of them."

"After we find them guilty of course."

"Of course."

"What can you tell me about them…the trip?" asked Inspector James.

"Sullivan came on board with a letter from Burgess—I believe it was Burgess although he hadn't signed the letter with that name—asking if they could travel free if they supplied their own food," said Captain Palmer. "I said they could not, but I would charge them a lower fare if they brought their own food. They had enough to pay for their fares."

"How much would that be?" asked Inspector James. George Dobson had carried six pounds in his pocket book, and he had found three of those pounds on Wilson.

"A pound each, so four pounds," said Captain Palmer. "They weren't using their own names, of course. I remember one—the man who came with the letter—as being Williams, but I assume he was Sullivan. Taller than the others, with a large face. All the names to be used on the tickets were in the letter."

"And they boarded at the Grey?"

Captain Palmer nodded. "They wanted to come aboard on the North Spit, on the other side of the river, but I refused to give them permission, so they boarded from the quay. And reboarded up at the Buller, where we stopped for a day to load coal. They needed new tickets from there."

"Did the four pounds take them all the way to Nelson?"

"Just as far as the Buller. They needed more for the rest of the trip.

I'm not sure where they found it, but I didn't charge them the full amount—or even half—there were fewer passengers from the Buller and any money I could get was helpful to the shipping company. I believe they paid two or three pounds from the Buller to Nelson."

"And they arrived in Nelson on…?

"June 6th." Less than a week before the Maungatapu murders.

"Did you see them during the trip?"

"Mostly Levy," said Palmer. "He spent the whole time playing cards in the saloon. "Sullivan hung around the saloon as well, although not as much as Levy. Levy won some money I think."

The crowds along Mawhera Quay were getting rowdy as he walked down to the skittle alley at the Alabama Hotel. A few wretched women were selling themselves to any men still able to stand straight, ready to do their business in the alleyways between the hotels. Greymouth was in desperate need of a Temperance Hall, like the one in Nelson. Once women got organized on the issue of temperance, the nights of drunkenness would be doomed. Although perhaps drunkenness would end on the same day women got the vote, both completely unlikely events in his view. Women would vote the same way as their husbands and the effect would be that married men would have two votes. Better that women concentrated on things like temperance and the poor.

The skittle alley was at the back of the Alabama Hotel, and he went down a narrow passageway to get to it, running the gauntlet of several drunken men leaning against the walls on either side, one with a woman crouched before him earning her shilling.

"What's going on inspector," said one, a skinny Irishman with a greasy bowler worn on one side of his head. "Not paying you enough then? Come for a bit of a gamble?"

James glanced at him and said nothing. One of his informants trying to look nasty. Might be useful to have a chat with him later. He found a boy at the door collecting fees, gave him a shilling for entry and another to hold Charlie.

"Where can I find the Greek boatman?"

The boy indicated a dark-haired, olive-skinned man who was just at that moment about to toss a wooden ball at the pins. "Two shillings if I knock down the copper," he called out, not realizing James was standing behind him. "You like to see a copper knocked down, don't you?"

Watchers melted into the darkness. The copper was the pin in front, and the Greek probably had no idea that an actual copper was standing behind him. The ball spun from his hand and rolled down the lane, hitting the front pin with a crack. The Greek leapt back, his arms raised, then realized he was alone with James.

"Where they all go?" he asked indignantly. "Gone with all my two bobs."

James handed him two shillings. "You knocked down the wrong copper, as far as they were concerned," he said dryly. "Here. Leave off a minute and talk with me."

"You a police?" asked the Greek. "You wanna talk about those boats that got their ropes cut? Six of them? I lost my boat…and the police don't…"

James displayed his warrant card. "That was unfortunate and we're looking into it. But for now I'd like to know how you came to lend money to Levy."

"Levy? Phil Levy the Jew?"

"I believe you know who I mean," said James. "Levy, Phillip Levy, one of the men involved in the murders up in Nelson. An associate of Burgess and Kelly."

"He was? I did not know that. Not Phil Levy I think. The Jews they don't kill…"

"He's been arrested in Nelson for five murders up there," said Inspector James. "And I think he was also involved in the murder of Mr. Dobson. Him and the others. Anyone who helped him will need to answer for it. Now…"

The Greek avoided Inspector James eyes for several minutes,

scratching his chin thoughtfully, then came to a decision. "I lend him three pounds," he said. "He pay me back before, so I think he gonna pay me back this time."

James did a quick calculation. Not enough for the tickets on the steamer, although they had the three pounds from George Dobson as well. "Anyone else lend him money?"

The Greek boat man shook his head. "He won some on the skittles. A few bob. I see him at the shooting gallery, another time. At Hilliard's. He make some there, maybe. He play cards too…pretty good at cards…"

"Did he tell you why he needed…"

"Course not," said the Greek indignantly. "I don't give him money to kill…"

"I mean, did he tell you he meant to go to Nelson with Burgess and Kelly?"

The Greek shrugged. "I do not know these Burgess and Kelly."

"How about James Wilson, or James Murray he is sometimes…"

"He's been here," said the Greek. "Curly hair? Sells papers sometimes? Not with Levy though. He's…*kako*…I think, a bad guy, but I don't know him much. He wanted to be in on things, to be a big man…"

The Greek was done giving information; he went back to his skittles. James returned to where the boy was holding Charlie, noticing that he looked nervous.

"Something the matter?"

The boy moved his eyes towards the door to the passageway, then back at James, shaking his head. "No sir."

James took hold of Charlie's leash and unhooked it.

"Stay."

The dog dropped obediently to the floor, his tongue lolling, panting, waiting for another command.

James drew his night stick from his belt, palmed it, and edged out the door. Fewer shapes lined the alley, and a sense of menace pervaded

GREYMOUTH, 1866: THE SKITTLE ALLEY

the area. He kept close to the wall and moved towards the street. Three shapes materialized, and surrounded him, pressing against him, two either side, a third in front. They wore floppy hats pulled low; glittering eyes showed above mufflers around the lower parts of their faces.

"I'll ask you to step back," he said calmly to the attacker facing him. "Unless you want to spend a week doing hard labour on the roads…"

One of the men at his shoulder shoved him. "Go on then," he said. "Arrest us. We'll come quiet, course we will."

The leader of the group, the most insolent, bent and picked up something from the ground. James turned and stared at him, saying nothing. The man's muffler had slipped, and his leering mouth revealed several missing teeth.

"Whatcha lookin' at?"

"I want to make sure I recognize you, the next time I see you," he said, tapping his night stick against his leg. "Hazel eyes, a scar above the left eye and through the eyebrow. Right eyelid drooping. Can't see with that eye I'd say. As you may have heard, physiognomy is a specialty of mine. Now, I'll ask you to put down that rock."

The man started to reply, then grunted and doubled over as James' night stick connected with his gut. The man to his front melted away down the alley, but the other went for the night stick, grabbing James by the wrist. As he wrestled for control, he could smell cheap spirits, mingled with the smell of strong cheese and rotten teeth. The man on the ground was recovering from the gut stab, and attempting to stand. James stepped on his forearm to hold him in place. Time to bring in the reserves.

"Charlie, attack."

A ball of black and white fur erupted from the door of the skittle alley and onto the back of the assailant, who clutched at James' sleeve in a useless attempt to prevent himself from falling; he hit the ground with Charlie on top of him, growling, teeth bared.

The man on the ground had pulled his arm free from James' foot and risen to his feet. He used his recovered stability to run away down the alley and off into the crowds out on Richmond Quay. James watched him go. He would catch up with him later. He had one of them, thanks to Charlie. He'd find this one in his files by his description and that file would contain his usual place of residence and the names of his known associates.

"Get him off me," said a muffled voice. Charlie had stopped growling and was shaking the attacker's head back and forth, scraping his face against the dirt and stones. James leaned down, pulled the muffler away from the man's face and took a good look at him. An ugly fellow, and fearful.

"Charlie, stand down," he said. The dog backed away and sat on his haunches, watching James attentively. The man scrambled to his feet and stood there swaying, eying the dog, afraid to move.

"All right then," said James. "It's off to the lockup for you. See what a week or two of hard labour will do for you. Attacking a police officer. I could ask for longer, but we'll leave it at that for now. Reduced by one week if you give me the names of your two partners in crime. Think about it tonight while you enjoy your meal of bread and water." He'd have a better meal than that, probably potatoes and gravy, but he didn't want to make imprisonment sound too easy. A ruffian like this would be terrified of hard labour after years of loafing. Slattery would put him on one of the road crews, probably, breaking the rocks for road metal.

He took his attacker out onto Richmond Quay and found one of his constables walking up and down, tapping his loaded stick against his hand, oblivious to what had just happened. The constable secured the man's wrists behind his back with a pair of cuffs, and Inspector James watched as the constable marched his attacker off in the direction of the police camp, his loaded stick threaded through the attacker's elbows to hold the man secure. He stroked the dog's neck in appreciation. "Good boy, Charlie."

It was dark when he arrived home, and he felt chilled to the bone.

He unlocked the door and gave Charlie a bowl of creamy milk, to reward him, as well as a nice piece of mutton bone left over from tea. He felt his way to the bedroom in the dark, not bothering to light a taper. Elizabeth stirred briefly, then went back to sleep, lying on her side. He pressed his body against her back and put his arms around her to warm himself, letting his hand rest on her belly. As he started to fall asleep he felt a sudden small flutter, and smiled. A boy then, with a kick like that. Elizabeth would be disappointed. But feeling the kick reminded him of the photograph he had seen in the window of the two children, one living, one dead, and he remembered in spite of himself the two small coffins they had left behind at the graveyard in Timaru. He found it hard to sleep with that memory, but eventually fell asleep in a sombre mood. In the other room, Charlie started to snore loudly, replete with the feast of milk.

21

Greymouth, 1866: The Criterion Hotel

Priscilla Fellows was determined to stick to her story. She looked down at her hands, which were nervously wringing a piece of cloth, refusing to look up at James. Her mother kept the Criterion Hotel on the corner of Arney and Gresson Street, not far from the police camp and James' own house. She was very young, probably not more than twelve, a plain child, but with a look of guilelessness about her that would sway any jury watching and listening to her. He had to make sure her account was accurate.

"Now Miss Fellows," he said. "May I call you Priscilla?"

She thought about it for a minute, then nodded her head without raising it, her hands continuing with the business of wringing the cloth.

"Thank you. Now, Priscilla, your testimony will be very important at the trial. You understand that?"

She nodded again.

"Can you tell me, then, when it was that you served James Murray, or James Wilson as I know him, his tea at this hotel?"

She looked up finally and stared defiantly into his eyes. "It was a Monday, the day after my brother went to Hokitika."

"I went to Hokitika on the Sunday, Sunday the 27th," said her brother, who was seated in the corner behind James. "My father was already there. He'd been there since the 21st. I was there for two days…"

"Are you sure it wasn't the second day after your brother went to Hokitika?" asked James. "The 29th, perhaps?"

He saw a momentary doubt flicker in her eyes and disappear. "I'm sure it was the 28th," she said. "I know it was, because my mother was away from home that day. That's why I was serving tea."

He nodded, keeping a look of understanding and belief on his face. "And your brother was unwell at the time, was he not? He had a cold?"

"Yes, he was. He slept with our mother…"

"The mother who was away from home at the time." He said gently.

He saw a tear slide down her face. "I…don't know. But I served Jamie…Mr. Wilson his tea on Monday night, I'm positive that I did."

"Now Priscilla," said her brother, whose name was Edward. He had already told James that he had not been home on the night that Wilson claimed he had taken his tea at the hotel, or the following night. "Don't say you're sure unless you are absolutely positive." He addressed James. "My mother was away one of those nights, but it could have been either night."

"Wilson says that you and your younger brother usually slept in the bunk over his head, but on the night in question, because your brother had a cold he slept with your mother."

"He had a cold when I left," said Edward Fellows. "I know that's true. And he tended to sleep with our mother when he was feeling poorly."

"Wilson also said he got up later than usual the next morning, and there was some concern over his breakfast…"

"Mother had a cooked breakfast for him, and he said he didn't want it, and she was annoyed. She asked him why he had said he wanted a cooked breakfast if he didn't intend to eat it," said Priscilla. "I know. I was there that morning as well."

"Now how did your mother…Mrs. Fellows manage to cook a breakfast when she was away from the house?" asked James. Wilson had spent considerable time creating an alibi for himself based on the mistaken idea that the murder had taken place on the 29th of May, harmonizing his story to that of a story in the Grey River Argus which had Dobson missing on the 29th. But once he realized that the 28th was the correct date he had attempted to wrench his account to an earlier day to fit the facts. It was understandable that Wilson would not know the exact date of the murder. He wasn't executing a business deal that required a document; he was up on the Grey attempting to rob someone and enrich himself, and had found himself an accessory to murder. That was why he had paced around in front of James' house for two hours, then come to see him.

Priscilla Fellows was looking sullen now. "I don't know how she cooked breakfast if she was away," she said. "I just know she was away when I served him his tea, and I did that on the day after my brother left for Hokitika. Can I go now?"

As she left, her brother stood up and came over to James.

"She's a good girl," he said. "She's usually very honest. But she's been swayed by a curly head this time I think."

"Wilson?" said James, surprised. "You think Wilson has attempted to pervert justice by…"

"No, no," said her brother quickly. "Nothing like that. But I think he appeals to her. He was nice to her…nice enough anyway, and she isn't used to that. You'll have noticed she's a very plain girl, and small for her age…"

"There's no understanding the female heart," said James. "Especially the young female heart." He and Elizabeth had been in their late twenties when they were wed, and the arrangement had suited them both. He couldn't remember feeling any rush of springtime yearnings, although he had admired Elizabeth from the first time he saw her at her brother's place in Port Phillip, with her strong face and her upright posture.

"Is there anything more you can tell me?" he asked. "When did Wilson arrive?"

Fellows looked thoughtful. "A couple of days before I left for Hokitika, I believe," he said. "The 25th or the 26th. He shared my room, as you've heard, with me on the top bunk. He rose very early—about half-past six, at break of day. On the Wednesday and Thursday succeeding his arrival he rose about half-past six o'clock ..."

"After the murder on the 28th?" asked James.

"Yes, that must be correct," said Fellows. "As I wasn't here on the days of the murder. Now let me see. On the Friday morning, he did not rise very early."

That would be the day he had come to see James.

"On the Saturday morning of May 26th, before I left for Hokitika I saw his boots, and did again late on the Tuesday following, the 29th, when I had returned. They were very light elastic-sided women's boots. When I observed them when I arrived home on the Tuesday evening they were wet, and so were his socks."

"Did you see any of the other members of the gang at your house?" asked James.

"I did. A man called on him on the Wednesday or Thursday following his arrival at our house when he was at tea. A tallish man with a large face...I don't think I heard his name at the time, but I've seen the allegoric lithograph done by Mr. Mabille, and I believe it was Sullivan."

"That's most helpful," said James. "And now, I need to speak with your mother..."

Fellows pulled out his watch. "She'll be home within an hour, I should think. She's doing the rounds paying the bills. Sometimes she gets talking, but..."

"I'll go home and have some tea myself, and return in an hour," said James. His house was less than a hundred yards away, and he needed something to eat. He'd met Mrs. Fellows before, and trusted her to give him an honest recital of events. A few weeks ago, she and her husband had taken in a boarder, one Samuel Symms, who claimed to be working for the Grey River Argus but was not. He'd told them he was waiting for his first pay which would come after two weeks. By the time they discovered he was lying, Symms had moved on. It wasn't the first time he'd obtained free board and lodging with similar stories, and had once even procured a loan of money from a store owner to buy a pair of knickerbockers, using the same devious plan of claiming to be someone he was not. James had spent time with the Fellows sorting that one out.

He crossed the street and went into his house, imagining as he did Jamie Wilson walking up and down the street in the rain, deciding whether to come and see him. Elizabeth was upstairs asleep. He went to check on her and found she was lying on their bed with her back to Harry, who lay facing the other way with his back against his mother's. He crept forward and pulled the blanket over them. Poor Elizabeth. Her pregnancy was tiring her out. He hoped this would be her last, and that she would have the daughter she longed for.

He returned an hour later, after finding a cold mutton sandwich made up for him in the pantry. Mrs. Fellows had returned and was sitting at her kitchen table with a receipt book and bills in front of her adding up a list of figures.

"The scoundrels," she said to James. "They think because I'm a woman they can take advantage of me."

She was a comfortable-looking woman around the same age as Elizabeth, but shorter and with less grey in her hair. He sat down at the table. "I spoke with your son and daughter earlier," he said. "I expect your son told you…"

"Priscilla is quite upset," she said, smiling. "She's very keen to take the stand at the trial and tell everyone all about Wilson. Of course, she doesn't understand how little she'll be saying…"

"Is she being honest, do you think?" he asked.

"She thinks she's being honest," said Mrs. Fellows. "She wants it to be true. She imagines herself as the heroine of her own story, saving the handsome young curly-headed bellman from the wicked police. He looks young for his age, Mr. Wilson, and he's small and fair…to her he probably doesn't seem very much older than she is…"

He laughed. "Well, I'm sure your story will be accurate," he said. "What can you tell me?"

"He came to the house sometime in May," she said. "Late May. He stayed for more than a week. I remember he did not have a swag when he arrived, but later in his stay he did have a swag...I noticed it under his bed."

"Was there a morning when he slept in?" asked James.

"On the Friday, I think. The Friday after Mr. Dobson must have been murdered. He was in the dining room and he said he was not particular about getting up early the next morning...said he'd been up early all week."

"Did he go somewhere in the mornings—those mornings that he got up early?"

"He said he delivered the paper - the Grey River Argus - but I take that paper and he's never the one who delivers it."

"What about right after the murder - after May 28th. Did anything happen that caught your attention?"

She tapped her fingers on the receipts for a minute, thinking. "I remember him washing his trousers," she said. "He put them on the line. That would be right after the murder I should think...I would say that in court if necessary. It would be important, wouldn't it? People, especially men, don't wash their trousers very often, do they?"

"That is important," said James. "Thank you."

"One other thing," she added. "He also said, before the murder, when he first arrived..."

"Yes?"

"He was standing at the door of the bar, and he seemed confused. He said, 'Mrs. Fellows, where's the police camp?'"

"And you're sure that was *before* the murder? Not after?" Wilson would know that the inspector in charge of the camp would live close to and most likely on the grounds of the camp; James' house backed onto the camp. It seemed strange that Wilson would want to know about the camp before the murder. Was he thinking of squealing on the gang even then? Or just worrying generally about the police.

"Did you ever see any of the others here?" he asked. "Burgess or…"

"Edward says he remembers Sullivan coming to see Wilson," she said. "But I can't say I remember him."

"Was anyone else staying here at the time? Someone who could help me with my enquiries?"

She opened her receipt book. "Let me see…there was a Mr. Kapau stayed here about the same time. A young half-caste from the North Island. He was down here looking for greenstone for his people up near Poverty Bay. We have excellent greenstone in this district, as I'm sure you know. The Maori use it for their carvings…beautiful work. I'd like to purchase some if I could."

"And he's returned to Poverty Bay, I suppose," said James.

"Yes. And I don't know exactly where he came from, so I can't give you any more information than that. I suppose you could have the police up there…"

"They rather have their hands full," said James "since the murder of the Reverend Volkner. And probably there isn't much he can tell us, this Mr. Kapau…what about this assertion of Wilson's that he was working at a shop?"

"He didn't tell me that he was working for anyone," said Mrs. Fellows. "Other than the lie that he delivered the Argus."

"George Coburn," said James, consulting his notes containing the statement Wilson had made to him after the inquest. "Wilson was up in the Grey until 11 o'clock on the 28th with Burgess and they had a drink at the iron shack with Kelly and Sullivan. He came back by himself carrying a heavy swag…the swag you saw perhaps, although he says he left it at George Coburn's place on Mawhera Quay." And the swag Wilson had later told him contained guns, although he didn't want to tell Mrs. Fellows about that. "He says he went to the barbershop and changed his trousers—left his old ones there." He stopped and looked up at Mrs. Fellows.

"The trousers he washed here," she said.

"Yes. Very strange. It sounds as if he's trying to change things by a day. He came home with the swag and trousers that had something on them—not blood, as Dobson had been strangled. Mud on his knees perhaps? From when they buried him? He came back here and had his tea, then went back to Cockburn's shop and took care of it until 8 o'clock. At that point, he came back here."

"I can't confirm or dispute any of that," she said. "I'm sorry to say." She pushed aside her receipt book. "Would you like a piece of pie before you go? I have a dessert pie with apples, nice and tart."

He left the Criterion and went along Gresson and Boundary Streets to Mawhera Quay to look for George Cockburn. Cockburn had a small grocery shop where he sold fruit and eggs from Nelson, butter and cheese from New Plymouth, and oysters from wherever he could get them. James eyed a barrel of fresh Bluff oysters as he stood waiting for Coburn to finish serving a customer. He wished he hadn't felt obliged to turn down the apple pie…

"Hello Mr. Inspector James," said Coburn eventually. He had a long, deeply-lined face which wore a permanently solemn expression. He looked trustworthy, but that appearance wasn't complemented by his actions. "Can I assist you with something? Perhaps a bag of oysters - just arrived this morning? Or a free sample?"

"Jamie Wilson," said James. "Was he here on the evening of the Dobson murder?"

"What day was that then?" asked Coburn.

"The twenty-eighth of May," said James.

Coburn made a show of thinking about it. "He did work for me from time to time," he said eventually. "But I can't say what days he might have worked for me in May. I can't be sure."

"Why does he work for you?" asked James. "Is it when you're extra busy, or for some other reason?"

"No. Usually he comes when I need to be at the wharf to pick up something, like these oysters here. Are you sure you wouldn't like some?"

"You can't tie his presence here to a specific delivery date?" asked James, ignoring the bribe. "Do you not keep records of your deliveries?"

Coburn shook his head. "I remember him being here sometime late in May, if that's helpful, but what usually happens, and I'm sure it did then, is he's around and I ask him to stop here for an hour or two while I pop down to the docks. I'm there all the time, and different people take care of the shop, so…"

"If you're called to be a witness for the defense at his trial," said James carefully, "would you say that you can't remember?"

"Of course," said Coburn. "Because I can't remember." Besides which, thought James, he did not want to be caught up in a trial with a member of the infamous Burgess-Kelly gang. Which meant Wilson's alibi rested entirely on the slim shoulders of young Priscilla Fellows.

He started to leave, then remembered something else.

"Did he leave a swag with you?"

Coburn avoided his eyes. "I think he did at some point. But he picked it up…and the possum rug that…someone gave him."

With that, James had to be satisfied.

A few days later the Hokitika Evening Star, having received permission from Inspector Broham, published an interview with Wilson laying out his alibi. It was "reliable as far as the accused himself was to be believed," the paper said. Wilson reiterated what he had said to James: he was up, on the Grey with Burgess, Kelly and Sullivan on the 28th, but he and Burgess parted with the other two at eleven to return to Greymouth; they met DeLacey and Burgess stopped to have a drink with him while Wilson carried on to Greymouth carrying the swag (he refrained from mentioning what was in the swag); he went to the barber shop and changed his trousers, leaving them there; he had tea at the Criterion; he went to George Coburn's shop and worked until eight.

He concluded his alibi by saying he had slept at the Criterion the night of the 28th, which Mrs. Fellows would confirm, as he had complained about his breakfast the next morning and she had made a sharp retort. All well and good, except for the fact Mrs. Fellows had not been there the morning of the 28th. He did not mention that he had been served his tea by young Priscilla, which would disappoint her. He could hardly use Burgess and Kelly as his witnesses, because not only were they his confederates, but also by then they had been hanged up in Nelson, Burgess, Kelly, and Levy, all three.[vi]

As he left the police camp at the end of the day he once more encountered Mr. Bain, the surveyor, with his assistant, George Sayle.

"Afternoon, James," said Bain. "George here has something he thinks you should know." He looked towards his assistant. "Tell Mr. Inspector James what you saw."

Sayle was a young, fresh-faced man not unlike his workmate George Dobson. He blushed pink, and took a couple of tries to speak. "It's…it's…it's…"

James saw a flash of irritation in Bain's eyes.

"It's about that man you arrested," Sayle said finally. "Wilson. I saw him."

"When was that?"

"I saw him on the last day of the month. I know it was that day because I had my monthly report on my desk, and I was hurrying there to finish it."

"Was he was doing something that caught your attention?"

Sayle nodded enthusiastically. "He was up near the tree, the tree that you marked where George's body was found."

"And this was after the murder? Or at least, the day we assume George was murdered?

"Ye…ye…yes," said Sayle. "That's what I said. Three days after the murder."

"That's not all," said Bain. "Tell him what, or at least who, you saw with him."

They waited patiently for several minutes. Sayle finally spit out his answer. "He was with Burgess and Kelly and Sullivan. And they looked very chummy."

"That's very useful thank you George," said James, and saw a red tide wash up Sayle's face from his neck.

"There's something else," said Sayle. "I've made a map, a map that you might find interesting." He pulled a sheet of survey paper from his pocket and handed it to James. "Can you see what I've done?"

James could. Every point where witnesses had seen something, and the times they had seen it, was plotted, with distances gives in miles known to the survey department.

"This is very useful, George," said James. "I've never seen anything like this before."

He had the satisfaction of watching Sayle's face turn an even brighter red.

"Mr. Inspector James," said Sayle, the praise apparently curing his stutter. "I hope you can punish everyone who took part in George's murder. He was the best chap you can imagine – all of us at the survey department miss him terribly."

"I hope I can, George, I hope I can," said James. He would have to find a way to include the map in the trial. It was the least he could do for poor Sayle and the many friends of George Dobson.

22

Hokitika, 1866: The Accessories

It was time to ride down to Hokitika and talk to Broham.

He rode around the lagoon, along the newly-metalled road, towards South Beach, passing the graveyard on the terrace side, towards Saltwater, where a small gold rush township had sprung up in the last few weeks. In the lagoon, the boatmen were ferrying diggers across the water at a great rate, probably making more than the men they ferried. He could see another stream of men flowing along the beach as well. A piece of land had been set out in Saltwater, and all that was needed was a mining surveyor to lay out some streets. One would arrive in due course.

At the Teremakau, which was flowing swiftly at high tide, he headed north looking for a better place to cross, not wanting to risk losing his horse. The tracks were still muddy from the rain and flooding in June, even washed away in parts. Just as he'd expected after reading Mr. Rochfort's meteorological observations in the paper that morning; almost fourteen inches of rain in June, with rainfall on all but twelve days in the month. He was getting accustomed to the permanently soggy state of the West Coast, and even enjoyed the damp blustery weather. Lucky for him he didn't suffer from rheumatism, often exacerbated by the variable climate of the West Coast, which tended to block the organs of perspiration.

After passing through the new rush at Camerons's, he arrived at

Greenstone, the oldest of the workings in the district. The town, which had been built on the dry bed of the Greenstone Creek, was home to about two hundred miners, mostly older residents who understood how to make a living from what they were doing. But the best days of the town had passed. Ramshackle wooden slat and calico huts lined the dry stony creek bed that stood in for a main street; James picked his way carefully between huge potholes and furrows, worried that his horse might lose its footing and throw him. What would happen if a heavy rainfall brought back the water to the creek and inundated the town? How would the townspeople ever escape, especially the youngest of them? Several unkempt, scabby children played listlessly in the dirt outside what seemed to be a store, staring at him with hollow eyes as he passed. A woman came out of one of the huts with a basket of washing on her hip, apparently intending to take it down to the stream, and called out to him.

"Are you the warden then?"

He reined in his horse. "No. Are you expecting Mr. Revell?"

"Bin 'specting him for more'n six months," she said. "But he never comes. Too many fights over claims, and they never get settled. We need the warden to come and sort everything out, tell us whose claim is whose."

"Could not one of your men come up to Greymouth to Mr. Warden Revell's office?" asked James. Mr. Revell was a busy man, what with being the warden of the gold fields who certified claims as well as the being the magistrate.

"Can't take the time nor the trouble," said the woman. "It'd cost too much for any of the men to take a day or two getting to Greymouth and back on the coach. There's no track there. And they'd lose the work of those days…"

"I'll let Mr. Revell know," said James. Elizabeth had made the trip to Hokitika with the children without a second thought, but she was a stronger woman than this one. "But he's a busy man. I can't promise he'll be down here for a while."

He rode on towards the Teremakau Valley, to a place where the river broke into several streams between gravel, and picked his way across. Further on, as he approached the Arahura River he came across a group of men building a water race—the McBride's Race. He'd read about it in the *Argus*. He watched for a few minutes as they laboured at their task. Westland was either flooded or in a drought, and without water for sluicing nobody made any money. No doubt the men who had put up the money for this endeavour would make plenty - one of the many ways money could be made from gold, and infinitely more acceptable than the way Burgess and his associates had chosen.

In Hokitika he made himself known to the constable at the rear gate leading into the stable, and left him in charge of his horse as he went in search of Inspector Broham. But Broham was away from camp; instead he found Sergeant Hickson, the same man whose infant son had died on the day James found George Dobson's body. Hickson was sitting bent over at his desk writing, a frown on his broad Irish face, his full, fair whiskers brushing his hand as he wrote.

James offered his condolences. "Sorry about…"

Sergeant Hickson sat back and gave a brief nod, his lips tight. "What brings you to Hokitika?"

"I need to hear what Broham has to say about one or two things. But no doubt you…"

An odd expression crossed the sergeant's face. James knew there was no love lost between the two Irishmen. Broham was ten years younger than Hickson, who, like James, had arrived at the mid-point of his allotted three score and ten years.

"I've been wondering how this robbery fits in…"

"The robbery at the police camp?" asked Hickson. "I can probably help you more with that than Inspector Broham could, although…"

A look of understanding passed between them: Broham would consider himself the most informed person no matter what the case being discussed.

"Let's go over to the mess and I'll fill you in," said Hickson. "The men aren't there now—the evening meal is at six—and we can get a mug of tea."

They settled at a table with a large mug and a plate of fancy biscuits. The men at the camp lived well. No wonder recruitment was so successful.

Hickson said, "You know we arrested Constable Carr—ex-Constable Carr—on a charge of stealing weapons and other goods from the camp?"

"We arrested him up in Greymouth and remanded him down here," said James, feeling he must correct Hickson.

"Yes, Yes," said Hickson. "Thank you for your assistance." He ran his fingers down his whiskers with a pincer movement. "I became mistrustful of him when he returned from Bruce Bay, on May 7th. I checked his kit, as I'm required to do, and found he was deficient in a pair of grips from his guns. He claimed he'd left them in Bruce Bay, and offered to pay for them…of course I said that wouldn't be necessary. I reminded him they were the property of the Provincial Government and it was his duty to report the loss immediately to his superior officer. He claimed the prisoner he was escorting turned violent, leading him to forget to report the grips to me. Then he attempted to pass off another constable's grips as his own. But I knew they weren't, as they were from a different manufacturer."

"Had it happened before?" asked James. "Did he regularly lose his equipment?"

"No," said Hickson. "Never. But he wasn't happy about his position here. He'd already tendered his resignation, but I told him he needed to give three months' notice. While he was waiting for the time to pass he offered his resignation two more times. His desire to leave was very strong."

"He has his wish now," said James. "When did you dismiss him?"

"June 9th," said Hickson. "Before we charged him with the robbery."

"And when did the robbery take place?"

"The evening of May 10th," said Hickson. He leaned back in his chair and gazed at the ceiling, remembering. "I gave Sergeant Moller a five-chambered Colt to clean on the morning of the 10th of May. Branded on the stock and on the case with a registration number, which I have noted in my book. That evening he asked me if I'd had taken the Colt from his room. And at the same time Constable Bolton, a mounted trooper, reported to me that someone had stolen his revolver and the case, as well as a sword-sling. Constable Bolton said it must have happened between eight and ten in the evening."

"And was Carr about at that time?"

"He was. It was his custom to stay up late, after ten, although the men were supposed to be in bed by ten o'clock. I reported him several times for that. He was in bed at ten o'clock that night, however."

"You checked his room?"

"I went into the mounted troopers' quarters to enquire about the matter of the missing guns. His room was next to the troopers' quarters and he heard me talking—heard what I said—and called out, 'Bolton, I would report the first man I found with them.'"

"What did he mean by that?"

"He meant it as a joke," said Hickson. "That was what I inferred anyway, from his manner of speaking."

"A nervous joke, perhaps," said James. "And not especially amusing. Did you search the camp?"

"Sergeant White, Constables Bolton, Moller, others, searched the Camp with me for the missing weapons, but before doing so I went into the various rooms and asked the men if they knew anything about them, but was unable to get any clue as to their removal. Carr assisted with the search."

"Rather audacious," said James. "And when were the trousers found to be missing?"

"At seven the next morning. Sergeant Wilson reported to me that a pair of pants had been taken from the washhouse the night before. A pair of Bedford-cord pants."

"Why anyone would want to steal trousers?" asked James.

"I'll get to that," said Hickson. "On the next day another constable, Constable Charles, returned from the Spit and reported the loss of his revolver—a Dean and Adams—as well as his sword, belt and pouch. Some blue jumpers were also stolen, but no one reported their loss to me. All the men have several jumpers and probably didn't notice they were gone."

"And you reported the matter to Inspector Broham?"

"I did. I also made enquiries with the sergeant at Bruce Bay as to whether Carr had reported the loss of his grips, and he replied that he had not."

"The loss of the grips made you suspicious of him," said James. "But how did you discover he had stolen all the other equipment? And what about the…"

Sergeant Hickson was in no hurry to get to the point. "Sergeant Dyer, another member of the force here, had been following a man whom Inspector Broham wanted kept under surveillance," he said. "Dyer watched the target all evening on the tenth. The man went to the Prince of Wales Opera House in company with another man and two women…"

James sighed. "And who was this man? Why was Broham…"

"Richard Burgess," said Hickson.

James leaned forward, interested now. "Burgess? Burgess was involved in the robbery of the guns?"

"I thought you knew," said Hickson. "We did a search of his place, even though we knew he had an alibi for that evening."

"And you found?"

"We found the two revolver cases," said Hickson. "And as I said, they were branded with the same registration as the revolvers, so we knew they were from the camp. I keep meticulous records…"

"You certainly do," said James. "You had him cold…how did you deal with the alibi?"

"He didn't steal anything from the camp himself," said Hickson. "We believe he had one of his associates undertake the theft."

HOKITIKA, 1866: THE ACCESSORIES

"Kelly," said James.

"Or Aldridge or Sullivan," said Hickson. "We took him to trial, and he had Aldridge, or we believe he had Aldridge, set up as a stooge. Aldridge came forward and said the two of them were walking along the beach—Burgess was going with him to look at the wreck of the *Maria*—and they kicked over some sand and found the cases. Burgess had convinced him that was what happened, although the weapons had been planted there to be found. And then Sullivan came forward, someone whom we did not know was an associate of Burgess, and testified to witnessing Burgess find the cases."

"He planned for the worst," said James. "He went where he knew he'd be noticed—the opera house—and then deliberately had himself arrested with his alibi and his witnesses in place." The clever bastard.

"Henry Brunetti from the Golden Fleece saw the two of them—Burgess and Carr—together at his place several times," said Hickson. "In company with another man named Chamberlain. This all came out later after Burgess was found not guilty. We still have Carr, Aldridge and Chamberlain in gaol, however. Carr even went to the Golden Fleece in his uniform at times. The man deserves to be given a long sentence with hard labour. He's a disgrace to the force."

"And the pants?" asked James. He'd been waiting patiently for the solution to the mystery of the pants.

"We believe they were planning to rob a bank dressed as troopers," said Hickson. "Sullivan was going to go in and talk to the bank manager dressed in the uniform, and hold the manager while the others robbed the bank. He's the tallest—the others were too short to qualify for the force and the manager would have suspected something was up."

"Where is Carr now?" asked James. Burgess certainly had an excellent imagination as well as an ability to sway people to the dark side with his discourse. He'd like to talk to Carr, to find out what he knew about the Dobson murder. "You have Carr in gaol still?"

"Yes," said Hickson. "As well as Aldridge and Chamberlain…and

Wilson, of course, since you remanded him here."

"Are they all together?" asked James, alarmed. Prisoners made an art out of exchanging information without the guards hearing them, to the detriment of reliable evidence.

"Carr and Wilson were together for a few weeks," said Hickson. "Carr is still here in the Logs…but we moved Wilson out to the new gaol in Seaview. I kept Carr here so I could keep an eye on him. You can talk to him if you wish…he's generally amenable to talking. I don't think he's a natural criminal. He married recently. His wife is a young Irish woman named Mary Reilly. And I believe he comes from a good Scots family. His father is a chemist in Berwick."

Outside Hickson led him to four log huts, known collectively as the Logs. Each one had a door with bars, and a small window high up on one wall - for air, presumably, and much too small for a man to squeeze through. "The men committed to trial were in these three huts," said Hickson, indicating the first three. Now we just use the one hut for everyone, as we have fewer of them.

"The convicted men as well?" asked James.

"Those have mostly been sent to Seaview," said Hickson. "We keep them under a warrant from the bench, and the debtors, lunatics and drunkards here. One hut does us for that."

"How many in the hut?"

"Five at the moment, but we can accommodate up to a dozen," said Hickson. The hut was about ten feet by twelve. It was a wonder prisoners had enough room to stand, let alone to sleep. "They have half an hour a day for exercise, and the door is left ajar during the day, on a chain of course. They don't suffocate"

"I prefer to make use of their time," said James. "Put them to work on the roads. Why have able-bodied men sitting in a cell doing nothing?"

"If we do that we take work from honest men," said Hickson. It was an argument that James had heard before. There was plenty of work in these new towns. No one need go unemployed. And building roads and ditches and telegraph lines meant more people came here, creating more jobs.

John Aitchison Carr was sitting on the floor of the log hut, his knees drawn up, his head slumped forward, his fingers scratching his scalp hopelessly through his thick dark hair. Prisoners often developed the itch in places like this, with no ability to keep clean, and crowded together with others. There were a handful of other men in the cell who looked at James with dull eyes, some with the wild gaze of lunatics. He could smell them through the door, the fetid smell of unwashed bodies and human waste.

"Carr," said Hickson through the partially open cell door. "Inspector James from Greymouth wishes to speak with you."

Carr's head came up, and he stared at them uncomprehendingly from dark eyes under heavy eyebrows. "What?'

"Inspector James would like to ask you a few questions," said Hickson.

"I don't have anything to say to Inspector James," said Carr. "Unless he wishes to free me from this hellhole." He had a cultured voice, almost free of the broad Scottish accent of someone like Mr. Fox. He put his head back on his knees.

"How do you find yourself in this predicament?" asked James, deliberately vague.

Carr's head rose again. "I don't know. I've asked myself the same question. If…when I'm free again I won't ever be here again, I promise you that."

"In the meantime," said James, "it would help your case if you could answer some questions for me."

Carr's head went down again, and he raised his broad shoulders to block out speech. "My solicitor said not to say anything to you…to any of you," he said. "And I don't intend to. You can leave, if you don't mind." He sounded as if he was dismissing them from his drawing room, and James smiled. A prison term would straighten him out, but it was a pity that a young man like that had fallen in with such a depraved person as Richard Burgess. He wondered if any of this would have happened were it not for the incomprehensible appeal of Burgess.

As they slogged back through the mud to Hickson's office, James asked, "How is Wilson dealing with his incarceration? Is he ready to talk do you think?"

"He complains all the time and feels very hard done by," said Hickson. "Seaview Gaol is better than the Logs, cleaner and more spacious—only half a dozen to a cell, with the debtors and lunatics in separate huts—but he's not happy and insists on his innocence. I doubt you'll get anything useful from him."

"I'll wait then," said James. "And see what he has to say at his trial."

23

Greymouth, 1866: Burgess Confesses

Inspector James returned from Hokitika to find there'd been a new confession. Now it was Burgess who had confessed to the murders, or at least to knowing about the murders, and being present at a convenient distance when they occurred. But he'd thrown the full weight of his near-deathbed confession at the feet of Joseph Sullivan. It was Sullivan, said Burgess, who was the perpetrator; he who had committed all those dastardly murders. Everyone else was innocent. Even Wilson.

Sergeant Walsh brought him a copy of the confession, published in the Nelson Colonist on August 10.

"You'll enjoy this," he said. "The gentleman has done his best to make Sullivan look like the mastermind of the whole affair. He's found the Lord and written his confession in 'his drear dungeon' settled on his knees in the dark."

"I imagine it is rather drear," said James. "What does he say about the Dobson murder, other than that he didn't do it?"

"Describes himself is 'a guilty wretch who has been brought through the instrumentality of a faithful follower of Christ to see his wretched and guilty state,'" said Walsh. "And that 'through the assurance of this faithful soldier of Christ, he has been led, and he also believes that Christ will yet receive and cleanse him from all his deep dyed and bloody sins.' Although, of course, he didn't really commit the bloody sins, according to him."

"And what does he say about the Dobson murder," asked James again patiently. Sergeant Walsh was clearly enjoying the extravagant style of the confession.

"Let's see," said Walsh, scanning through the article...foully murdered...bloody drama...spare the effusion of innocent blood being shed...he has quite a way with words, does Burgess. Now, Dobson, Dobson, ah, here it is...Burgess talks about being in gaol in Hokitika for suspicion of the robbery at the police camp." Walsh ran his finger down the column. "He was discharged...here's what he said:

'...I must leave Hokitika for a while, at all events, so with that we proposed going to the Grey. We arrived there on the Saturday, the 26th May. I took up my residence at the Provincial Hotel. Sullivan began drinking, and spent what money he had, which was very little. He left the Greymouth township on the Sunday night, and did not return till the Tuesday following, late in the day.'"

"Sullivan wasn't a heavy drinker when I knew him," said James.

Walsh continued reading. "During this time, Mr. Dobson, the surveyor, was murdered. He came to town, and sent the man Wilson, now charged with the murder in Hokitika of Mr. Dobson, to find me and to go to the Bridge. I went to the Bridge indicated, and there I saw Sullivan. He told me they had made a great mistake in stopping a man whom they took for a banker, but who turned out to be only a surveyor. He said, 'he was such a nice young fellow, but after we stopped him we could not let him go, so took him off the road about 100 yards, and there I 'burked' meaning choked him. He said, laughing, as I was taking him into the bush, 'did you think I was a banker? Here is all the money I have, some £6 odd.' He said, 'I buried him, compass and all—he had a compass with him.' He has since been found, I believe, by the murderer Sullivan telling where he was buried. Mark the atrocity of his acts. He has since charged an inoffensive man, Wilson, with complicity in the murder, who is as innocent as the babe on its mother's breast."

Walsh stopped and looked at James, who was rubbing his eyes. He was feeling sick. Poor, poor young Dobson.

"Do you believe all this?" he asked, shaking the paper.

"Yes, I do," said James. "The gist, anyway. All he had to do was change one name: he's replaced Kelly with Sullivan. And, of course, he has made sure he was not on site. Everything he knows about the murder was told to him not by Sullivan, but by Kelly. Sullivan wouldn't use the term burked. That comes from the London slums. But the actions ring true, I think."

"You don't think he was there when Dobson was murdered?"

"I think Kelly and Wilson murdered Dobson," said James. "Witnesses saw two short men, one dark, like Kelly, and one fair, like Wilson. It was probably Kelly who strangled him, but it would have taken two of them to tie his wrists with leather straps, take him into the bush, and hit him around the head with rifle butts. Sullivan may have been up the track looking for Mr. Fox, as he says. I don't know, and it doesn't matter. What matters to me is that Wilson is found guilty."

"Perhaps we should walk it out," said Walsh.

"Walk it out?" asked James. "You mean go back to the scene of the crime? Good idea. We can see how long it takes to walk from Arnold Township to Greymouth, and how we think everything happened. Look at it from the point-of-view of the crime, rather than a search for a body."

They took a flat boat up to the Arnold and walked back to where the murder had taken place. It was a difficult walk and took almost two hours. Clearly Dobson was a fit, healthy young man. The site of the murder had almost disappeared, the ferns thickening and the bush as dense as ever. James had left a ribbon nailed to a tree near the murder site and a slight indentation remained in the ground where the body had been buried. He stared at it for a while, then walked back to the track, about fifty yards away.

"Now, if you were Kelly and Wilson, where would you put up a tent?" he asked Walsh.

Walsh pointed up the track another fifty yards. "There's the obvious place," he said. He walked towards it. "There's a flat area here, and a good view along…" He bent down. "And look at this." He jerked a stick from the ground and handed it to James. It had been sharpened at one end with a hatchet or knife. "A tent peg."

"Good find," said James. "Although not proof in any way." He stood by the hole from which Walsh had pulled the peg. "So here they are, waiting for Mr. Fox. One of them, Wilson I think, was inside the tent, and the other, Kelly, was outside. They were alerted to his approach by a signal from Sullivan." He stared up the track. "Walk back along the track, Walsh, then turn and come back towards me."

Walsh complied. As he walked towards the tent site, James could imagine it was Dobson, walking with a spring in his step, no cares in the world other than the repairs that need to be made on his track. A healthy young man enjoying a brisk walk in the bush.

Walsh reached him and stopped, smiling in a friendly way. "Good afternoon sir," he said. "Can you tell me how far I am from the coal pits? Dobson said that to Sullivan, so I imagine he also said something to Kelly – how far was it to the coal pits, did he think it was going to rain… Making conversation, as one does on the road…"

"If Kelly was standing here, outside the tent, as witnesses said," said James, "Dobson would have been below him slightly and Kelly could have jumped down onto him. But it wasn't their practice to jump people. And Dobson was taller and younger than Kelly. Kelly would stick him up." He picked up a branch and pointed it at Walsh. "So, I'm sticking you up."

Walsh raised his hands. "Then he'd call on Wilson," he said.

"And Wilson would come out of the tent, bringing the two leather straps. Dobson was facing a rifle and would comply, probably thinking he was going to be tied up and left in the bush…the usual practice in stickups. Like Mr. Walmsley was, although Walmsley ran for it…"

Walsh put his arms behind his back. "Did they hit him on the head now, do you think, or did they take him into the bush first?"

"They took him into the bush first," said James. "He laughed and asked them if they thought he was a banker at that point, so he was still on his mettle. He was probably nervous, but not afraid. Thinking his way through it, wondering what to do."

"He was hit over the head several times," said Walsh. "Do you think they did that after he spoke?"

"Perhaps he made a run for it, like Walmsley," said James. "I'd like to think that he did. I can't imagine that he would just stand there, or walk to his own death…"

"They said he was afraid, that he died of fear," said Walsh. "Perhaps it was an impulse, the surge of energy a soldier has in battle, and they saw that as fear."

James nodded. "I think you're right. He tried to run and one of them hit him over the head with a rifle butt. He couldn't move fast with all this undergrowth and the ferns. He fell, and they hit him again…several times."

"Then Kelly strangled him," said Walsh.

"Yes, it was definitely Kelly," said James. "If you remember, he used his left hand when he tried to throttle Sullivan at the Provincial Hotel when we rushed them there. And Dr. Foppoly and Dr. Strehz both thought the strangler was left-handed." He stared at the ground, imagining the scene. "And that was when Wilson realized what he had just taken part in. He probably hadn't expected to murder anyone. He thought it was a robbery. But he had to go along with it after that. It took him two days to come and see me at my home."

"That makes him an accessory still," said Walsh. "Could you charge him as an accessory?"

"I could," said James. "But only if he confesses to being an accessory. He still insists he had nothing to do with it. He either tells me the truth or he goes down for murder, with malice aforethought."

24

Wanganui, 1888: The Executions

"Do you remember that time we heard the explosion and rode up the coast to see what is was?" asked Crozier suddenly. He had been walking ahead of James, and had slowed down to turn back. Perhaps he'd been trying to think of something to talk about, not realizing that James was in his own world, a world of the past.

"Of course," said James. It had happened just two years ago. His memory hadn't failed to that extent. "The eruption of Tarawera…we thought it was a ship in trouble…"

Three of them had ridden north up the coast looking for a ship. It wasn't until they returned that they learned the mountain up near Rotorua had exploded. In Wanganui, two hundred miles away, people had heard the blast and later had felt the earthquakes. The noise had been heard as far south as Blenheim in the South Island and Auckland to the north. In Auckland, the flashing lights in the sky raised fears that it was an attack by Russian warships.

A cloud of ash had hung in the air for days across the country. He'd forgotten that Crozier had been with him that day. He should have remembered…Crozier was always the man you sent when a good horseman was needed. Funny how he hadn't risen in the force. Perhaps he preferred a quiet life, and didn't want to be a leader. Ambition was a strange master, as he had found to his own disillusionment.

"One hundred and fifty people dead," said Crozier. "Maori villages buried. Day turned into night. It was like something out of Mr. Lytton's description of The Last Days of Pompeii, or so I was told." He moved the testimonial to his other hip and added, "I've always been afraid of being buried alive. One of my worst fears, especially with all the earthquakes in this country."

They were almost to the railway bridge, away from the town and all its buildings, and he could see a steam train pulling several cars rumbling over the tracks looking like tumbrels on the way to the guillotine. His house on Sydney Place was in view, and he could see the the new house on Halswell Street, which was costing him over two hundred pounds, behind some trees a short distance further on. He could rent out the house on Sydney Place for ten shillings a week - he had the lease for three more years, and it was paid in full already. With a mortgage of five-percent a year on the new house, the ten shillings a week would help keep him afloat for two or three more years, unless one of the children decided to wed.

"Of course, I'm also afraid of being strangled. Or hung. My mother said I was born with the cord around my neck, and that's why I'm afraid…"

"You're more likely to be buried alive," said James. "You haven't committed any crimes that would get you hanged, have you?"

"I suppose you're right," said Crozier. "Have you seen anyone hung, Inspector James?"

"Just one, in seventy-one. Anthony Noble, in Hokitika, the first man to be hanged there. He murdered a young girl of eight or nine—violated her, then cut her throat with a tomahawk. Deserved to be hanged…"

"How dreadful," said Crozier. "A young girl…"

"He was a coloured man," said James. "From Baltimore in America. We'd had him in gaol in Hokitika for assaulting a woman, but he'd recently been released. The girl's father was unemployed at the time…he was in poor health…and the mother was making ends meet by taking in washing. They went into town to make some purchase, locking both doors—the back and the front—before they left, leaving the children—three girls—asleep. They returned home to find the doors unlocked and a trail of blood leading from the bedroom. I was sent for and searched the area with neighbours. We found her near a swampy area not far from the cottage. It was one of the ugliest things I've seen…"

"And they hung—hanged him," said Crozier, who was a fast learner.

James nodded. "If I had to see anyone hanged, he was the man. Other than Dobson's killers of course." Now that he thought of it, Noble was also caught because he was left handed. He'd used a left-handed tomahawk, as slashes on the head proved. "Noble didn't die easily. He struggled for several minutes. Didn't say anything…no last words of apology or sorrow for what he had done…although he left a letter…"

"But you didn't see Burgess and the others hanged," said Crozier.

James shook his head.

"My uncle's friend went to watch the hangings," said Crozier. "He was up on Church Hill overlooking the prison yard before dawn, hours before the execution, but all he saw was the tops of their heads, the three of them, when they stood on the scaffold."

"I heard about it later," said James. "They all went to the scaffold in a different manner. Burgess was the most…the most dignified, I suppose you could say. He thanked all his gaolers and Mr. Shallcrass, shook their hands. Blessed them for their kindness. Claimed he been led to seek the mercy of God, and would go to his drop 'as cheerfully as to a wedding.' He imagined he would find eternal bliss. Why he should think that I don't know. Eternal damnation, more like."

"I would think so," said Crozier. "And what about the others?"

"Well, first about Burgess," said James. "He also swore at the end that the murders had all been committed by Sullivan, even Dobson's murder. Kelly and Levy were innocent, he said. He admitted to having knowledge of the murders, although he wasn't there for Mr.

Dobson's murder—which was true—but that the others weren't there either. They were innocent, all of them, he said. Of course, that was in his so-called confession. What he really wanted was to see Sullivan blamed for the murders, because he'd turned on them. Even facing death, he had the presence of mind to plan a revenge. A cool customer until the end. But Kelly, he was incoherent with fear. They said his mind had gone. He hadn't slept and had terrible diarrhea that morning. They gave them all brandy, of course, but that only goes so far… He'd written out something and insisted on reading it, delaying the hanging. He claimed he'd not murdered anyone since he was born, and blamed Sullivan, whom he called the demon of the West Coast and the Maungatapu Mountain Assassin. Levy was calmer, but still trying to litigate his crime. He complained that the government had denied him the money - twenty-five pounds—that would have allowed him to call witnesses who would prove his innocence. Said that the government spent a lot of money on the approver Sullivan, including a promise that he would be pardoned and sent somewhere else in the world, with his wife. Levy said he heard the superintendent promise him that."

"And was he?" asked Crozier. "Sent somewhere else?"

"Was he…oh, you mean Sullivan? Yes, yes, not long after the hangings. They were taken to the scaffold, the murderers. Burgess kissed the rope and said it was a prelude to heaven. Levy was composed, but Kelly kept insisting he was being murdered, asserting that he was innocent, right up to the last minute. He managed to buy them an extra thirty minutes of life with his protestations."

"They died sweetly, then," said Crozier.

Inspector James had heard that comment before. It was a reference to something attributed to the wife of Jack Ketch, the executioner in James II's reign, who had given his name to all future executioners. Although anyone could do the job, she said, her husband alone had the ability to help a culprit die sweetly. Executioners were still sometimes called Jack Ketch.

"Who did the job?" asked Crozier. "They wouldn't have a regular hangman in a place like Nelson, would they?"

"A man named Michael Clarke," said James. "He was awaiting trial for robbery at the next session, and they offered him his freedom if he would do it. He did it well, considering it was his first time. He took the next steamer to Sydney. I wondered afterwards what became of him. Not a pleasant task, hanging three men all at once. And Burgess recognized him under his hood…"

"What about last words?" asked Crozier. "Did any of them admit to murdering Mr. Dobson? Or did they all say it was Sullivan, like Burgess?"

"Kelly insisted that Sullivan and a man named Ned had poisoned Dobson with strychnine. But we knew that was a lie. I saw the autopsy myself, and the doctor, Dr. Foppoly, said there was no strychnine burn in the throat…but he'd been beaten around the head and strangled by someone with a predominant left hand."

"Then who do you think murdered Mr. Dobson?" asked Crozier.

"It was Kelly, the left-handed one, with the assistance, or at least complicity, of a man named James Wilson."

"Was he found guilty, this Wilson?"

"He went to trial for feloniously killing and murdering, without malice aforethought," said James.

He remembered it well, as if it had all happened yesterday. All that time it took to get Sullivan down to Hokitika for the trial of Wilson and the others. Months of work, and then finding out that a warrant hadn't been received in Nelson. Because Burgess, Kelly and Levy had gone to the gallows with the help of Sullivan's testimony, James was determined to get him down to Hokitika, and use his testimony to help convict Wilson, Carr, and the rest, but especially Wilson.

It was several weeks after the executions and a full six months after the murder before Sullivan arrived in Hokitika. In the interval, the whole country was treated to a deluge of salacious information about the murders. Casts of the hanged men were taken immediately after their deaths by Tatton and Knight, under the supervision of the well-known phrenologist, A. S. Hamilton, who studied the heads and pronounced on them in lectures and made a career for himself from the information—information James found totally spurious. Copies of the casts went on sale at Tatton's Chemist shop, and were snapped up eagerly. Even the Sherriff of Nelson gave way to the degenerate desires of the public by auctioning off the "relics" of the gang, including a gun and some possum rugs. Plays and tableaux were performed and wax effigies went on display.

Sullivan, in particular, came in for approbation. The Nelson newspapers were full of angry letters about Sullivan's self-satisfied demeanour when he walked through town as part of a chain gang, and papers further south picked up the stories. When Sullivan was eventually brought to Hokitika for the trial, the whole town was in an uproar and ready to lynch him, having tried him in their minds and found him guilty.

25

Greymouth, 1866-67: Sullivan Returns

Preparing for the Trial

In early November of 1866, months after finding the body, Inspector James had at last received word that the Supreme Court in Nelson had issued a writ of habeas corpus ordering the Nelson gaoler to send Sullivan to Hokitika to give evidence in the trial of James Wilson. Both he and Broham had communicated with the Nelson police several times, but the Nelson police had done nothing, had not even replied to the communications. By then, Carr and the other conspirators had been discharged by the magistrate, on the grounds they had been in gaol too long while awaiting Sullivan's arrival, notwithstanding the constant remand requests from Inspector Broham. Carr, represented by Mr. Rees, asserted that he did not want his case discharged for that reason as he preferred to wait for the opportunity to prove his innocence, but the magistrate discharged him anyway. And still Sullivan did not come.

James was in the stable yard of the police camp preparing to ride to Nelson to see where things stood, when one of his constables found him. The constable had been running and was out of breath.

"Mr. Inspector James, sir..."

James finished tightening his horse's girth and turned. "Yes?"

GREYMOUTH, 1866-67: SULLIVAN RETURNS

"We just had word from the signal station…the Airedale was spotted off the coast on its way to Hokitika, and Sullivan is aboard."

"Does anyone else know about this?" asked James.

"I, um, don't think so," said the constable, his shifty eyes giving the lie to his statement. He'd probably been bellowing the information to everyone he passed as he ran to the camp.

"Ask Sergeant Slattery to send a telegraph to Inspector Broham," said James. "Tell him to say Sullivan is on his way and should arrive tonight. I believe he has a plan to protect Sullivan from the crowds."

"Yes sir," said the constable.

"And tell Sergeant Slattery that I'm on the way to Hokitika with all haste to assist. I'll be back tomorrow."

As he arrived at the spot on South Beach below George Dobson's burial site, the Airedale appeared at the horizon moving steadily south at 15 knots. The tide had just started to come in but the beach was open; the Teremakau would still be low when he got there in an hour. He settled his horse into a steady trot. He should reach Hokitika before the Airedale and have a chance to help stop any riots that would occur when the populace found out the despised Sullivan had arrived. Hokitika was a hot-blooded town, with all the Irish there. Last New Year's Eve they had rioted at Bracken's Hotel; Carr, who was still a police constable back then, had accidentally shot himself in the leg while attempting to make an arrest. There were even suspicions that some of the rioters were Fenians, although the word Fenians was a standard insult flung at anyone who was Irish.

He crossed the Teremakau on the ferry punt, his horse swimming behind, and arrived at Hokitika an hour later. He headed straight towards the transit shed on the river, where the boat would normally dock. The area was alive with uniformed constables who had formed a chain, arms linked against a throng of angry men—as many as two hundred, it appeared.

"Is Sullivan arriving here?" he asked a constable he recognized from his previous visit.

"He's coming in at the spit," said the constable, as he struggled to maintain a foothold against the jostling, angry mob. "Sullivan is. They sent out two detectives in the harbour master's boat to bring him in. We're just here to confuse them, make them think he's coming here."

A tall, thin-faced man with a cloth cap and long mustaches overheard, and yelled, "He's coming in at the spit. He's coming in at the spit…"

"Let's get him," yelled another. "Let's get the bastard…"

The crowd surged back and half of them ran towards Spence Brothers right-of-way to get to the beach. The other half, not understanding what was going on, kept the pressure on the line of constables, yelling obscenities at them. One of them spat at the constable near James, who grabbed him by the collar and pinioned him against his saddle. "Arrest him," he said to the constable.

He followed the crowd on horseback to the beach, thinking he could place himself between them and the detectives holding Sullivan, but the crowd and the muddiness of the right-of-way held him back. The surge of bodies took him towards Revell Street and the police camp, in time to see Sullivan, a detective on each side, being pushed through a human passageway of three sergeants and the harbour master into the police camp.

The crowd groaned loudly, and began to hiss and wave their arms above their heads. Several yelled curses at Sullivan, pounding on the backs of the men forming the barrier. The door to the station opened suddenly, and Inspector Broham marched out, his back straight, his eyes an icy blue, and his red hair gleaming in the sunlight; the crowd silenced for a moment and fell back, awed, then slowly began to roar again; but in the brief period of calm the two detectives managed to bundle Sullivan into the station.

James took his horse around to the stable entrance, showed his warrant card to the constable on duty, and was directed to the station house. He found Broham pacing up and down angrily. Sullivan had already been taken out to the Logs.

"How did they know he was coming in today, and at the spit?" he demanded of James, without greeting him.

"He was seen off Greymouth," said James. "I telegraphed you…someone else could have done the same thing. The paper, perhaps?"

"You should keep better control of your town," said Broham.

"That was not the only way anyone could have found out," said James mildly. "Someone on the harbour master's boat could have…" It was probably best not to mention that a constable had revealed to James that Sullivan was coming in at the spit, down at the transit shed. He doubted the constable would be broadcasting that piece of information. Inspector Broham would have his stripes.

"Well, we have him now," said Broham. He waved a folded newspaper at James. "And today I received this…this self-serving lie from the police in Victoria. A letter published in the Inglewood Advertiser that Sullivan wrote from the Nelson gaol. It's to a resident of Wedderburn in the Victoria goldfields. He claims to have first met Burgess and Kelly in Hokitika, and mentions some of the previous crimes they have committed. I doubt he ever lived in Wedderburn in his life. He's…"

"Actually, sir, I happen to know he did," said James. "I met him there in the late fifties. He and his wife kept a half-way house between Wedderburn and Inglewood. It's definitely the same man."

"You could have mentioned that to me before," said Broham, frowning at James. "But he's lying about meeting them here in Hokitika, at least. He met them in Otago—he was convicted with them, but sent back to Australia."

James took several seconds to reply, but his honesty finally overcame him. "No, as it turns out, that was another Sullivan," he said. "Not our Sullivan. Our Sullivan started using his first name, Joseph, when he arrived in New Zealand, for some reason, and that confused the Otago force. He was known in Wedderburn as Thomas Sullivan…"

"Inspector James, you need to keep me better informed," said Broham.

"I assumed you would…"

"Never assume," said Broham sharply. "Now, as it seems he may be telling the truth about that at least, there are some other details in the letter that we could consider."

James waited.

"This may not be relevant, but Kelly has a brother—under the name of Noon, his real name—in gaol in the Mount Eden Stockade. Sullivan claims the brothers are the last surviving members of the gang of Captain Melville, the notorious bushranger. He says they were tried in Melbourne in 1854 for a murder at the Ovens goldfield, two years earlier. They were acquitted, apparently, because of the passage of time. They could no longer be recognized…"

"After just two years?" asked James. "I recognized Sullivan after a passage of over ten years. People don't change that much."

Broham nodded. "I agree. And then of course he mentions Otago, which we knew about already…at least I was under the impression that I did…and the Nelson police found the revolver he said he hid, still fully loaded, and some strychnine…"

"How does he say he met Burgess and Kelly?"

"At a billiard saloon in Hokitika. Sullivan says he found them to be decent men, although they spent money freely," said Broham. "But someone robbed Sullivan and he reported it us. We apprehended the thief but couldn't find Sullivan to confirm the identification, so we had to let him go. Apparently the robber was an acquaintance of Burgess's, and Burgess had prevailed upon Sullivan to hide with them to avoid giving evidence. They gave Sullivan five pounds to cover the cost of the robbery. After that, he says, he was their slave. He'd lied to the police and the gang held it over him. Ironic, really, considering what happened in Nelson."

"I believe he's weak, rather than immoral," said James. "But I also believe that what he says is true, for the most part. What does he need to lie about, other than his own part in the affair? And he mostly admits to that—enough to get him hanged at least."

"Let's hope he's convincing enough for the jury to convict Carr and Wilson," said Broham. "Although I may have to try conspiracy to rob for Carr."

"For Mr. Fox?" asked James.

"Indeed," said Broham. "Although Sullivan mentions Carr in relation to the robbery and their plans specifically in his letter. Not by name, however. He refers to 'a policeman connected to them.'"

"And, of course, it was Sullivan who was the witness when Burgess was arrested for having the pistol cases of the stolen guns under his bedclothes," said James.

"He mentions that in his letter," said Broham. "He felt that he was even more under their power after he did that."

"He stumbled into the lesser crimes, and before he knew it he was implicated in the murders." Said James. "He claims he acted as lookout for all the murders, including George Dobson's."

"I'm beginning to feel that although he's a despicable person, perhaps we should trust him for the facts, at least," said Broham. "Thank-you, Inspector James, for clarifying some details for me."

James felt he had been dismissed, so he left.

Outside, the crowds remained, and a carnival atmosphere had taken hold. The tall thin man with the long mustache approached him and said with a sneer, "In trouble, are you? You and that loud-mouthed constable at the transit shed…" James thought he heard a faint German accent. Not a Fenian, at least. The Germans were one thing, but he remembered the Irish from the Eureka stockade…and now with the Fenians spreading around the world…

He brushed past the German and walked down Revell Street, looking for a place to spend the night. Revell Street, like Mawhera Quay and other streets in Greymouth, was crowded with hotels both small and large. He walked by Bracken's Hotel, where Constable Carr had shot himself in the leg during the New Year's Eve riots, and decided against that, finally settling on the Kortegast brothers

Exchange Hotel. A board outside noted:

Kortegast Bros. have great pleasure in announcing to their friends and patrons that they have made such alterations as to enable their hotel to be considered one of the most comfortable in New Zealand. Several new bedrooms have been added; and as none but the choicest liquors are kept, the supremacy this hotel has always maintained will still be maintained. Excellent accommodation for Boarders. First-rate Billiard room, with Thurston's table. Stabling is now added.

That sounded exactly what he wanted. He would have a decent meal, perhaps a game of billiards if there were any players in residence, a good night's sleep, and return to Greymouth at his leisure the next day. He might even ride inland, stop at Kumara and Greenstone again to see how the inhabitants of those towns were managing—and if Mr. Warden Revell had been for the promised visit.

He was met inside by a young woman with the pale, freckled skin and round face of an Irishwoman. She was wearing an apron covered in flour and looked as if she had just come from the kitchen.

"Is Mr. Kortegast about?" he asked.

"He's down at the wharf…buying some fish. He'll be back soon. I'm Mrs. Kortegast."

"Ah," he said, feeling guilty. He had assumed she was the cook, or perhaps the maid. "I'm looking for a room for the night."

"We have a room," she said. "Let me show you."

He followed her up the stairs and along the hallway to a pleasant-looking room at the rear of the building.

"This is a nice quiet room," she said. "Will it suit?"

"It will suit very well," said James. Certainly far better than sleeping on the floor of a store. "And perhaps a fish dinner, if your husband returns with a catch?"

"We do a beautiful smoked fish pie," she said, winning her way to his heart instantly. "I have a wee piece in the kitchen if you'd be liking it now. The crust is nice and fresh…"

He sat at the kitchen table and enjoyed the pie, possibly one of the best he had ever tasted. What a pity that Elizabeth…well, one couldn't expect her to excel at everything. And there was always Jack's Nonpareil when he fancied a tasty piece of pie.

"Now what would you be doing in Hokitika," Mrs. Kortegast asked as he polished off his meal with a large nobbler of Irish whiskey and a slice of good cheddar from New Plymouth.

"I'm the police inspector in charge of the Greymouth camp," he said. "I came down to talk to Inspector Broham about…a matter of importance."

"That Mr. Sullivan, no doubt," she said. "The whole town is talking about him. And Mrs. Sullivan, his wife. They say she's in Hokitika, although I've never seen her…I heard she came in on the Gothenburg a few weeks ago and said she was looking for her husband who had last written to her from Okarita."

"More than one Sullivan in town," said James. "Especially in an Irish town like this…"

"I expect so," she said. She picked up his plate and took it over to the sink. "Now talking of Sullivan, who escaped the hangman with his lies…"

James wiped his lips with a napkin and waited.

"They have their heads in town…"

"Their heads? Whose…"

"Oh, of the rest of the gang," she said. "The casts of their heads I mean. Mr. Hamilton, the phrenologist, opened a museum down the street a ways. I went to a lecture he gave about the gang. He understood them very well."

"What did he say?" asked James. He could probably give as good an accounting of the three men without resorting to running his hands over their skulls, but he thought it prudent not to say so.

"He had casts displayed on the stage," she said, patting imaginary heads with her hands. "He turned them around and pointed to all the different organs. He said he thought Burgess was the most remarkable example of a criminal he had ever seen, and stood alone in 'completeness of polished and successful ruffianism.' Levy and Kelly were both small in the organ of conscientiousness, but Kelly had the advantage intellectually over Levy. I was surprised to hear that. I thought Levy was supposed to be the planner."

"I thought so," said James. "Although I never met Levy so I can't be sure."

"But you met the other two?"

He nodded, but said nothing.

"I don't suppose you can talk about it. Look at this." She picked up a folded-back copy of the West Coast Times from the table, and pointed to an advertisement on page three. He took it from her and read:

Practical Phrenology. A. S. Hamilton twenty-eight years Practical Phrenologist, in England, Scotland, and Ireland, has arrived, and may be consulted at his Phrenological Museum, Revell street. Casts and Skulls of the heads of Burgess, Kelly, and Levy, and many other murderers and bushrangers may be seen at the Museum. Charges: Verbal delineation of character, five shillings; written analysis, with directions for the improvement, correction, and profitable application of the intellectual powers, one pound.

"Remarkable," he said, keeping his voice neutral. "You're interested in seeing the heads?"

She pulled a face. "Not at all. They were unpleasant characters by the sound of it. But I'd like to have Mr. Hamilton…have him delineate my character…"

"You feel you need to know more about your character?"

She nodded, pleased that he seemed to understand. "My husband thinks I'm foolish, but I've always believed the shape of a person's head must prove something. I believe my forehead," she tapped herself above the eyebrows, "shows that I'm benevolent."

"I could have told you that," he said, and saw her face fall. She turned away and began washing his plate in the sink.

He sat there for a minute, and was about to say something placatory when the door flew open and a man strode in.

"William," said Mrs. Kortegast. "Here is Inspector James from Greymouth come to…"

William Kortegast glared at James. "What are you doing here then?" he asked. It was the tall thin man from the transit shed and the station – the German with the long mustache. James nodded to him and rose from his chair. Time to make a strategic withdrawal and see if anyone was in the billiard room.

26

Hokitika, 1867: The Trial: Day One

The Crown Prosecutor began his case on January 28th, 1867, eight months to the day from the murder of George Dobson and more than three months after Burgess, Kelly and Levy had hanged for the Nelson murders. He rose in front of the court wearing his black robes and scruffy grey wig, his thumbs hooked into his buff-coloured waistcoat, looking like a man who could not possibly lose any case, no matter how complicated. But he was opposed by two consummate defenders: Mr. Rees, brother of the late suicide Mr. Rees of the Bank of New Zealand, and Mr. Button. Mr. Rees was a competent defender, but James was worried about Mr. Button: an accomplished musician who conducted the Church of England choir, Button also gave lectures on electricity, performing astounding experiments, and at both proceedings he routinely held crowds in the palms of his large expressive hands. The two defenders had eschewed the stuffy robes and wigs, and were dressed in smart charcoal suits with dark vests, looking for all the world like wealthy businessmen.

The West Coast had changed in the last eight months. A tramway now ran from Greymouth to Saltwater and would soon carry on to Hokitika. The boatmen on the lagoon, who watched as their lucrative livelihoods disappeared, had other ideas; earlier in the week someone had placed rock on the track, almost causing it to overturn. It was not the first such dastardly act of sabotage the boatmen had—allegedly—performed. Earlier in the month a wedge had been pulled from a sleeper and placed on the track, but had been found immediately.

James had gone down to the boat launch at the end of Arney Street and had a friendly word with the boatmen. He saw them now, watching him with narrowed eyes beneath the brims of their floppy hats as he rode past on his way to the trial in Hokitika. His job had also changed since the death of George Dobson, becoming more difficult; bushrangers were again at work in the area, three men having bailed up a man named Nicholls. They had stolen poor Nicholl's gold, belted him to a tree, gagged him with a stick, and left him fifty yards off the track, too terrified to call for help because they'd threatened to shoot him if he did. Burgess had laid a pall over the crime of bushranging: before he'd arrived on the scene everyone understood a robbery to be a robbery, and not a robbery/murder, but now victims had to assume they might die. To complicate things for James, the Governor was due in Greymouth and they would all have to parade before him in full dress uniform. He hoped he'd find the time to meet with His Excellency, keep an eye on the boatmen on the lagoon, stay alert for bushrangers, and still attend the trial every day.

Some minor associates of Burgess had been tried and convicted in the past few weeks, including one for perjury for his false testimony on the robbery at the police camp, who had been sentenced to penal servitude for a term of four years; James hoped that the general feeling of antipathy towards the minor gang members would extend to James Wilson. It very much depended on who had been assigned the task of magistrate for this Supreme Court sitting.

William DeLacey, the stable man who had ridden past Inspector James when he escorted Mr. Fox up the track, had been convicted of conspiracy to "stick up and rob Mr. Edward Burton Fox," and sentenced to two years. All was going well. Now, if only Mr. Justice Gresson was not on the bench. Three supreme court judges were assigned to the South Island: Gresson, Arney, and Johnston. Gresson, who lived in Christchurch not far from Edward and Maryanne Dobson, George's parents, would go out of his way to parade his impartiality and fairness. James had given evidence in front of Gresson several times in Timaru, and had seen how his dedication to fairness caused problems for the police. He was, like Mr. Button, a committed member of the Anglican church, and had been for most of his fifty-seven years. And an Irishman, as well. He'd been in New Zealand from the early days, arriving at Lyttelton on the Nelson, and walking over the bridle path to Christchurch. James remembered reading that the Gresson family, in the manner of King John losing his clothes in the Wash, lost all their baggage on the Sumner bar as it followed them to Christchurch. People repeated the story when they wanted to mock him.

He arrived in Hokitika to discover Mr. Justice Gresson seated at the bench, ready to start the trial of James Wilson. Justice Gresson was wearing his black robes, with white bands at his throat, and a short wig, looking as if he had been magically transported to Hokitika from the Old Bailey. The courtroom was packed and quiet, most of them intimidated by the illustrious presence before them. Wilson sat in the prisoner's box, his curly hair combed flat, wearing a nondescript brown suit. He had shrunk since his incarceration, and looked less dangerous than he had on the night he'd come to James' house on Arney Street – in fact, scarcely dangerous at all.

The Crown first called Mr. Anderson, who affirmed he had seen Dobson at his store in Maori Gully on the 27th of May, and walked up the track with him and Mr. Fox to Arnold Township the following day, the 28th of May. He'd last seen George Dobson heading down the track towards Greymouth.

Edward Burton Fox then gave evidence. The reporters in court leaned forward and took notice, partly because this was the first time he'd spoken in court, but also because of the difficulty they had in understanding his thick Scots accent. Mr. Fox told the court he had been with Dobson on that last day, and described the clothes he was wearing and the compass strapped around his body. The last time he had seen him, he said, at about eleven o'clock, Dobson was going down the track towards the Grey. He continued with his own movements:

"I went from the Arnold Township to Greymouth in a boat, and reached the latter place at about a quarter to three. If Dobson had walked at his ordinary pace, he ought to have reached the Grey at about half past five in the evening... I never saw Dobson alive after leaving him at the Arnold."

Mr. Button stood up and coughed quietly into his hand. "Was it a dry day, Mr. Fox?" he asked. "How fast would Mr. Dobson have been walking?"

"I am not certain whether the weather was wet or dry on the 28th May," said Fox. "Dobson was a very good walker, and was considered a first-class bushman. I think he should have walked from the Arnold to the spot where the body was found in about two hours. He could have walked from the spot to Greymouth in about two hours and a half. It is nearly six miles from Greymouth to where the body was found."

His lack of memory about the weather was worrying. After eight months, many of the details might have faded, not only from Mr. Fox's mind, but also from the minds of other witnesses. James was also annoyed that neither men had been given a chance to bring George Dobson to life for the jury. Sympathy for the victim often played a part in a conviction.

Mr. Fox stepped down from the witness box. Sullivan was escorted to the box, accompanied by a loud murmur and some hissing from the room. Sullivan greeted the hissing with a smirk, straightening his necktie. Mr. Justice Gresson banged on the desk with his gavel. "I'll ask you to be quiet please, so the court can hear what the witness has to say."

Sullivan wore a dark suit with a velvet waistcoat, a sky-blue necktie at his throat, his large face surrounded by newly trimmed whiskers, and looked as if he were about to partake in a stroll along Bond Street.

He'd been the centerpiece of several trials, and clearly enjoyed being the focus of everyone's attention, even when that attention was mostly negative.

The prosecutor began by asking him how he had met the prisoner.

"I first became acquainted with the prisoner on Friday, 11th May, at the Arahura, about six miles from Hokitika," said Sullivan, looking towards Wilson with a smile; Wilson glowered back at him and raised his hand towards his neck, to indicate throat-slashing, but thought better of it and let his had drop. "I was in company with a man named Kelly. I returned to Hokitika leaving the prisoner with Kelly. I had a conversation with the prisoner-that day. The prisoner said he was going to the Grey with newspapers, and would accompany Kelly and help to carry the swag."

"And later you went to Greymouth?" asked the prosecutor. "All of you?"

"Yes. Well, the three of us. The prisoner came the next day."

"And when would that have been, when the prisoner arrived?"

"I was at Greymouth on the 26th of May. Kelly and Burgess were with me. The prisoner arrived at Greymouth the next day, Sunday."

"Did he say anything to you?"

Sullivan nodded. "I had a conversation with him. I asked him why he did not start from Hokitika with us, and he said because he had to get some money."

"And once in Greymouth you had a plan to go out onto the track and accost..."

Button sprang to his feet. "Objection."

"You later met out on the track" said the prosecutor.

"Yes," said Sullivan. "It was arranged that Burgess, Kelly, Wilson and myself were to go out on the road. We were all four to meet at the iron hut on the Arnold track early on the following day, Monday. Kelly and I went out on the Sunday night, and slept at the iron hut. I met the prisoner about half-past ten on the following morning, about a mile on the Greymouth side of the iron hut. We remained at the hut about half-an-hour."

James listened carefully. Sullivan was much clearer about the days than he had been earlier. Now his testimony fit the evidence given by others very neatly, placing the murderers in the vicinity of the murder on the correct date – May 28th.

"I went with Kelly and the prisoner, and we went in the direction of the Arnold," Sullivan continued. "We proceeded about four miles. There is a bridge over a ravine, where Kelly stopped; it was an open part of the river. We reached there about one o'clock, and I remained there about half an hour, and then left Kelly and the prisoner, and proceeded myself in the direction of the coal-pits."

"The others remained there at that spot?" asked the prosecutor.

"Yes, they did," said Sullivan. "Kelly remained there because he had a cut on his face, and Mr. Fox would know him. I went along the road to watch for Mr. Fox, who was supposed to be coming from the Arnold. I might have gone on a distance of three-quarters of a mile towards the Arnold after I left the prisoner and Kelly."

"And what were you to do when you saw Mr. Fox coming," said the prosecutor, careful not to put the suggestion into Sullivan's head that they were waiting to rob and kill Mr. Fox.

"I was to alert them," said Sullivan. "But Mr. Fox did not come."

James felt his fists clenching. Here it was. The moment of the killing.

"I met a young man on the road; he was dressed in dark clothes and was carrying a greatcoat something like the one now produced. He also wore a strap, similar to the one in Court, He had leather outside his trousers but I cannot say whether they were leggings or boots. I spoke to him in an ordinary way, and he proceeded down the road, and went on. It was about half a mile from where I left Kelly and the prisoner that I met the young man."

A sigh ran through the court. They all knew what was coming next. Here was George Dobson, walking along the track, encountering Sullivan, on his way to his own doom.

"I went on about a quarter of a mile towards the Arnold, where I stayed about ten minutes, and then returned to the spot where I had left them. Kelly and the prisoner were putting up a tent when I left them, and it was up when I returned. The door of the tent was closed. I saw Kelly as I approached speaking to someone, and when I got to the tent he was standing with his hands behind him...I asked Kelly where the prisoner was, and he said in the tent."

"I heard some voices, and just afterwards saw a man and woman coming up the track. I went, by request, and had a conversation with them, to delay them. They stopped about three minutes, and then walked on, and I returned to the tent. The man Martin Mullins is the man I met with the woman. When I got back to the tent I saw the prisoner and Kelly. The prisoner was on his knees, gathering up some papers. They had made a fire about four yards from the tent. The prisoner had a large new pocket book in his hand, and Kelly threw the papers into the fire. I caught one of them up, and saw that it was an order to pay £45; The names of Revell and Dobson were on it. I threw it in the fire, and it was consumed."

"Did you say anything to Kelly or the prisoner?" asked the prosecutor.

"Kelly asked me if I had met anyone," said Sullivan. "I said, yes, that I had met a young fellow —neither a man nor a boy...I asked why they put him up, and they said because they thought he had something."

"Did you ask either of them where the young man was?" asked the prosecutor.

"I asked whether he was tied up," said Sullivan. And the prisoner said, 'Oh yes, he's right enough.' I was invited by Kelly to go into the bush and see him, and the three of us then went into the bush. We had some difficulty in finding the man. I heard the prisoner say, 'here he is,' and I went forward and saw the young man whom I had seen on the track about an hour and three-quarters before."

"He was merely tied up?" asked the prosecutor. "Or was he..."

"I thought he was dead," said Sullivan. "And said so to the prisoner and Kelly. He was sitting in a crouching position. His head was lying over his right shoulder, and his face was turned upwards and discoloured. Kelly said he died from fright, and the prisoner confirmed the statement, saying that they were going to tie him up when he dropped down dead."

"Did you ask them what they intended to do?"

"I asked what they were going to do with the deceased, and Kelly replied, 'leave him there.' He said Dick and he, alluding to Burgess, did a man like that once before; that they would roll him up in blankets, and if ever he was found it would be thought that he died from exhaustion."

"But he was buried when he was discovered by Inspector James," noted the prosecutor. "Did you assist the other two in the burial?"

"Kelly asked me to keep the road while they dug a hole to bury the deceased," said Sullivan. "I took a double-barrelled gun and went along the track about a hundred yards towards Greymouth…I heard some voices coming from the direction of Greymouth, and made a noise to attract the notice, or what is called, 'give them the office,' to warn Kelly and the prisoner to stop what they were doing."

"What did you do when you perceived the coast was clear?" asked the prosecutor.

"We proceeded into Greymouth, having planted our swag on the road. We had some disagreement about dividing the things and money taken from Dobson. The prisoner wanted to take a gold watch and Kelly objected and I agreed with him."

"Did you tell anyone what you had done, once you reached Greymouth?" asked the prosecutor.

"I advised them not to tell Burgess of what they had done that day, but to keep it a secret amongst the three of us," said Sullivan. "But Kelly said there were no secrets amongst mates, especially between him and Burgess. The prisoner said Burgess was a very nice little chap, but that Levy was a hound."

"When did you part from the pair…Kelly and Wilson" asked the prosecutor.

"On the quay," said Sullivan. "I then proceeded to the Provincial Hotel, where I saw Burgess playing at cards with a female named Rosa. Kelly and Wilson arrived, and Burgess gave the prisoner three £1 notes and a half-sovereign, and gave me a £1 note and ten shillings in silver. I did not see Burgess give Kelly anything."

Dobson's money had helped them in their escape to Nelson on the Wallaby, as James had thought.

"And did you leave them at the hotel…the Provincial Hotel, was it?" asked the prosecutor.

"It was arranged that the prisoner should fetch the fire-arms that we had 'planted' into town, and he said he would leave them with George Colburn, a restaurant keeper in Greymouth, and an old mate of his at Nelson. I offered to accompany the prisoner to fetch the firearms into town."

"That same day?"

Sullivan shook his head. "No, on the following day. It was arranged that we should all sleep at different hotels that night. On the following morning, I started at about half past five, and went to the iron hut. I saw the prisoner that morning about a quarter of a mile on the Arnold side of the iron hut. This was about eight o'clock. Kelly was with me."

"Did the prisoner say anything to you that morning, as you fetched the guns?"

"He told me that the 'bloke,' meaning the deceased young man, was a surveyor. I asked him how he knew it, and he said by reading his papers."

He had learned that from James, of course, and not on the day after the murder. And the papers had mistakenly given the date as May 29th. Sullivan was squeezing facts to fit with the narrative, but not enough to influence the jury.

"Do you have anything else important to tell us about what you saw that day?" asked the prosecutor.

"I saw some pieces of old cloth brought to the iron hut by the prisoner for masks," said Sullivan. "But Kelly introduced a better

HOKITIKA, 1867: THE TRIAL: DAY ONE

idea - that of using pocket handkerchiefs."

"And these are the pieces of cloth?" The prosecutor pointed towards the evidence table.

"Something like those I refer to, but I cannot identify them," said Sullivan He sounded almost apologetic. "We planted the pieces of cloth near the iron hut."

"Thank you," said the magistrate. "Now, one more thing…"

Sullivan pulled out his watch.

"It's one o'clock," he said, a hint of complaint in his voice. "Time for lunch."

The magistrate frowned. "No, Mr. Sullivan, it is not yet time for…"

"It is by my watch." Sullivan waved his watch in the direction of the magistrate, and looked around the court, seeking agreement. "I won't give any further testimony until I have my lunch."

The magistrate's lips tightened to a thin line. "As it happens we are done with you," he said. He picked up his gavel and whacked it on the desk, as if Sullivan's head was on the receiving end. "We'll adjourn for lunch."

James went down Revell Street looking for a cup of tea and a sandwich. He returned afterwards to find Brohan standing outside the courthouse having a pipe.

"Going well so far, James," he said. "We should be able to convict on the strength of that testimony. Very solid, I thought."

"It seems very solid," said James. "But the people of this town despise Sullivan. Not just here, but in Greymouth and everywhere else. He must be the most hated man on the coast."

"That's true," said Broham. "Do you know, he actually demanded English porter with his lunch. The local porter wasn't good enough for him apparently. If the locals found out…but the jury will ignore those sentiments. They'll know better than to let emotions influence them. And Mr. Justice Gresson will direct them to ignore such feelings."

"I hope so," said James. His experiences in Timaru did not give him the greatest confidence in Justice Gresson, however.

"Shearman thinks we did well," said Broham after a pause. He had a self-satisfied look on his face. "Sent me a letter the other day, congratulating me on finding the body, and conducting the investigation." He must have seen the consternation on James face, and added, "You were very helpful of course. Couldn't have done it without you." He knocked the pipe out on the heel of his boot. "I suppose we'd better return to court."

The next man up was Mr. Bain's articled pupil, George Randall Sayle, one of George Dobson's mates who had been present when the body was exhumed. He'd been with James and Bain when they went up to Stillwater to look for the cloth masks Wilson had mentioned, and was determined to present the map he had given to James. He'd done so at the pretrial, but had not aroused enough interest in it to present it again. He gave his brief evidence and stepped down.

George Windhover, the next witness, who had passed the tent on May 28th, claimed to have seen two men there; one fair and the other dark.

"Is the man on the dock, the prisoner, the man you saw that day?" asked the prosecutor.

"The prisoner is something like the fair man I saw at the tent," said Windhover, staring at Wilson. "But I cannot swear to him."

Mr. Button rose to his feet. "Mr. Windhover, did you not say you should know the prisoner? That you had seen him before?"

"I don't recollect that," said Windhover, avoiding looking at the defender.

James winced. A stronger statement would have been helpful.

"And the dark man, could you say definitely that he was not the dark man you saw at the tent?" asked Button.

Windover was more positive of this answer. "No, he was not."

The prosecutor stood up again and asked, "Did you speak with the men?"

"I remarked that it was a queer time to put a tent up," said Windhover. The dark-complexioned man spoke to me."

"And after you left the tent, did you see anyone else?"

"I met a young man…he wasn't wearing a watch."

William Gilby, a miner from Maori Gully was then sworn in. He too had seen the tent on the 28th of May on his way from Greymouth to the Arnold. He'd seen two men, one erecting the tent, the other filling a billy with water. One was fair, the other dark, and both were little men.

"Is the prisoner the fair man you saw?" asked the prosecutor.

"I can't say," said Gilby. "Something similar. He—the fair man—asked me if it was going to rain, and I said I doubted it. He asked me if I would pitch a tent, and I said I wouldn't."

Mr. Button rose again. "Is the man Sullivan, now in court, either of the men you saw that day?"

"I can't be certain, but I don't think he was."

"After you left the tent, did you see anyone else?" asked the prosecutor.

"I met a young man with a coat over his arm, and a belt over his shoulder," said Gilby. By now, everyone present recognized the description of George Dobson, and there was a soft groan from the room. Justice Gresson rapped his gavel against the desk and the witness stepped down from the stand.

John Mullins, husband of the married couple James had sent for the day he found the body, was called to the stand. He recalled seeing two men at the accommodation house a mile and a half from the Grey, one fair and one a half-caste. Kelly was dark, but not a half-caste, so he'd probably seen someone else. He and his wife had stopped to eat dinner at Alabaster's store near the coal pits. Then, about two miles on the Arnold side of Alabaster's store, he had met a man coming towards the Grey. He was near the tree bearing the mark of George Dobson's grave, not far from a bridge.

"Did you speak to this man?" asked Mr. Button.

"He said something to us," said Mullins. "But I did not speak to him. If he said I spoke to him for three of four minutes, then he's sworn falsely."

"And do you see that man in court today?"

"It was Sullivan," said Mullin, pointing in Sullivan's direction.

"And you did not see a tent or a fire on the road that day?"

"No I did not."

Disappointing testimony, thought James. Mullins had testified at the inquest that he'd seen two men putting up the tent. Enough to confuse the jury and throw some suspicion onto Sullivan, which the defense would want. But why would the prosecutor bring it forward? What was he thinking? Surely he did not want to prove that Sullivan was the guilty man here.

The next testimony was even more disappointing. David Duncan had left Greymouth on the morning of the 28th of May and returned the same day. He had seen Wilson, whom he knew, having shared a room at a hotel with him, coming towards Greymouth carrying a swag. He was with another man who had a cut under his eye. The man could have been Sullivan but he wasn't sure. He remembered having told Constable McIlroy that he had seen Wilson rolling up his swag near the iron hut. That put Kelly and Wilson together, as Kelly was the man with the cut under his eye, as the final witness asserted.

Benjamin Barnard of the Provincial Hotel was the last man to the stand. At this point, apparently, the prosecutor was attempting to verify that Wilson knew the members of the gang. Kelly, Burgess, and Sullivan had been at Barnard's hotel; he had seen them in his bar talking to Wilson on several occasions. Kelly had a black eye and a cut under his eye a day or two before the murder. He was not sure about dates, but he was certain about one thing: Burgess had been at home all day on May 28th.

The court adjourned for the day.

27

Hokitika, 1867: The Trial: Day Two

Inspector James was up early the next morning, feeling a trifle irritated. The trial had gone reasonably well so far, but the prosecutor seemed to have strayed from a strict indictment of James Wilson and was muddying the waters with testimony pointing to Sullivan and Burgess. Burgess was dead, and Sullivan had been convicted of the murder of Jamie Battle, by his own admission. He hoped the evidence of the second day, including his own, would improve matters. He ate breakfast and walked down to the spit to watch the tide coming in up the river. As he neared the wharf he could see a crowd of people yelling vociferously, some even throwing rocks as a steamer, the *Atlantic* by the look of it, attempted to dock. Voices were calling out to someone on the boat to come ashore, and not to be afraid.

"What's going on?" he asked a short, thickset man who was standing at the rear of the crowd, grinning broadly.

"It's some Celestials," he said. "Come from Sydney to inspect the coast on behalf of a group of their countrymen. When we yelled at them they dived under the hatches, and now they won't come out. If we encourage them come here they'll go home and bring more."

"Is there some problem with having Chinamen here?" asked James, puzzled. He'd respected the Chinese in Victoria, especially their willingness to carefully rework depleted diggings. A good living could be made from the tailings, and the shopkeepers in Carisbrooke had reported that Chinamen could be trusted to pay their tick. He pushed his way to the front of the rowdy group and waved them off, but they ignored him and continued yelling. The atmosphere was more like a fête than a riot; no mere police inspector was going to dissuade them from their entertainment. Eventually they would grow tired of the excitement and leave, allowing the Chinamen to find their way ashore. He gave up and returned to the courthouse, where he was the first person called to the stand.

He told the court the whole story of his involvement with Wilson, spending most of the morning telling it: the visit to his home on the night of the 30th of May when he had taken Wilson to see Mr. Warden Revell; the trip up to the Twelve Mile the following day with Mr. Fox and the undercover constables, when they had been spotted by the gang; the letter from "Incognito" asking James to meet him at the hotel in Blaketown, when Wilson had told him how the gang had returned to Greymouth after spotting his party.

"I next saw the prisoner on Friday at nine in the morning, when I finally had warrants to arrest Burgess, Kelly, and Sullivan."

"Did you arrest Burgess, Kelly, and Sullivan?" asked the prosecutor.

"He told me they had left town," said James. He waited for the inevitable question, asking why they had left town, but it did not come.

"What did the prisoner say to you?" asked the prosecutor.

"He asked me about the missing surveyor, and when he had last been seen last alive," said James. "He speculated that Burgess and Sullivan had 'put him away.'"

"This was on the day you arrested him?" asked the prosecutor. "Did he make a statement at that point?"

"Prisoner then made a long statement, that on the 28th of May, a Monday, he and Burgess left Greymouth, proceeded as far as the Arnold track, and arrived there, about nine o'clock in the morning. They met Kelly and Sullivan there, and had a drink of hot tea together. They then proceeded up the track, and selected the spot where they intended to meet Fox. After remaining an hour there, it came onto rain, in consequence of which the whole four returned to the iron hut. The prisoner and Sullivan remained there, and Burgess and Kelly proceeded into Greymouth, reaching there at 5 o'clock. The prisoner slept at the Criterion Hotel that night, and did not rise until very late on the following morning, a Tuesday. On going into the main street, he met Kelly who asked him where Dick was and gave him a swag containing firearms, which he took to George Coburn. I then arrested the prisoner on the charge of conspiring to murder Fox, and on our way to the lock-up the prisoner said I had no right to arrest him, and that nothing would induce him to divulge anything further."

Mr. Button rose, looking disinterested, as if attending to a minor point. "He said he was up the track with Burgess, Kelly and Sullivan on the…" he consulted his notes briefly, as if he needed reminding of the date, "on May the 28th?"

James confirmed that it was, realizing that he too had muddied the waters of who was where when, and on what date. The dates may not have been important, but lack of precision could take them off the table. The jury might start to think the confusion was their own, and blank the dates from their minds.

"You searched him at the station in the presence of Sergeant Slattery?" asked the prosecutor.

"Yes. We found three pounds and some silver on him." The exact amount Sullivan claimed Wilson had been given by Burgess. He hoped the jury had noted that point. They were looking somewhat bored, unsure of what had happened.

He was asked about the clothing used for the masks that he and Mr. Bain had found. Then, at last, he came to the point where he had found the body, and the toe of the boot that had led him there. The jury woke up and paid attention again.

"The compass, in the case produced, was also on Dobson's body, which was in a state of decomposition. The pipe and other articles produced were found on the body. I had the body taken into

Greymouth where it was identified, and an inquest was held, at which I was present."

James saw the jury sink back as a man. Not enough lurid details for them. What about the skin falling off the hand, and the face that looked as if it might have been gnawed away by rats? They had read of such things in all the papers and were hoping to hear more. He then gave details of the confession Wilson had made regarding the arrangements to intercept Mr. Fox, and put the confession into evidence.

"Did you ask the prisoner about any involvement of the gang with Mr. Dobson's murder?" asked Button.

"I asked the prisoner whether he thought Burgess, Kelly and Sullivan were involved in the murder of Mr. Dobson, and he said he did not know," said James. "At that point, the three, along with Levy, had been arrested in Nelson for the murders on the Maungatapu Track. He asked me if he thought one of them would confess, and I told the prisoner that I thought Sullivan would very likely give information as I saved his life at Korong when he was in the hands of a party of Germans who were about to stab him, and when I interfered and he got clear, he ran off and left me in the lurch. From this I inferred that he was a coward."

At that he was asked to stand down, and he did so, feeling as if had more to say, more that would implicate Wilson, would show him for the villain that he was. But he had to answer only the questions he was asked, to be guided by the prosecutor.

Mr. Revell, the warden of the gold fields and the Greymouth magistrate, was called, and confirmed the story of the night James had taken Wilson to the courthouse to make a statement.

"He made a statement to the effect that Burgess, Kelly, and Sullivan were going to stick-up Mr. Fox and murder him, and that he, the prisoner, was one of the gang; that he was acquainted with Burgess and Kelly in Otago, who each got three and a half years in gaol there; that when they came out of gaol they were escorted out of the province by instructions of the Commissioner of police."

"Please continue, Mr. Revell," said the prosecutor.

"The prisoner also said that the movements of Fox were well known to them all. That a man named Billy, Billy DeLacy, a stableman, was connected with them, and the way he managed to get information was by asking Mr. Fox what time he was going out to the Arnold, and would he take letters. He also said that Burgess and party were fully determined to carry out their purpose of robbing Mr. Fox, and if they got possession of their fire-arms they would not be taken with their lives."

"Who did he consider was in this party of Burgess's," asked the prosecutor. "This gang."

"Burgess, Kelly and Sullivan," said Revell. "And another man named Levy…one of the men hanged in Nelson, as you may recall. He said that the party were living in town and spending money at the rate of three and four pounds per day, and that some person must be underground for it."

"Underground?"

"Dead," said Revell. "Dead and buried, presumably."

"What had he to say in his own defence?" asked the prosecutor.

"He said he had never done any roguish action himself, but he had committed robberies, and had never gone so far as to take a man's life. That was why he wanted to make a statement. He also asked me for a sum of money to enable him to leave the province, but I replied that it was not in my power."

"Did you see the prisoner again?"

"About a week after the first interview I again saw the prisoner at my office after he was remanded for the attempted murder of Mr. Fox. At this time, George Dobson was missing. I said he'd been seen on Tuesday the 29th of May on the Arnold track, and was I afraid that he'd fallen into the hands of some of the gang. Prisoner denied all knowledge of it, and stated that he had been out on Monday, the 28th May, to the iron store, in company with Burgess, Kelly, and Sullivan, for the purpose of waylaying Fox; that it came on to rain, and that Burgess and himself proceeded to town, and left Sullivan and Kelly behind. Prisoner said he slept at the Criterion Hotel that night, and did not get up till late the next day, when he walked on to the town, and met Kelly with a swag on his back, who asked him where Dick, meaning Burgess, was."

James resisted the impulse to stand up and say, 'Don't you see? Going by Mr. Revell's account, Wilson is giving himself an alibi for the wrong day. He admits being on the track on the 28th and has covered himself for the 29th, the day he says he slept in and saw Kelly in town.' Wilson was making that claim because the newspaper reports of Sullivan's confession had been a day off, originally at least. Now, all that was happening was the two days were converging, confusing everyone.

Charles Todhunter should have been called next, but he was at home in Christchurch, too ill to attend. His medical practitioner was present and swore that to be the case; an earlier statement he'd made at the inquest, identifying the body, was taken into evidence. He had also made a deposition as to the interview in the cell, at which he had been present. Button requested that James be recalled.

"What did the prisoner say to you in the cell?" he asked.

James had a copy of the paper ready, and handed it to the clerk. "The prisoner told me on the 5th of June that he had seen it reported in the paper that morning that Dobson had been missing since the 29th May, and was last seen between the Arnold and Twelve Mile. I am certain the Grey River Argus was published on Tuesday, the 5th of June, and that it contained a paragraph relative to the missing George Dobson." He emphasized the word 29th, but the prosecutor failed to notice. It was the best he could do.

The final witness for the prosecution was called. Dr. Strehz came forward to testify about the autopsy, as Dr. Foppoly had left the province. Strehz gave his opinion that George Dobson had died from strangulation. He was not asked about further injuries.

At that, the prosecution rested and the court retired for refreshments.

He returned to the court after another cup of tea and found Mrs. Fellows and John Heron talking to each other near the door. Neither had been called to stand so far.

"Are you appearing for the defense?" he asked Mrs. Fellows.

She shook her head. "Edward and Priscilla are," she said. "I was told I wasn't needed."

"Blast," said James. "I thought you would have been an excellent witness, whereas..."

"Priscilla will just help Mr. Wilson," she said. "I know. But I was here yesterday and was sent home. I've told Priscilla she must tell the truth, but you know what she thinks the truth is."

"I was supposed to appear for the Crown," said Heron. He looked upset. "I was at the preliminary hearing in December, and I thought my evidence was important..."

Heron had testified that the gang had been at his pie shop before the murder, four men, Sullivan and Burgess who he knew, and two fair men. They'd asked to leave a swag and a shovel at his place. Later, he'd picked up the swag and found it to be "fearfully heavy." His evidence had been useful to paint a picture of the gang, and—possibly—to put guns and a shovel in their hands, but he'd been unable to identify the two fair men. He was not therefore useful as a witness against Wilson.

"You came down from Greymouth on the off chance...?" James asked.

"I came to see justice done," said Heron. "I heard they might try Sullivan again as well. I'd like to see him in front of a jury in this town, I very much would."

"It's not likely to happen," said James, earning a glare from Heron. Stories about Sullivan's possible retrial were running through town like a bush fire and were difficult to put out.

Mr. Rees began the case for the defence by calling James McElroy, who had been a constable at the time of the murder, and present at the discovery of the body. He testified that he'd put together the evidence for Inspector James, and that David Duncan had told him he'd seen the prisoner on Tuesday 29th of May with another man, folding up their swags at the iron shanty.

William DeLacey, the stable man who'd kept the gang informed of Mr. Fox's whereabouts, shuffled to the stand in shackles. He was serving two years for his part in the conspiracy to rob Mr. Fox. The defence asked him if he knew either of the men in court.

"I know 'im," he said, nodding towards Sullivan. "Sullivan. I seen him a few times with the others." He cast a look of triumph at Sullivan, who straightened his necktie and smirked in the direction of the prisoner.

"Did you remember seeing the men on May 28th?"

"I was up the track looking for some lost horses," said DeLacey. "Mr. Anderson 'ad lost them. I saw them—Sullivan and Kelly—in front of the iron hut rolling up their swags."

"You are sure it was Kelly you saw?"

"He 'ad a black eye and a scar on 'is face," said DeLacy. "I went away after the 'orses, and when I came back they was still there."

"What time was this?"

"Between one and two o'clock," said DeLacey. "I mounted my horse, and rode down the track towards Greymouth. I met Mr. Duncan," he pointed towards David Duncan. "He asked me to assist them in putting the cattle across the river, which I did. I then continued my journey down towards Greymouth. Before I got to the bridge, which is about one-and-a-half miles from Greymouth, I saw the prisoner and Burgess."

"And you are certain it was them?"

"I'm certain as to the identity of the prisoner. I afterwards met them again at the accommodation house, a few hundred yards from where I previously saw them and spoke to Burgess, I met them again just as I got into town, and a third time, between six and seven o'clock in the evening, at a fruit shop in Greymouth."

"How fast were you riding?" asked the judge. "How long would it

HOKITIKA, 1867: THE TRIAL: DAY TWO

take you to ride from the iron hut to Greymouth?"

"About three miles an hour, so an hour and a half," said DeLacey. "Course that was <u>riding</u>…"

Justice Gresson held up his hand to silence DeLacey. "You can only testify to what you know," he said sternly. "Now, you may leave the stand."

Edward Fellows was called, and testified that he was the son of the proprietor of the Criterion Hotel and that it was their custom to serve tea at five or six o'clock in the winter season. "My sister attends to the bar and tea tables at times," he said. "My father came to Hokitika on the 21st May. I left Greymouth for Hokitika, on a visit, on the 27th May."

One more person-Coburn- testified before the person James was dreading, Priscilla Fellows, came to the stand. Coburn, while insisting he was not a friend of the prisoner, said he had known him in Nelson, had lent him money, and had employed him at times in his store.

"I know the prisoner at the bar," he said. "I recollect the 27th May on a Sunday. I saw the prisoner at my house on that day. He had dinner with me. I saw him on the following day walking down the main street, alongside the river. I believe it was about half-past 2 or 3 o'clock, The prisoner has been in the habit of serving in my shop, but I cannot say whether he served on the night of Monday, 28th of May."

"And you are quite sure that you saw the prisoner between half-past two and three o'clock on Monday the 28th of May."

"I am positive that I saw him at that time on Monday, 28th of May," said Coburn. "Quite positive."

A juror raised his hand. "Was he carrying a swag with him when you saw him on the street?" he asked.

"Yes," said Coburn. The prisoner was carrying a swag when I saw him on the street on May 28th.

Coburn left the stand, grinning in the direction of Wilson. Not friends indeed. He may have just saved Wilson's neck. James would be paying more attention to the perjurer Mr. Coburn in future.

The door to the courtroom opened, and Priscilla Fellows entered. She was wearing a pale blue dress and had spent time perfecting her hair, which was braided tightly on the top of her head. She took the stand, clasped her hands on her lap, and lowered her eyes.

"Miss Fellows," said Button. "Can you tell us who you are?"

"Priscilla Fellows," she said in the softest of whispers. "My mother is Caroline Fellows, proprietor of the Criterion Hotel." She raised her eyes briefly and glanced in the direction of Wilson, then blushed bright red.

"Miss Fellows," said Button, "Are you acquainted with the prisoner?"

"He stayed at the hotel in May last year," said Priscilla. "I served him his tea."

"Do you remember one particular day, Monday, May 28th?"

She nodded. "I remember the Monday the 28th May that followed the Sunday that my brother went to Hokitika. The prisoner at the bar had his tea at our house on the Monday night I speak of. I am positive of it, because I served him, and I have never had any doubt on the subject."

"And why are you so sure?" asked Button.

She raised her head and stared at the courtroom, and said firmly, "The cause of my recollecting it so clearly is because my mother was not at home at the time."

"And you are sure of that?"

"I'm very sure," she said.

And with that, the defence rested.

The defense and the prosecutor then each addressed the jury. Mr. Button began on behalf of Wilson, giving an able summary of what the witnesses had said. He talked for two hours. James took time to leave the courtroom and walk up and down Revell Street. It was all out of his hands now, and there was nothing he could do or say that would make a difference. When he returned, the prosecutor had just risen to his feet to reply to the defence.

"I would like the court to note that the prisoner was first to give information to the police," he said. "He did so in order to protect himself, and as has been proved, in the hope of getting a guarantee of free pardon for the crimes he had committed."

This was good, James thought. Exactly what needed to be emphasized.

"It is not difficult to imagine why he did not take advantage of the reward offered by the Government to anyone who confessed, inasmuch as he was well aware that the privileges of reward, and etcetera, offered in the bill, would not extend to the principal in the crime. There was no doubt that the prisoner had been one of the principal malefactors of the desperate gang to which he belonged, but had become frightened at his own deeds. As to Sullivan, he could have no possible interest in saying anything more than the truth against the prisoner, and in proof of which his evidence was in many parts corroborated by the prisoner."

The prosecutor finished, and James looked around the court and at the jury. The jury's faces were unreadable, but the people in the court had sneers of contempt on their faces. Not a good sign. Now Justice Gresson must direct the jury well.

Justice Gresson put on a pair of spectacles and read from his notes without looking at the jury, summing up the case for them.

"I would remind the jury," he said, "that the case now before you is a most important one, involving, as it does, a question of life and death. I am aware that you have already given considerable attention to its hearing, even at considerable personal inconvenience. I concur with the learned counsel for the prisoner in warning you against the influence of prejudice. Deeds that are well known to the world, crimes, the very nature and magnitude of which are sufficient in themselves to excite the indignation of every right-thinking person, have been perpetrated by the gang of which the prisoner was an associate, and the peculiar atrocity of the particular murder of which the prisoner is charged is certainly alone sufficient to create a prejudice in the case."

Not just for the prisoner, thought James. The jury must also feel the strongest of prejudices against Sullivan. He waited for Gresson to make that point, but he did not.

"I hope the jury will try hard to disabuse their minds of any such feeling, and judge the case simply by the evidence you have heard." He stopped, and looked at the jury over the top of his glasses. "According to law, I am quite justified in expressing an opinion in my charge to you. I would ask you to look upon it merely as one opinion, and give the preference to your own conclusion, which will be the opinion of twelve men."

What was his opinion, then? James was not clear at this point and was getting increasingly worried about what it might be.

"I look upon the evidence of Sullivan as one of the cardinal points in the evidence upon which you must form your verdict; I will, therefore, read to you the law relating to accomplices, and leave it to you to judge whether there was sufficient independent evidence, leaving Sullivan's out of the case, to bring the crime so near home to the prisoner, that you can entertain no reasonable doubt as to his guilt."

Damn. This was not heading in a good direction. If they were asked to disregard Sullivan's evidence they would be left with a potpourri of conflicted versions.

"This is a case in which the independent evidence, as it was termed, is required to be stronger even than in ordinary cases of less magnitude. The principal evidence in this charge against the accused is given by probably as tainted a witness…"

James felt his jaw clenching, his heart pounding, and his face reddening. Gresson was feeding into the worst prejudices of the jury.

"…as ever entered a court of justice one who has been convicted of murder, and out of his own mouth perjury. I would therefore ask the jury to take the principal features of evidence for the Crown, apart from Sullivan, and see if it is sufficient to convict the prisoner beyond any reasonable doubt.

James listened as the magistrate read the principal features in the

HOKITIKA, 1867: THE TRIAL: DAY TWO

evidence, commenting on each one.

"I will leave it for the jury to consider your decision. If you take the circumstances detailed by other evidence, that of independent witnesses, as conclusive to the prisoner's guilt, you will, no doubt, credit the evidence of Sullivan, but if you come to a negative conclusion you will throw it aside. In conclusion, I will leave the case in your capable hands, assured that you will give the whole of the evidence your careful consideration, and sincerely trusting you will arrive at a correct decision."

With that, he raised his gavel and tapped it once forcefully on the table.

The jury left, and returned thirty minutes later with their verdict: Not Guilty.

James left court with his mind in turmoil, not looking where he was going, and almost knocked over the reporter from the Grey River Argus.

"Mr. Inspector James," said the reporter. "I must convey my condolences..."

James brushed him aside. He had no time to bother with the reporter right now. He was just surprised that he wasn't gloating about the defeat.

28

Greymouth, 1867: A Letter to the Editor

He arrived back at the police camp in Greymouth still feeling sick at heart. Not guilty. How could it be possible? How had the jury not seen that the circumstance of James Wilson's visit to him within days of the murder of George Dobson as a sign of his guilt? And that the gang of reprobates who had stepped up to tell the lie that Wilson had been with them on the day of the murder were not to be trusted—not a single one of them. Coburn, DeLacey, even Priscilla Fellows.

James had ridden from Hokitika in a white fury, not waiting to talk to anyone, even Broham. He'd been stopped at the Teremakau for two days waiting for a fresh to subside, but the forced rest had still not cooled him down. No doubt Broham would already be shifting the credit subtly back in James' direction. Shearman would hear a new version of the story, of how James had kept Broham in the dark, had not followed up on clues, had not found sufficiently convincing witnesses or evidence.

He went into the station expecting to find Sergeant Slattery, but he was not at his desk. Someone had left a copy of the Grey River Argus on James' desk, and he sat and flicked through it, trying to calm his anger, waiting for Sergeant Slattery to return, turning the pages angrily and barely focusing on what was there.

It was hard to get away from news of the Dobson murder trial, however. News had been telegraphed to Greymouth after the trial, and a special edition rushed out. Not Guilty!

The editorial on page two discussed the unlikely possibility that Sullivan would now be tried for his role in the murder of George Dobson. "Some idea has prevailed during the last day or two," it said, "that this particular unhanged murderer Sullivan would have another chance of getting his deserts through the information laid against him for the 'doing-to-death' of Mr. George Dobson: We are sorry to say that there is very little chance of the claims of justice being thus met." This hatred of Sullivan was the very thing that had freed Wilson. That Sullivan had gone free – or free enough to avoid the noose – had enraged everybody, not least because he was a traitor who had turned on his partners in crime. "The man is already, velvet waistcoat and sky-blue necktie notwithstanding," the writer continued, "sentenced to penal servitude for life; and the warrant by which he was sent back to give evidence at the recent trials contains a provision to the effect that he will be sent back whenever his services as a witness shall have been exhausted. So far as the purposes for which he was sent down are concerned, Mr. Sullivan's presence in Hokitika may now be dispensed with…we shall breath more freely when the atmosphere is cleared of him."

He flipped to another page and found an article reprinted from the West Coast News. He did not want to read it, but his eyes were drawn to it. How often had he been angry at what he read in the paper about his actions? But this time, the editor seemed to agree with him: "It is not for us to question the verdict of the jury, further than to express an opinion that had the jury been able to return an open verdict of 'not proven' this was eminently a case for such a verdict being recorded. But the law of English criminal procedure lays down the maxim that a man must be declared guilty or innocent, and that unless the proofs of his guilt are complete any doubts are to be interpreted to the favor of the accused."

The writer went on to say that there was no doubt that Wilson had been up on the track on the day Dobson was murdered, and that although the chain of evidence was weak, Sullivan's "intelligible and precise" history of the proceedings had generally been supported by other evidence. What had Sullivan to gain by lying about Wilson, the writer asked? Did that mean he was also lying when he implicated Levy, who had gone to his execution vehemently protesting his innocence? That was too difficult for any decent human being to believe, that they had sent an innocent man to his death. James read the argument and smiled grimly. Whatever the world thought about Sullivan, he knew that the police in Nelson had been convinced of his reliability in this at least. As for Levy, perhaps he had considered himself innocent, because his hands had not been around another's throat. But he had been a willing participant in the robbery and certainly present at the murders in Nelson.

The writer went on to argue the very point that James thought was important: the fact that Wilson had "voluntarily placed himself in the clutches of the police almost immediately after the day on which the murder had been committed, and although offers of pardon and other inducements were held out to him he did not make any confession, but on the contrary reiterated his denial of any knowledge of the missing man."

He was about to close the paper when he noticed a letter to the editor with the heading, The Dobson Murder. He debated with himself about reading yet another letter, probably from the opinionated *Scrutator* or someone of his ilk. But glancing at the bottom of the letter he saw with shock that the letter was signed James Wilson. He read it with growing annoyance:

> *Before this frightful tragedy, in which I was so unfortunate as to get mixed up I was always of opinion that if the police did fall across any evidence that could tend to establish my innocence they would only be too glad to bring it forward; instead of that they have acted quite the contrary. In two instances that have come to my certain knowledge, and can, if necessary, prove, they have*

endeavored to get witnesses out of the way, when Mr. James knew that they could swear, positively that I was in the Grey at the time that the villain Sullivan swears that I was with him engaged in the murder of Mr. Dobson.

How dare the paper publish such a self-serving letter from this criminal. He scanned the rest of the letter, his heart heavy. It went on to give what sounded like specific examples of Inspector James bribing witnesses or forcing them to leave town. Many would believe Wilson's claim. Once more his career would be compromised through no fault of his own. Albert Kapau, wrote Wilson, had been willing to testify he saw Wilson at four in the afternoon, and had tea with him at five thirty, but Mr. James had gone to see him and told him his evidence would not be needed. And Priscilla Fellows had served him his tea when he was supposedly on the track with Sullivan murdering Mr. Dobson, but James had gone to the girl's mother and tried to pay her off. It was libel of the worst kind. In fact, it was the crown prosecutor who had told Mrs. Fellows that her evidence would not be wanted for the prosecution, why he did not understand. The rules of service forbid him to send a letter to the paper, and he therefore had no way of refuting this nonsense.

He threw the paper on the table and rested his head in his hands. Sergeant Slattery came in and said softly, "Good evening Mr. Inspector James, I'm so sorry to hear about your unfortunate loss…"

James looked up at him. Sympathy for the loss of the Dobson case was almost worse than criticism. "Thank you," he said. "Nothing to be done about it, I suppose. Sullivan was not a good enough witness for the jury…"

He saw the expression on Sergeant Slattery's face change. "Ah, yes," he said. "The Dobson case…a terrible miscarriage of justice…will you be returning home soon?"

James stood up. "Yes, I'd better be off home, I suppose. Elizabeth must be wondering where I am…I was stuck at the Teremakau for forty-eight hours."

Sergeant Slattery nodded awkwardly. His face had turned a bright red, and James wondered what was the matter with him. Slattery was a portly man. Perhaps his heart was giving him a problem.

"Are you alright, Sergeant Slattery?"

Sergeant Slattery nodded and pretended to sort some papers on his desk.

"Quite…quite alright thank you Mr. Inspector James."

He left the station house wondering about his sergeant. At least it had taken his mind off the maddening letter from Wilson.

As he reached the corner of Arney Street he saw Mrs. Bain and another woman—Mrs. Heron, John Heron's wife, he thought—leave the Bain house and enter his own. Mrs. Bain and Elizabeth frequently met to gossip over a cup of tea, but seeing two women visitors was unusual. He increased his pace. Could Elizabeth have gone into labour? It was still a few weeks until she was due, but it would not be the first time a baby had arrived early. James, their first little Australian boy, had been two months early—probably why he had died within weeks of his birth. He was starting to feel uneasy.

Louisa was standing on the verandah, her back pressed again the door jamb, the door open. She held a small blanket close against her lips, her normally rosy cheeks were a deathly white, and her eyes were wide and filled with horror. He ran up the steps and grabbed her by the shoulders. Charlie sprawled on the verandah beside her, his head on his paws, looking forlornly up at his master.

"Louisa? Louisa? Are you well? Has something happened?"

She took a long time to answer. It seemed almost impossible for her to speak, but finally she said in a whisper, "Am I going to die papa?" Then she began to sob.

29

Greymouth, 1867: A Cold Wind Down the Grey

He stood on the verandah, his feet frozen to the spot, unable to move or speak. Who had died? Perhaps the newborn child, come early? God forbid that it was Elizabeth. He wanted to demand of Louisa, "Who has died?" but she was too shaken to speak. It was not fair to ask her.

He heard a creak and looked up to see Dr. Morice standing before him, his hands clasped in front of him. Dr. Morice had arrived from Dunstan in Otago in November to take up the position of surgeon to the Grey River Hospital that became free when Dr. Foppoly returned to Italy. He was a man of about thirty, of a military bearing, and seemed to know what he was about. But he was not an accoucheur like Dr. Foppoly or Dr. Strehz, who had also left Greymouth. He was a surgeon and worked mostly at the hospital, mending broken bones, binding wounds, and taking care of the sick and insane.

James could not speak, but stared at Dr. Morice. Dr. Morice cleared his throat a couple of times, and said, "You have a new son, Mr. Inspector James."

He felt the rush of relief that resembled a fresh coming down the Grey. "A son?"

Morice nodded. "Yes…a son. But I'm afraid I have something I must tell you…"

"Harry died," said Louisa in a flat voice that he hardly recognized. "He was sleeping and I went up to his room, and when I touched him he was cold…"

"Harry? Harry is dead?"

"I'm very sorry, Mr. James, but I'm afraid he is. It happened on Friday, and the shock brought on your wife's contractions early. She gave birth early this morning"

He pushed past Morice and towards the door of the bedroom. Harry, little Harry Timaru, who had been conceived in sorrow when Mary and Henry had died within weeks of each other in Timaru…they could scarcely think of a name to give him, and had used another form of Henry and the name of the town where they lived. James had been away at the goldfields and had come home to find his lovely Mary Elizabeth dead of pleurisy, at just eight years old. And Henry, not long past his second birthday had died a few weeks later. His body had swollen up until it was unrecognizable—dropsy—something he had never heard of in a child, a disease that affected men who drank too much, not an innocent child. The doctor had said it was his heart.

"I think it must have been his heart," said Dr. Morice, echoing his thoughts. He had his hand on James' chest, preventing him from entering the bedroom.

"His heart? Henry…"

"Your son," said Dr. Morice. "Harry, was it not? Had he been tired, languid…?"

"Yes…yes, he had," said James. Why had he not realized that it was not natural for a two-and-a-half-year-old boy to be sleeping constantly?

"And perhaps you noticed a blue tinge to his lips on occasion?"

James remember the blue he had seen in Harry's lips when he carried the child home from the coach, and how cold he had felt. "Yes, once at least."

"Ah then," said Morice. "His heart, I expect. Not a strong heart. At least you can take comfort from knowing that there was very little we could have done. A child born with a weak heart is not likely to survive..."

"I take no comfort from that," said James. He brushed away Morice's hand and pushed open the bedroom door.

Elizabeth lay in the bed, her face away from him, looking at the wall. Beside the bed, Mrs. Bain and the other woman he had seen with her—a wet nurse he realized now, as Mrs. Heron had also recently given birth—were tending to the baby, trying to get it to attach itself to the breast of the wet nurse.

"William," said Mrs. Bain sadly. "I'm so sorry you have to come home to this. Elizabeth has refused to hold or feed the child..."

"Elizabeth..."

She turned to look at him, her eyes dark and empty like stones.

"He's just going to die William," she said. "This boy is just going to die like all the others. I knew Harry was going to die, I knew he was ill..." She turned her face back towards the wall and began to cry.

He could no longer stand to be in the room. Pushing past the doctor he ran out onto the verandah and down the steps. His chest felt constricted, as if his own heart was about to fail, like Harry's. He hurried along Richmond Quay, away from his house, the police camp, the Criterion Hotel, from everything he wanted to forget. At the end of the quay a rocky spit jutted out into the ocean and he made his way along it, stepping from rock to rock. When he had gone as far as he could he sat and looked back up the river to the town.

A barber, a dark mist that presaged an icy blast of wind down the river, was forming between the ranges and he could already feel the chill in his bones. He put his hands under his arm pits and huddled down. The tide was coming in, and dark waves crested in front of him, the same incoming tide that had slowed him on his way from the Teremakau less than an hour ago, but a lifetime past. This was how it felt when all emotions had been drained from you. He understood why Mr. Rees had cut his own throat, and why so many other men—and women—had commit suicide when all alternatives seemed impossible. The dark water drew him forward, and he imagined himself sinking into it, and into forgetfulness. But he did not move towards it. How would Elizabeth manage without him? And what would happen to Louisa, already wounded by the loss of her sister and brother in Timaru, and now another brother? He could not leave Elizabeth alone with Louisa and their new son.

Five children he had lost.

The newborn James in fifty-five, up in Carisbrooke, and then one-year-old William in fifty-eight, in Korong, of diarrhea. They had left the gold fields and the force, taking Henry and Mary Elizabeth, their surviving children with them, and gone south to Melbourne. Louisa was born in Sale the following year. Then Shearman had recruited him to the new Canterbury force, and they'd come to New Zealand, with the two girls and Henry, to start afresh.

But in Timaru, less than a year after they arrived, Mary Elizabeth had died of pleurisy, followed within weeks by an already-weak Henry with dropsy. Elizabeth had been desperate to leave Timaru, had wanted to return to Victoria to be with her sister Susan. But he wouldn't return to Australia. He would get ahead in New Zealand, he knew he would. Eventually she'd agreed to him requesting the posting to the gold escort. Now, here they were in Greymouth and another child had died. Where could they go? Could he start anew one more time?

The cold wind of the barber had started to intensify. If he sat here much longer he would die of pleurisy himself. He looked back at the town, with the half-built seawall already crumbling from the constant onslaught of the river, Mawhera Quay lined with hotels overflowing with drunken diggers, smoke rising from iron chimneys that might catch fire at any minute, and everywhere, normal working people going about their business who needed to be protected from the likes of Burgess and Kelly. It was not the most beautiful town in New Zealand, but the sense of responsibility he felt for it was overwhelming. He would stay in Greymouth and he would continue to do his very best to make the town another Ipswich, or Plymouth, or Swansea or Blackpool. He would see a newer, better England built in this new land of his. Once more, he would make Elizabeth understand.

He walked briskly back towards his house. Elizabeth would endure, as she always did. And he would do his best to make sure his two surviving children led better lives than their parents.

Dr. Morice and Mrs. Heron had left, and Mrs. Bain was seated awkwardly in the kitchen holding a tiny bundle in her arms, rocking him from side to side.

"Hello William," she said. "Did you want to see your new son?"

For a moment, he felt the way Elizabeth must feel. Why should he hold the boy? He would just die. But he fought off the feeling and held out his arms. The boy looked up at him for a few seconds, with an intense blue gaze that he recognized as his own, then his eyes drooped and he was asleep.

"Thomas," said James, looking down at his son. "Thomas Harvey. That's a good honest name." He took the baby into the bedroom where Elizabeth lay, now fast asleep with Louisa beside her, pressed against her mother's back, and sat on the seat by the window. When Elizabeth awoke, he would hand her the boy, tell her the name he had chosen, and insist that she put him to her breast. He would remind Elizabeth how strong she had always been and how she must continue to be strong. She might not love the boy, but she would do her duty to him, to both of them. She always did.

30

Wanganui, 1888: Memento Mori

He was home finally. His legs were aching again and his stomach churned as it tried to digest the cheese and onion sandwich and the ginger beer. As he had half expected, Elizabeth was sitting on the steps of the verandah of the new house on the corner of Halswell Street, a stone's throw from the old house, a shawl around her shoulders to keep out the cold. Her hair, steel grey now and held back in a loose bun, had kept its colour more than his, but her face was deeply lined from the strong New Zealand sun. She looked beautiful. Charlie, as always, was flopped by her side…not the same Charlie he had owned in Greymouth, but his seventh Charlie: an Australian Shepherd, as the dogs were now called.

"There's Mrs. James," said Crozier. "She looks very contented."

"Would you like to join us for…" he had been going to say a drink, but remembered Crozier's dislike of alcohol, so said instead, "for a cup of tea?"

Crozier shook his head. "I'd best be getting back," he said. He nodded and smiled at Elizabeth and placed the testimonial beside her on the step. "Best of luck for the future, Mr. Inspector James. And I hope I didn't bother you with all my questions."

"Not at all," said James. "I enjoyed talking with you. Thank you for carrying the testimonial home. I shall think of you every time I see it. And…take care of those boys of yours now." He sat down beside

Elizabeth.

Elizabeth turned the testimonial towards herself. "This is very nice," she said. "And look—everyone has signed it. You must feel better, William, knowing that your men hold you in such high regard."

James caught her eye, and she smiled. She was laughing at him. She, more than anyone, knew how much he felt the irony of receiving a testimonial when he'd been pushed from his job.

"Well old girl," he said. "You're going to see a lot more of me for the next while."

She put her hand through his arm and squeezed. "You know I'll enjoy having you at home with me. You can work on the new garden…there's a lot to be done. Oh…there's a letter for you from the council…I put it on your Davenport. Perhaps they have some work for you."

"I did request an appointment as Justice of the Peace," he said. "I'll look at it later."

She reached behind herself and pulled out an old newspaper. "I found this on your Davenport. An old Lyttelton Times. Have you been reading it? It seems so long since we were in Timaru. Twenty years, it must be."

"Twenty-three," he said. "Yes, I found it this morning when I was clearing out the desk. I put it there when we were in Timaru, found it again in Greymouth, and put it back, intending to read it later. It's an old report to the government on the best route for the road across the mountains. Written by George Dobson, before we went to Greymouth, before we had any idea that we would be going there…"

She looked at the date on the paper. "You must have put it there just after Mary died," she said. "When I was so desperate to go back to Victoria, and you thought we should move forward not backwards."

He took her hand in his. "It hasn't been so bad since then, has it?"

"Not so bad, no," she said. "Although it seemed that every time I fell pregnant we moved somewhere, so I hope this move…"

He laughed. "We're getting a bit old for that."

"Anyway, I was reading this paper…have you read it yet?"

"Read it to me," he said.

She folded the paper in half and held it away from her face. "I'll try. My eyes aren't what they were. I'll read the part at the end. It's his daily notes I think, and reads like an adventure—something from *King Solomon's Mines*

March 7. After breakfast Anderson asked if I would give him enough provisions to carry him to the diggings, which I consented to do, knowing the uselessness of arguing with a man touched with the yellow fever. Russell, however, determined to stay with me, and see me back over the range. I was much pleased with his conduct, as, had he left me, I should have been obliged to give up all further explorations and return alone. Taking with us a week's provisions, we followed up the east branch of the Otira, where for a long way up we had easy walking; but the hills at last closing in, a rough scramble of about two miles, over boulders and through bush, brought us to the foot of a saddle, up which we had to climb on our hands and knees. On reaching the top I saw by the character of the bush, that we were looking down the east side of the range, so followed down the creek, which rises from the saddle, until we came to the bush where we camped. This saddle, which I have called the 'Goat's Pass,' must be immensely high, as the bush does not grow to within several hundred feet of the summit.

She stopped and looked at James. "Shall I continue? There's more…"

He nodded, his eyes closed, and she read on:

March 8, —Followed the creek bed as far down as possible, and then took to the bush, but, unfortunately, taking the wrong side of the creek, became entangled amongst a mass of cliffs covered with thick bush out of which we had some difficulty in extricating ourselves, having to throw our swags down through the bush, and lower ourselves after them by the branches of the trees. On getting into the open river-bed, I saw that we were in the east branch of the river Bealey, and throwing away the remainder of our provisions, we started off at a good pace, determined to reach Messrs. Goldney's station that evening, having walked from the Teremakau in two days. From this place, I was obliged to drive to town, having lost my saddle horse, and being delayed by heavy rain on the 9th and 10th, which caused an unusually high fresh in the river Kowai; did not reach town until late in the evening of Saturday, the 11th of March." Dobson's Exploration., Lyttelton Times, Volume XXIII, Issue 1372, 14 March 1865

"He goes on to recommend Arthur's Pass—the route he named after his brother," she said. "He sounds like a bright young man, doesn't he? And very brave and strong."

"I think he was," said James. "I wish I'd know him. I always felt drawn to him, almost as if he was my son. I've been thinking about his…"

Elizabeth squeezed his hand. "Best not to dwell on the bad parts of the past. I saw him, you know, when he was alive."

"You did?" asked James, surprised. "You never said…"

"Didn't I? I suppose we had some other things to think about then, didn't we? Yes, I saw him with his crew. There must have been twenty or thirty of them. They were passing through town towards the lagoon…going to repair the Hokitika road, I think. Or perhaps that was when they were building it, I'm not sure. Some of the men were on horseback, and some in drays with the equipment. Mr. Dobson was walking with another man at the rear of the procession. They were talking very animatedly, and he was waving his arms around. I thought he looked like such a lively, confident young man. He had his shirt sleeves rolled up to his elbows, and he was wearing a broad brimmed hat, and his face was quite rosy from the sun…but the thing I noticed the most was that although he seemed so much younger than the man he was talking to, that man, whoever it was, seemed to be deferring to him. You could tell that he…Mr. Dobson…was the man in charge."

He wanted to talk to her about the past, about all the dead boys, and Mary Elizabeth. They had never really talked about it. "We had some hard times…" he began, and he saw her frown.

The door behind them opened and a young woman came out. She was dressed in a pink muslin dress with a morning wrapper on top, and was carrying a large feather duster.

"What on earth are you two doing, sitting on the step holding hands. I quite thought it was a pair of young lovers I saw here."

"Annie," said James. "I didn't know you were here."

"I came to help mum clean out the cupboards, but I sent her outside. I can work faster by myself," she said. Elizabeth Mary James, known as Annie, born two years after Thomas, when Elizabeth was forty-one. Their miracle daughter.

Elizabeth reached up and pulled at Annie's skirt. "Sit with us for a minute," she said. "We were about to get maudlin, thinking about the past, and you must stop us."

Perhaps it was for the best. He moved over, and Annie sat down between them.

"Now, you can each hold one of my hands, and stop looking like a pair of foolish old lovers. Just so wrong at your age."

"Just wait until you and your Mr. Field reach our age," said Elizabeth. Annie blushed scarlet and pulled her hand away. "Frederick…Mr. Field means nothing to me," she said. "Just because I danced with him…"

"We'll see," said Elizabeth.

James could see his daughter biting her lip, her cheeks still red. A wedding coming up. Better get moving on the Justice of the Peace request. He was clearly going to need the money.

"Here comes Thomas," Annie said suddenly. "You can tease him about who he's been dancing with…"

James eyes weren't as sharp as his daughter's. He put his hand over his eyes to shade them and peered down the path along which he had so recently walked. The sun was in his eyes but he could see the faint outline of a man walking towards him. He was walking briskly, and carrying something over his shoulder. A compass case? No, it was an architect's blueprint tube, held on a leather strap. He smiled to himself and thought, "Neither man nor boy."

It was his son, coming home.

31

Afterword

William Henry and Elizabeth James moved to Auckland a few years after he was forced into retirement, first selling most of their furniture at auction. My impression of him grew partly from the two pianos and the many paintings and sculptures he owned and put up for auction. I also found several mentions of his pen and ink sketches and an article about him painting scenery for a backdrop of a play his daughter Annie was involved in. Notably, Louisa's son, and the James' grandson, Sir Erima Harvey Northcroft, was one of eleven judges on the International Military Tribunal for the Far East after the World War II.

Elizabeth died in Auckland in May, 1904 at "the good old age of 78." After she died, James moved back to Wanganui* to live with his son in his Durie Hill residence. His son was by then an architect, and a very nice building he designed can still be seen on Victoria Street across from the old Bank of New Zealand. James died in Wanganui on April 3, 1907 of asthenia and cardiac disease after two years of suffering (according to his death certificate). He is buried in the Heads Road Cemetery, one of the oldest in New Zealand. I visited him there in 2017.

George Dobson's brother Arthur (Sir Arthur Dudley Dobson) went on to have a spectacular career as surveyor and engineer, spending the last twenty years of his working life (1901 to 1921) as the city engineer of Christchurch. He was knighted in 1930, partly as a recognition for his family's impact in opening up the South Island to road and rail, and by exploration.

Two of George Dobson's younger brothers, Herbert and Robert, moved to Gisborne and Napier on the east coast of the North Island. Robert died young in 1893, aged 41. But his son, Ralph Boyd Dobson, married Rhoda Graham, my grandmother's sister. I did not know of the familial connection when I began this book.

George Dobson is now little more than a footnote to history: the man who was killed by the Burgess gang before they committed the murders on the Maungatapu, the oldest son of an illustrious New Zealand family who is known mostly for his early death. I have tried to bring him back to life in this book, and hope I have succeeded.

*Wanganui is now spelled with an H - Whanganui. I have used the older spelling which was used in the nineteenth century.

If you would like to see photos of some of these people, or have any questions about what became of them, please visit my website at www.wendymwilson.com

www.ingramcontent.com/pod-product-compliance
Lightning Source LLC
Chambersburg PA
CBHW060518080526
44586CB00012B/527